Blues Before **Sunrise 2**

MUSIC IN AMERICAN LIFE

A list of books in the series appears at the end of this book.

Steve Cushing

Blues Before **Sunrise 2**
INTERVIEWS FROM THE CHICAGO SCENE

UNIVERSITY OF
ILLINOIS PRESS
Urbana, Chicago, and Springfield

© 2019 by the Board of Trustees
of the University of Illinois
All rights reserved
1 2 3 4 5 C P 5 4 3 2 1
♾ This book is printed on acid-free paper.

Library of Congress Cataloging-in-Publication Data
Names: Cushing, Steve, interviewer.
Title: Blues before sunrise 2 : interviews from the Chicago
　　scene / Steve Cushing.
Other titles: Blues before sunrise (Radio program)
Description: Urbana : University of Illinois Press, [2019] |
　　Series: Music in American life | Includes index.
Identifiers: LCCN 2019021416 (print) | LCCN 2019021876
　　(ebook) | ISBN 9780252042829 (hardcover : alk.
　　paper) | ISBN 9780252084652 (pbk. : alk. paper) | ISBN
　　9780252051685 (ebook)
Subjects: LCSH: Blues musicians—Illinois—Chicago—
　　Interviews. | Blues musicians—Illinois—Chicago—
　　Biography.
Classification: LCC ML394 .B647 2019 (print) | LCC ML394
　　(ebook) | DDC 781.643092/277311 [B]—dc23
LC record available at https://lccn.loc.gov/2019021416
LC ebook record available at https://lccn.loc.gov
　　/2019021876

*Dedicated to my father, Richard Cushing (1925–2015),
who, when he saw the first book, asked if he could help
and wound up transcribing the majority of the
interviews in this book.*

&

*Farewell to that generation of African Americans
ostracized by our parents and grandparents.
Thanks for sharing your music and
your recollections of the era.
Our time together was too short . . .*

Contents

Introduction   ix

PART ONE TALKIN' 'BOUT YOU
Abb Locke Talks about Two-Gun Pete   3
Brewer Phillips on Memphis Minnie   8
Louise "Mattie" Johnson   17
Dick LaPalm Talks about Nat King Cole   25
Grady Freeman   35
Theautry Jones   42

PART TWO AMEN CORNER
Clarence Small   47
Reverend F. W. McGee   75
Pastor Donald Gay   82

PART THREE BRONZEVILLE
Andrew Tibbs   101
Bill Samuels   114
Marl Young   131
Scotty Piper   149

PART FOUR SHORT-ORDER CHICAGO
Little Brother Montgomery   161
"Robert Jr." Lockwood   170
Sippie Wallace   179
Johnny Lewis   187
Homer Harris   196
Blind John Davis   201
Arbee Stidham   207
Collenane Cosey   217
Roosevelt Sykes   220

Index   225

Introduction

This is *Blues Before Sunrise 2: Interviews from the Chicago Scene*. All of the interviews in this book were prerecorded, edited, and produced (music was mixed in, interspersed with the conversation) before being broadcast on the nationally syndicated public radio program *Blues Before Sunrise*. This is the second volume of transcribed interviews, and a follow-up to *Blues Before Sunrise: The Radio Interviews*, published in 2010. The book is presented in four sections, with the interviews in each section presenting a specific category or interest.

Talkin' 'bout You

This section presents artists and personalities who spoke at length about artists other than themselves. Chicago tenor man Abb Locke discusses his years spent living with and serving as "running-buddy" to Chicago's notorious "Two-Gun Pete," a legendary black Chicago policeman reputed to have killed more than a dozen people in the line of duty. Then blues guitarist Brewer Phillips speaks at length about his adopted "mother," blueswoman Memphis Minnie, discussing the later years of her life and career. We have an interview with Louise "Mattie" Johnson, an administrator in the Indianapolis public school system. Louise talks about her mother, Flossie Franklin, an Indianapolis schoolteacher who during the 1930s helped famed blues pianist Leroy Carr write lyrics for some of his most famous tunes—including "Blues Before Sunrise." Ms. Johnson also discusses the career of her brother, Guitar Pete Franklin, an acclaimed bluesman based in Indianapolis. This section also includes an interview with Dick LaPalm, who as a white college student in 1950 decided he wanted to work for Nat King Cole. He had never met or seen Nat Cole but was resourceful enough to win a job as a trusted member of Cole's personal staff, a job he held until Cole's death in 1965. And finally we present a pair of short chapters, first with Grady Freeman, who was a childhood friend to Chicago bluesman Jr. Wells, and then we wrap up the section with a thumbnail interview with Theautry Jones, who worked for a very brief time with Chicago harmonica genius Little Walter Jacobs.

Amen Corner

This section contains interviews with artists who made religious recordings. There is an extensive interview with Clarence Small, a longtime member of Wings Over Jordan. This world-famous black choir was founded in Cleveland in 1936 and spent the next two decades touring and performing nationwide. Wings Over Jordan were heard on their own national radio broadcast every Sunday morning on the CBS radio network. Clarence talks at length about touring and performing during the 1940s as black artists in a world of segregation. Also included: an interview with Rev. F. W. McGee Jr., who talks about his father, Rev. F. W. McGee Sr., a popular Chicago clergyman who made more than forty recordings for the Victor label during the 1920s. Finally in this section we talk with Pastor Donald Gay, the younger brother of Chicago's fabulous Gay Sisters. The Gay Sisters, Evelyn, Geraldine, and Mildred, were popular recording artists, touring and recording extensively during the 1950s and 1960s. Pastor Gay tells the story of his sisters, their career, and their recordings.

Bronzeville

This section presents conversations with artists and personalities from the famed area of Chicago's black South Side known as Bronzeville. Artists featured in this section were raised in Chicago—as opposed to the stereotypical southern émigré found in postwar Chicago Blues—and they often played a style of music that displayed a higher degree of jazz influence than classic postwar Chicago blues. There is Andrew Tibbs, who had a series of hit recordings for the Chess brothers. We also present a series of interviews that serve to create a profile of Billy Samuels, a pianist/vocalist and leader of a trio called the Cats 'n Jammers who, during the 1940s, recorded for the Mercury label. Billy died in 1964, but we are able to reconstruct his career and life through the reminiscences of family, friends, and fellow musicians. Also in our Bronzeville section is Marl Young, a Chicago-based pianist/arranger who lead bands at a handful of South Side Chicago nightclubs, including the El Grotto, the DeLisa, and the Rhumboogie Club—simultaneously! In later years Marl moved to Los Angeles, where he led the band for Lucille Ball on *The Lucy Show* and was instrumental in merging Los Angeles' black and white musicians unions during the 1960s. Finally, in this section we present an interview with Chicago's Scotty Piper, known as "The Dancing Tailor." Scotty won his fame as tailor to the biggest names in black entertainment, from heavyweight boxing champion Jack Johnson to Duke Ellington, and even made a suit in 1940 for a young athlete named Harold Washington. In addition to his stories on the world of black entertainment,

Scotty has firsthand stories of the 1919 Chicago race riots and running away to join the Ringling Brothers circus.

Short-Order Chicago

This final section contains a handful of my earliest—and shortest—interviews, done in the days before I got truly comfortable with long-form interviews. Ironically, this section includes some of the biggest names interviewed on my radio program, so while these interviews may be brief, they're chock-full of interesting stories. We hear from blues pianist Little Brother Montgomery, bluesmen "Robert Jr." Lockwood, classic blues singer Sippie Wallace, Blind John Davis, and several others.

Blues Before **Sunrise 2**

Part One **Talkin' 'bout You**

Abb Locke Talks about **Two-Gun Pete**

Blues writer Paul Oliver was, almost from the beginning, the number 1 advocate of listening to the music's lyrics. Paul maintained that blues lyrics—both prewar and postwar—profiled and reflected the activities of everyday life of African Americans and helped document special events as well as notable individuals in the black community. Chicago's "Two-Gun Pete" was just such an individual. His real name was Sylvester Washington. He was a notorious black Chicago policeman, reputed to have killed more than a dozen people in the line of duty. Pete had such a fearsome reputation in the black community that legend says he would arrest thugs on the street, and instead of handcuffing and dragging them off to jail he would simply instruct them to report to the station house— and they would! Two-Gun Pete was mentioned several different times on blues records, and from time to time stories of his career or tales of personal run-ins with Pete were part of the conversation among blues musicians. One of the major Chicago newspapers ran an article on him and *Life* magazine had published an impressive photo of Pete on duty. I was fascinated to hear that there was such a character on the Chicago scene. After reading the printed articles and hearing the stories I asked around to see if anybody in particular had more stories about Two-Gun Pete. Dick Shurman said the man to talk to was Abb

"Two-Gun" Pete. Photo courtesy Scotty Piper Collection, Chicago History Museum.

Locke. Abb was a regular on the Chicago blues scene working as a tenor player in the bands of Howling Wolf and Otis Rush. Abb had rented a room in a tavern/boardinghouse owned by Two-Gun Pete and was running-buddies with him for a few years—so all the stories were firsthand.

This interview was recorded May 28, 2013. Abb Lock died in March 2019.

■ ■ ■

I contacted Abb and we met in the office of Delmark Records in Chicago.

Abb, when did you first meet Two-Gun Pete—what year was it?

About 1958—somewhere in there . . .

And was he still a cop when you knew him?

No—the last person he killed, the church got him off the force because he was killing too many people. . . . But he still had power [*laughs*] because he originally got many of those people at the Police Department jobs. I had to find me a room because I was sleeping with a buddy of mine from Cotton Plant, Arkansas—that's where I'm from, Cotton Plant, Arkansas—and they went back home and I had to find me a room. Well another friend of mine was still here and he stayed with Two-Gun Pete. He told me I could get a room over there in Pete's place. Pete had a tavern with rooms for rent upstairs. So he took me over there and I met Two-Gun and I got a room there. Then the very next week that same buddy and Pete got into it; but you don't really get into it with Pete—you just talk nice and get on away from there [*laughs*]. So when my buddy left, Pete asked me if *I* was leaving. I didn't have nowhere to go—and it was a nice room, I had me a little TV up there and nobody bothered me. You didn't have to worry about *nobody* bothering you because nobody came up there. After my buddy left, there wasn't anyone there except me and Pete. Pete—he'd be drunk everyday—everybody's scared, too scared to be around there. Pete's place was right there by the lake—Thirty-Ninth and Lake Park. Some people be going to the lake and the guy stop by to get a beer with his wife, and Pete—by him being drunk and mean, he might call your wife a bitch and then say, "Now tell your husband to defend you!" See, Pete's ready to shoot him—and the guy's scared to death. Both the husband and wife are scared to death. Then Pete might go in the backroom and get something and they'd both jump up and run out of there [*laughs*]. The truth is, I didn't have nowhere else to go, so whatever he said to me, I said, "You-are-right!" If he cussed me out I said, "You-are-right!"—nothing but "You-are-right!" I'd come downstairs and I'd go into the bar and he'd say "Now, you know you ain't got no money—whatcha doin' in here?" And I would say "You-are-right!"—and

I left back out. Maybe the next week I'd go in there two or three times and then he got to like me. "Locke, you're all right!" Well, yeah! And he got crazy about me then. So I wasn't goin' nowhere—because I didn't have nowhere to go. . . . I was paying $15 a week—well that was a lot of money then. Anyway, he got to like me and I was his buddy then. If I didn't have my rent money he'd say "Don't worry about it, Locke! You know you ain't got to worry about it." "Yeah—but I got to pay you." [*Laughs.*] "Naw, don't worry 'bout it!" Then, he had me behind the bar—and he'd be over there half-drunk and asleep and he put a pistol down there—I wasn't gonna mess around with that pistol—I don't care what happened! He'd be over there asleep and I'd have to watch over him while he slept and make sure nobody came in there and messed with him. And he'd cook everyday—about eleven or twelve o'clock he'd call "Locke!—C'mon down!" And I'd get up and go down there and he'd done cooked—greens and beans and meat. He cooked! And he had a Thunderbird convertible and he took me with him everywhere he went. He'd go downtown to pay his bills, down to the bank there before you get to Woodlawn before you get to Sixty-Third Street—he'd go to the bank and do his banking, you know? Then we'd go downtown, go down and eat and stuff, all in that convertible. He treated me nice—I was his righthand man. He could trust me. "Locke, I like you. You're all right!" We got along good, he liked me and he wouldn't let nobody mess with me. I was playing with Howling Wolf, and Wolf came over and parked his truck there, came in and said he was looking for Abb Locke. Pete pulled his gun and put it up against Wolf's neck and started shouting "What do you want with Abb Locke? What do you want with Abb Locke?" And I walked in and yelled "Wash!"—I didn't call him Pete—I called him Wash. His real name was Sylvester Washington, and I called him "Wash" for short. I said, "Wash, he came to pick me up. That's Howling Wolf!" And Pete's saying, "Oh, oh, oh" with the gun under Wolf's neck [*laughs*]! He wasn't going to let anybody mess with me—"Nobody messes with Abb Locke!" And when we got in the truck Wolf says, "I ain't never goin' back in that God-damned joint anymore! You be outside when I come by here!" [*Laughs.*]

People call him Two-Gun Pete to his face?

NO! You didn't do that—not to his face. I knew him about three years and I never heard anybody call him that. In fact, I don't remember anybody calling him Pete. I always called him "Wash."

How many people did he kill?

I've heard everything from seven to seventeen but I think it was actually eleven. Now, you know, he didn't like policemen. Yeah, he was a policeman—but he didn't like policemen. A policeman came in there and got smart with him.

A white policeman came in and got smart with him in his own joint—and Pete whupped him and dragged him outside, leaned him up against the wall bleeding, right by the door. Pete was kind of rough—you know? He was a brute. He could kill you with his bare hands. I got scared and I said, "I better get out of here. Somebody's gonna blow this place up." He looked a lot like Red Foxx, you know, Fred Sanford? Picture Fred Sanford, only a couple inches taller, looked just like him. And Pete kind of walked like that, too—drawers with suspenders and no shirt and both guns on his waist. When he was a policeman, he'd walk down the street and there'd be a lot of thugs on the corner. And he'd tell them all "I want you all off this corner"—he'd say it real low. And when he came back, if they were still on that corner, that gun would come out—and that stick—and he's whupping heads with that gun on 'em. I mean whupping heads! [*Laughs.*] His daughter was on dope. Somebody put her on dope and she came in there crying, and he'd say "Look at this bitch!" and he'd be mad. She came by there crying a lot of times, but he never did find out who put her on dope. And Pete's wife left him for the coal man. Yeah, she was scared and she just wanted to get out of there—and she left with the coal man. [*Laughs.*] Pete had a girlfriend, a lady about forty years old. Pete wanted to be a big lover, and they'd go upstairs. He'd come down and say "Locke, I been up there two hours on that woman!" He'd go back in the bar somewhere and his girlfriend would say "Two hours shit! He's been up there asleep!" [*Laughs.*] My buddy came up from Memphis. His name was George Coleman. You can hear him blow the alto solo on B. B. King's record "Woke Up This Morning." And George didn't have anywhere to stay, so I got him a room at Pete's place. Anyway, somehow or other he and Pete got into it, arguing, and Pete was gonna kill him. My room was up on the second floor and I told my buddy, "Stand beneath that window. I'm gonna throw your clothes out that window. You get them clothes and get away from here or that man's gonna kill you! You got no business arguing with that man" [*laughs*]. And he got away from there. He's living in New York city today.

When you hung out with Pete, were you at all concerned about possibly being in the line of fire?

Well, I thought about it—but I didn't think about it too long because, really, nobody wanted to mess with Pete. But yeah, it might have been dangerous—like you say, in the line of fire [*laughs*]! He had a buddy who was a policeman from St. Louis. He came and stayed with Pete for about a week on vacation—and he had *his* two guns on behind the bar. Both of them had their guns on—both had one in the front and the other gun in back, you know, big holsters all around.

Having known Pete for some time, did you have any idea what made him so mean-spirited?

Something was wrong with him. I think he was worried about all those people he killed, that's why he kept those pistols. He was afraid family or friends of the people he had killed would try to retaliate—take revenge—and he wanted to be ready. So he kept the one gun in the front pocket and one in the back—just to be ready—even when he went to bed at night and got out of his pants, he laid those pants out right by the bed so he'd be ready. All that fear built up. He wouldn't let anybody know, but I think deep down inside he was afraid.

What finally convinced you to move from there?

I was on the road with the Wolf and we come in from Florida. When you came into Pete's place, one door—you'd go in the bar; and the next door, located right next to it there—you'd go upstairs. When I came in, I hollered at him, I yelled, "Wash!" He was walking on upstairs and I thought he heard me so I opened that same door going upstairs behind him. When I opened that door behind him, he turned and put that gun dead on me. He said "Locke! You know better—you know to say something!" I said "I hollered at you—I thought you heard me." But he didn't hear me. That shook me up. I had to get out of there. I left the next day . . .

Abb Locke. Photo courtesy The O'Neal Collection.

After you moved out did you ever come back to visit?

I never went back in there but I'd drive by there on my way somewhere else and see him sitting out there. I'd stop and wave at him—and he'd wave back. I might stop and holler at him "How you doing!" He'd always say, "Locke, You're all right! I wish I could be like you!" After I left, the little girl he was going with, he used to whup her every day. I don't know why—but he used to whup her every day. And one last day he whupped her, and she stabbed him—and he died . . .

Brewer Phillips on **Memphis Minnie**

One of the real delights of postwar blues is the second-line guitar. The electric bass wasn't available until around 1958. Before that time, many bands would feature two guitars—one playing the lead, the other playing a complementary second part, usually consisting of rhythmic "lumps," combined with chording and appropriate finger-picking lines. It was a genuine skill onto itself, a real rarity, and there were a limited number of players on the Chicago blues scene accomplished in this role—Jimmy Rogers, Johnny Young, Lee Jackson, and Brewer Phillips. Brewer worked with Hound Dog Taylor, playing second-line guitar to Taylor's slide guitar leads. I saw a lot of Hound Dog and, therefore, a lot of Brewer. Brewer was an accomplished second-line guitar in a very rough-and-tumble fashion, a way that was in keeping with his overall image as a person. Brewer cut sort of a menacing figure in a down-home way. He wasn't evil, slick, and calculating; his threat was a sort of out-of-control personality freshly emerged from the back alleys. He had very few teeth left, and the couple that remained reminded me of pumpkin seeds inserted in available vacancies up front. He had kinky black hair styled in a comb-over that resembled a black sock draped from one side of his head over to the other, with a handful of coins bulging in the toe. Since I mostly saw him on the bandstand, he was always drunk, loud, and profane—usually spouting off

Brewer Phillips. Photo courtesy James Fraher.

about his sexual intentions or about the money he had recently begun to make now that their band was playing out on the road. I worked in Magic Slim's band playing drums—and Slim and Hound Dog were friends. Whenever Hound Dog and Brewer fell out with some bandstand dispute, Hound Dog would ask Magic Slim to play second guitar in Brewer's place—which Slim did reasonably well. Also, Slim and his band had taken over the Sunday matinee gig at Florence's, long hosted by Hound Dog and band, so when Taylor and the guys were back in town, they would visit on Sunday afternoons. Also, during my early days on the blues scene I was sort of a nighttime running buddy with Hound Dog for a while. Apparently, Hound Dog had such a tragic childhood that even as a sixty-year-old man he was still scared of the dark and wouldn't go to sleep until the sun rose. So he spent weeknights in Chicago visiting the clubs that supported live music, and I spent a series of Tuesday nights out on the town with him. I knew Hound Dog well but only saw Phillip on the bandstand, and what I saw convinced me to keep my distance—until an incident about two years later. During my time with Magic Slim on the Southside, I was the victim of a shooting. I was shot pointblank with a .38 pistol, just barely survived and spent a good deal of time in the hospital recovering—a week in intensive care and another three weeks as a recovering patient. During that time I was visited at the hospital by Hound Dog, which surprised me, but we were friends—and by Brewer Phillips, which amazed me. They showed up together—and it wasn't just the visit that surprised me, it was an entirely different Phillips than I had previously seen. He was quiet, sober, and benign—I was touched. And while Hound Dog was busy trying to pick up my mother in my hospital room, I made sure I thanked Phillips for coming by, and from that point on we were friends. During one of our conversations Phillips mentioned that as a young man he spent a good deal of time in Memphis under the musical tutelage of Memphis Minnie—and that he regarded Minnie as a mother figure. It sounded like an interesting story to me, and we made arrangements to do an interview for the radio program. For some peculiar reason, which I can't remember at this late date, I arranged to record this interview at Bob Koester's Riverside Studio.

■ ■ ■

What started me really, my mother would sing spirituals when we come out of the cotton field. I was too young to work at that time—I was the baby of the family. I'd get wood and water for her so she could make lunch for the rest of the family. She would sing and I'd play. That was back in '39. My brothers had a guitar, but when they went off to the service, they took it with them—so I didn't have a guitar. I had an acoustic guitar—it didn't belong to me—it belonged to a friend girl of mine. I was a little halfway slide man. We had a blues guy there in my hometown—Greenwood, Mississippi—named Bobby Hines, and he was working out of Bunker Hill Music there. During that time when I'd go to my old uncle's house—he had one of those phonographs—we'd get those 78 records—Sonny Boy and things. I heard them once and—the blues—you're born with them.

Did you hear any Memphis Minnie records?

No—I didn't have sense enough to realize I'd heard her records—when I did realize, I think it was sometime in '46. Then in '49 I heard "Kissin' in the Dark"—"Honey, that's my birthmark." And it took from 1949 until 1956 before I met her.

When I first met her, Memphis Minnie was in a little place right out of Memphis they call Walls, Mississippi—out on 51 Highway. She was living there with a cousin about eleven or twelve miles south of Memphis. There was a night club out there and she was with some people—they told me that was Memphis Minnie. So—I got a chance to meet her. Then I guess she got some money and she moved back to Memphis—on Third Avenue.

So this guy that I was dealing with, James Walker, he got me a job at Memphis Cotton Sales—I was a truck driver: he was a truck driver, and he got me a job on the haul with him. So on Sunday, he knew how to get in touch with Minnie, so we went over to her house. And I had met her already. We picked her up and took her back to his house—her and her husband. We'd have everybody over and give them a few bucks—it was something like a project. All the people would come around and hear her and Son Joe play at James Walker's house on Sunday. This was in 1956, so I was about twenty-five years old.

When I did meet her, she was a good woman—she was kind but she was in bad shape. So I was working—driving a truck for Memphis Cotton Sales—a buck an hour. In the evening when I got off of work, I'd go by her house. I'd bring food for her and her husband—and I'd stay there until she put me out. But she would teach me how to play—she'd thump me on the head and teach me. She would teach me time—she was like a mother to me.

When you say she was in bad shape—do you mean financially?

Yeah—she was in bad shape finance-wise—she didn't have anything! And she was living on the welfare at that time. I didn't know anything about welfare—they was getting money from the government; I used to get her guitar out of the pawn shop—it was her guitar—she and her husband, Little Son Joe. I'd get paid and after they took out income tax and Social Security and everything, I'd have a few bucks left and get her guitar out of the pawnin' shop—on the weekend.

What make of guitar was she playing at this time?

It was a Gibson—an old make of Gibson—a good guitar at the time. On the old make they didn't have the cut in the neck—it was just a plain neck. Made like an acoustic but it was a good model—it was a hollow box—and it was a Gibson. The next one she bought had the cut in it.

I don't understand what you mean when you say it had the cut in it.

With the old box the fret board stopped right at the top of the guitar box— all right, but when they made the one where you could get down to a low E, then it had the cut in the box. The fret board extended into the body of the guitar—the cut in the neck. That was an expensive guitar at that time—very expensive—especially if it was made by Les Paul Gibson. And she could get more money for that at the pawnin' shop. If you could get $15 or $20 you knew it was a three-hundred-dollar guitar—and no pick-up on the guitar—just acoustic. She was a better guitar player on the acoustic than she was on an electric.

You saw her play on an electric?

Yeah—oh, yeah! Around '59 or '60—the last meeting I had with her—I met her in Syracuse—and she was old and failing, she had to sit down—well mostly she sat down all the time when she played—but to see her do a good show—an amplified show, at the Royal Theater there on Beale Street in Memphis—that's the first time I seen her stand up and play. And do you know how much money she was making? Two bucks. I was backstage with her—A. C. Reed, WDIA there in Memphis, Rufus Thomas—man—it's been so long—I forget.

What did she show you on guitar?

She showed me a D chord—and a C chord. And that was up at the end of the neck—not in the middle of the neck like B. B. use—she showed me how to use those chords up there—I can play a lot of Memphis Minnie but I never had nobody to work like she did. "Come On and Be My Chauffeur" and "I'm Gonna Buy Me an Airplane." Every evening when I'd get off work, I'd go straight to her house—and stay there until she got tired of me and she'd put me out [*laughs*]. And I didn't have far to walk. She was living on Third Avenue there in Memphis—right down from Bobby's mother's restaurant.

Most of the time—she mostly stayed to herself. Now I know that—we were out 41 Highway, almost to Georgia—a school had booked a gig—with Rufus Thomas. James Walker, me, Memphis Minnie, and her husband—and Roosevelt Sykes! We drove out there—and they had to fight the mens away from her—"This is Memphis Minnie!" And she was signing autographs and things at the time, you know—for the young kids—and the old mens were standing back admiring her, you know? And Son Joe [*laughs*]—We always called him Son Lemon because he was always begging—she was the one who gave him that name! [*Laughs.*] You call him Lemon cause he could be squeezed—he'd do anything for a drink [*laughs*]. I just wondered how in the hell he could hold on to her—a beautiful woman like she was—with all those men pulling at her. And as far as I know, she was very faithful to him—she loved him. It's amazing.

Was Son Joe in bad health at that point?

No, he wasn't—he just was a little older than she was—and couldn't get around as well as she could. Sometimes—if she got out of the chair—she could kick her legs for a few minutes! We had one of those guys there that had an old wire recorder—worked off of wire. Sometimes on Sunday we'd get him and we'd all get together. Remember that "One Black Rat—someday I'll find your tail." You ought to hear them work it in person—Boy!—some of the most beautiful music I ever heard. And he could work with her. But I didn't want to follow her—I wanted to play like her and let him follow me! [*Laughs.*] That's why she was interested in showing me.

When they played together—was there a lot of talk between them as they played?

A lot of times! He'd be saying "Yeah, child—Yeah, honey!" And we'd be listening to how he followed her—and how she'd be playing the guitar—and talking! And when she said "Yeeaahh"—her voice had a tremble in it at all times. A bunch of us would be dancing and having an outdoor fest. On a Sunday evening—just a fish-fry out in the country—no electricity—just mules and wagons and the people would come out and have a fish-fry—but it was more like a bug-fry. [*Laughs.*] You got the pot setting outdoors—firewood around it—the bugs would come to the light of the fire—and wind up in the pot along with the fish! [*Laughs.*] And Memphis Minnie was right down that road—they'd go out in the country. You know, Minnie—for a woman singing the blues—I think she was the best!

When you saw her, had she lived in Chicago?

She had lived in Chicago about three years—before she went back to Memphis.

I read that when she was a kid, she ran away with the circus. Did she ever talk about that?

I remember that she told me she was in a circus at some point—and she played a showgirl. I've heard her say that, and she said they cut her out because they wouldn't allow her to take her husband with her—and she never did do anything without her husband.

She told me that, but I never did pay any attention—she was drinking wine at the time. You could buy her a fifth of Wild Irish Rose and she and Son Joe would come to your house and play just like they were in the studio. She'd sit and talk when she used to cook those beans—have them ready for me when I got off work in the evening. We would sit and talk—but I was interested in the guitar. At that time she was getting sort of up in age—back in the late '50s and the early '60s—but she still had the spirit. At the time she had the meningitis—I think that was in '60 or '61. She was at John Gaston Hospital; she had meningitis—yellow fever—and the doctors gave up on her. There wasn't any cure for her. Well, her son went and got her a quart of corn whiskey—and that saved her! She stayed in the hospital on charity—and you know how it was in the South—she got treatment *sometime*—and during that time she went into a coma. They pushed her into a backroom there—to die. And they covered her with a sheet. But the next morning that whiskey had sweated the fever out of her—the sheet was yellow and everything—but she survived. That whiskey cured her! [*Laughs.*]

She was mostly Creole—not like I am [*laughs*]—and she was just as *country*! She'd have on different stockings and flour all over her shoes and her hands and things. She was just real country. She didn't wear any perfume—a little Mum deodorant—that was it! No lipstick—no powder—no perfume. She had soft hair—black! She could fix it any way she wanted, and Boy—she used to look good! She'd just use lard and water: she'd wash it with bar soap—known as P&G—rinse it with spring water and then put hog lard on it.

She showed me some pictures when she was twenty-one and twenty-two years old—you'd jump out of an airplane for her, man!

Did Minnie chew tobacco?

Yeah!! She didn't only chew tobacco—she dipped snuff! Her brand of snuff was Copenhagen. Now her tobacco was Brown Mule. She lived on the ground level but people lived beneath her in the basement—so you would call it the second floor. When she sent me to the store for that fifth of Wild Irish Rose, she'd say "Phillip—bring me a Brown Mule." "I can't get him up the stairs Minnie!" [*Laughs.*] She'd chew the tobacco and dip the snuff—and when she was at home she'd get a little twig, get the ends off and dip it down in the bottle and then put it in her jaw. And that chewing tobacco—she'd put that in her jaw, and a lot of times she had that tobacco in her jaw while she was singing—and she used to spit tobacco while she was on stage into a cup—or what-so-ever! [*Laughs.*] You'd see her reach down and (pretends to spit into a cup) set it back down—a lot of times! She never did smoke that I knew. She used to drink that Wild Irish Rose—and corn whiskey—as much as she could get. Bourbon and Canadian whiskey? We didn't know anything about it. But that homebrew—you make it out of potatoes and yeast cake—like that—and wine!

Did she ever wear glasses?

Yeah—after that sickness her eyesight wasn't as good and she started wearing glasses. But she never could read—maybe comic books—she could look at those—but to just sit down and read a book—no, she couldn't.

When black folks of that era needed glasses, did they go to the eye doctor?

No—they just went to the dimestore. They'd try a pair and if they couldn't see good through those, they'd lay those down and try another pair. [*Laughs.*] They had them all in a drawer!

Did Minnie know how to drive?

No.

How about Son Joe?

Yeah.

Did they ever own a car—or talk about a car they had owned—or discuss buying a car?

No—never! You had to go pick them up and take them. Now Joe Hill Louis—when they played with him, if he booked a gig somewhere, out in Alabama or Georgia—you know, not too far a drive from Memphis—he would pick them up. And a lot of times I would take her.

Did she have electricity?

At that time—when she was in the city—yeah.

Did she have a radio or a TV?

A radio—but no television. Not even a record player. She had a little old radio there—and it worked off a battery. She had the battery sitting outside of the window—but she did have electricity.

What would she listen to?

She would listen to something like M Squad—you know, Lee Marvin. She'd listen to WDIA—Rufus Thomas—and we had another station WLOK—Hunky Dorey. And he played mostly blues—maybe you've heard of WLOK—now maybe sometime she'd listen to that once in a while.

Did she have any of her records around the house?

The only record that I knew she had a copy of [was] "Be My Chauffeur." That was an old 78 and that was scratched up so bad—and she didn't have anything to play it on in the first place. Mostly, if you wanted anything by Memphis Minnie, you had to go to the record store. We bought her records there in Memphis—sometimes she'd listen to them and sometimes she wouldn't. Sometimes she'd tell you who all was there on the record and who was doing what—why this one made a mistake here and what he should have done—and then she'd say "Well I should have got in there—but I was too late." She always would tell you about her mistakes.

Did Minnie ever go to church?
In all the time I knew her I think she went to church once—or twice.

Was that in Memphis?
No—that was in Arkansas. We used to go to WDIA on Sunday morning—and she and her husband rode to Hughes, Arkansas. We met a group that was broadcasting there on WDIA on Sunday mornings. James Walker and I went there that Sunday morning—and they were singing in a church that Sunday evening out around Hughes, Arkansas. So Memphis Minnie and James Walker's wife and Son Joe and I rode over there that Sunday night. That's the only time I could say that she ever walked inside a church. We went inside to hear the jubilee quartet—just to hear the boys sing.

So she never sang church songs?
No—never.

Did she ever go fishing?
She never went fishing that I know—but I know she liked them. I know she'd clean whatever I'd catch. If I went fishing, she would clean them and she would cook them—and we would eat them!

During my time with Memphis Minnie she didn't have *anything*. During my time with Roosevelt Sykes *he* didn't have anything. All the good times he'd had—they all got away from him. Roosevelt Sykes—now he and Memphis Minnie were buddy-buddies. I met him in Memphis—that's when I started playing with him was in Memphis—but I met him in Mississippi! After I ran across him there in Memphis—living in a kitchenette—and Minnie was living in the same kind of place, but at least she had a bathroom. She and Roosevelt Sykes used to sit and talk about what good times they *used* to have—and how they were going to get their good times back—sure they did. She and Roosevelt Sykes were the main ones who talked about how much they used to get for a gig and how many gigs they had and how they couldn't get around to all the gigs, how much money they used to make—and then "Wham!"—it all fell off!

Why do you think that happened? Why did it all go away?
Well, if I have to bring this in—maybe at the time they didn't know anything about agents, and if you got in a dispute with an agent or fell out with

an agent—and he'd drop you "Snap!"—just like that. No more—you were just through.

Do you think her style of blues went out of style?

No—because everybody liked it. Everybody tried to play it. And the reason it wasn't as famous as it should have been is that nobody ever learned it. She had a different style of guitar from everybody. Do you hear anybody imitate Memphis Minnie? No way—because nobody played the way she did!

Did she ever talk about Big Bill Broonzy?

Oh yeah! She'd always mention him and said he was a sneak and that he was a crook. He wanted all the money—you never could pay him. She'd always tell me, "Don't be like him." I don't want to say anything bad about him—but he wasn't like Robert Jr. or Sunnyland Slim or Joe Hill Louis or Roosevelt Sykes. He was just a different guy. I've heard her say that over and over again—about Big Bill Broonzy. And this other guy John Lee Williamson—he came up back in the '30s—and Memphis Minnie, she was in her prime back then and she used to tell me about what a nice guy he was. They never did record together but they were on a lot of tours together. And we had this girl, Bonnie Raitt, that Dick Waterman had—she recorded a lot of tunes by Minnie in the late '60s and early '70s, and she asked me how to get in touch with Minnie. She had royalties that she wanted to pass on to Minnie and she asked if I knew how to get in touch with Minnie. But after I left Memphis I wasn't ever in touch with her anymore—but the last three or four years that I was there she wasn't getting any bookings at all—she was just playing little clubs every so often. She used to tell me—and sometimes I thought she was telling me the wrong things—"Child, I been all over the world—New York, Chicago, California." And I'd say, "Aw—you ain't been nowhere!" [*Laughs.*] And she'd say, "You just try to get there—Do like I tell you and you might make it."

Louise "Mattie" **Johnson**
(with her sister, Dorothy)

Every other Friday was payday. I would cash my paycheck and set off on my well-worn route of the Chicago record stores. First stop was Jazz Record Mart, which was still located on Grand Avenue at the time. As I walked in, owner Bob Koester was at the cash register cashing out a customer, which was unusual. As I passed by, Bob called out to me: "Hey Cush—here's somebody you ought to meet." His customer was a well-dressed, middle-aged black woman. "The two of you ought to get together—this woman has a story I know you'll find interesting." And, turning his attention to his customer, he said, "This is Steve Cushing. He does an overnight blues radio program here in Chicago called *Blues Before Sunrise*. His program is one of the few shows that plays blues from the twenties and thirties. Cush, this is Louise Johnson; her mother was Flossie Franklin, who helped Leroy Carr write some of his tunes. In fact, she helped him write a couple of his biggest hits—if I'm not mistaken?" "That's true. You mentioned the song "Blues Before Sunrise," well my mother helped Leroy Carr write the lyrics for that very tune." Bob suggested

Louise Mattie Franklin (Johnson). Photo courtesy Lester Johnson Family Archive.

that we should get together to do an interview, and she gave me a note with her name and phone number. Louise lived in Indianapolis, where she worked as an administrator in the Indianapolis public school system. I believe I called that following Monday and made plans to drive down and do the interview on Friday of that week. Indianapolis is a four-hour drive from Chicago, and I'll never forget the trip. Over a foot of snow fell that morning into mid-afternoon, and the state police actually shut down Interstate 65 for an hour to give the snow plows a chance to go through and clear the highway. I arrived at Louise's house about four in the afternoon, where both she and her sister, Dorothy, were waiting to do the interview. They gave me a quick tour of the house, including a table stacked with vintage blues 78s—mostly Leroy Carr Vocalions but with a few Bumble Bee Slim records mixed in. I'd never seen so many blues 78s in one place before, and it made me envious. We settled in the front room, and I set up a high-quality cassette deck with a condenser microphone. I think I was there the better part of three hours altogether while they relived the days when Leroy Carr, Roosevelt Sykes, and other noted bluesmen came to their house.

This interview was recorded January 19, 1987. Louise "Mattie" Johnson died on Mother's Day, May 13, 2000. Dorothy Shockley died 1993. Theirs was a stop-over house/boardinghouse 1930s–1950s for blues and jazz. Pete Franklin died in the 1970s. Pete recorded at the University of Wisconsin at Madison, 1962–1968–1974.

■ ■ ■

Louise: Our parents were born in Tennessee. My father was born in Gallatin, Tennessee—he was one of a family of seven, and his father (in other words, our grandfather) was a Baptist minister, the Reverend Thomas Franklin. My mother was born in Nashville, Tennessee, and her mother was an evangelist of Apostolic faith. Somehow or another both families ended up in Indianapolis, my parents met—and they married—and this is where they brought their family up. All of us grew up in Indianapolis—and when I say all of us, I mean my brother Sylvester, my brother Pete—his real name was Edward Lamont Franklin—my sister Dorothy, and I. We all were born in Indianapolis, and this basically is where we lived, except for military stints done by both of my brothers: Guitar Pete was enlisted and in World War II—he was stationed in Japan and then he re-enlisted, and again I think he was in the Pacific. My brother was in the navy and stationed in the Pacific. Our mother was just a housewife and a mother—she was that old-fashioned type who believed if you had kids you were supposed to stay home and bring them up—and that's just exactly what she did. But she loved music. Both my parents loved music—my father played piano by ear. My mother would say, "I can bang out . . ." and she would bang out a few little tunes—mostly blues, by ear—and her brother, Charles Woods, could play some blues on a harmonica and almost make you cry. So both families—for whatever reason—just seemed to have that love for music.

So there was no conflict between their religious backgrounds and their involvement in blues?

Louise: I don't think it mattered—for one thing, both of my parents had lived a life of enough restrictions to the point that they were glad to be liberated from the religious backgrounds that they'd had. I can tell you one little anecdote about my father: now, he knew very well that he wasn't supposed to be around a tavern, but he was a little boy and filled with curiosity about the sounds coming out of the tavern [*laughs*]. He knew very well that his father would have got on him good, but there was an older lady in the neighborhood that used to say "Come here, Jul"—that was for Julius. "I'll give you a penny to go down to the tavern and get me a bucket of beer." They sold it by the bucket. My father would always say that when he went down there and knocked on the side door, a man would say, "Whadyawant boy?" He'd tell him he wanted a bucket of beer for Mrs. Who-ever-she-was. But he said he was trying to see everything he could when he got there because he heard ragtime and blues coming out of the tavern—and he said he used to hear the feet shuffling in the sawdust on the tavern floor, and he was just filled with curiosity about that.

So blues was no stranger in your house?

Louise: Oh, are you kidding—a stranger? We woke up by blues—we had blues all day long—and when we went to bed, we heard blues, and it lasted as long as whoever was playing them—usually my mother and the record player. Unless she had people over, like Leroy Carr and Scrapper Blackwell, Peetie Wheatstraw, the Devil's Son-in-Law, whoever—Jesse Elry. One morning in this very house I woke up and heard some *terrific* piano playing, and it was Roosevelt Sykes—early in the morning. I don't know how he got here or when he arrived. I was asleep, and I heard this piano thundering; I came downstairs and took a peek—and there was Roosevelt Sykes. We had his records, you know, and they were played and I liked his style of playing that piano because he played with much gusto and enthusiasm—at least he was that morning when I awakened. I liked his music, so when I heard that piano, I said, "My goodness—who is that?" I came downstairs, and my mother had a baby grand piano—and there he sat! And she was beaming with joy and happiness because blues was what she liked.

How did the connection with Leroy Carr come about?

Louise: I was small—and I really don't know how it happened, but I think he came to our house after "How Long Blues"—was that 1928? She met him not too long after that. He was at our house every day when he was not on the road or in Chicago recording. Interestingly enough, the Melrose brothers would try to locate Leroy, and they would always come to our house. I remember thinking whether Melrose was one name or two—Mel Rose. But we'd just call him Mr. Melrose. He'd come sometimes when he wanted to locate Leroy and talk about recording sessions, and I wish I could find that promotional picture of Leroy. The Yazoo label has a reproduction of that picture on their flyer—that's the same one I had in the little book my mother used to write poetry. But they took that picture in our home. I'm trying to remember where we lived at that time—Eudell or Twenty-Fifth Street. But at the time there was a red velvet stool—a wrought-iron bench is what it really was—and that promotional picture was taken in our home. They would always be seated in the kitchen—and mama had a notebook. He would play melodies, and he had the words for them sometimes; other times she would listen and say, "How about this Leroy? This might be better." And she'd have a line that she would contribute. Or sometimes she would say, "Leroy—I was thinking while you were gone—what can you do with this?" And she'd read off the words to some blues. He'd say, "Yeah, I think that'll work." And that's the way they worked it. Now, please don't think I'm trying to say that my mother wrote all the words—the lyrics—she did not. But I know she collaborated with him—an example is "Blues Before Sunrise."

Flossie Franklin. Photo courtesy Lester Johnson Family Archive.

Do you know any other titles she contributed?

Louise: Well—I said this—and the man, who was a deejay said, "Oh, come on now!" My mother helped to write the words to "In the Evening When the Sun

Goes Down." And he acted so ridiculous about it that I thought, "Well—maybe I'm wrong." But I thought she did. I guess this man thought I didn't know—or maybe he thought I was just lying, making it up! He was the program director of a local radio station—I will not call his name, however. [*Laughs.*]

What were the big ones for Leroy?

Dorothy: "Prison Bound."

Louise: And the one that put him over—"How Long"—right!

Dorothy: Didn't he have a tune called "Shady Lane"?

Louise: Now, mama helped with that—yeah, part of that was hers.

How about "Low Down Dog" and "Sloppy Drunk"?

Louise: She didn't have anything to do with those. She never sought any recognition at all. She was just thrilled to hear the kind of music she liked. She was a creative person.

So she never received composer's credit on any of his tunes?

Louise: Not to my knowledge—we never thought to look. If it had been, it would have been Flossie Franklin.

Dorothy Franklin. Photo courtesy Lester Johnson Family Archive.

Dorothy: A lot of people around here called him "Aggravatin' Papa"—and when we were little, we'd say "Mama—here comes Mr. Aggravatin'!" [*Laughs.*]

Louise: It's funny but that aggravatin' was from a blues song he put out before we met him called "Aggravatin' Papa." I don't know how it got started—who started calling him Aggravatin'—but we were taught to call adults mister, so it became MISTER Aggravatin'! I don't think we even knew what the word aggravating meant! [*Laughs.*]

Did he pay much attention to you kids?

Louise: I think his mind was on those blues and music. But he may have.

Dorothy: I think we were more interested in listening to him and what he was playing. We'd stand around the corner—or wander in and out—but no, he really didn't pay any attention.

So he wasn't the type to have fun with kids or tease them?

Louise: No—I thought he was a gentle type of man but I think his main interest in life was the music that he produced—and if you notice, in his style of playing he was not one of those singers who sang with gusto like some of the country blues singers; he has a more urban, mellow, smooth style of playing and singing. He was very appealing to a lot of people but as far as we were concerned, we were mostly in the background, observing and noticing. He had a daughter I met just once named Maureen Carr. She was older than I was—I would say I was around twelve and she may have been sixteen. Sixteen-year-olds don't have too much in common with twelve-year-olds. To my knowledge that was the only offspring I ever heard he had.

What about Scrapper Blackwell—what was he like?

Louise: Now, I can say less about Mr. Scrapper Blackwell. He was big to us—I would say he was a big, raw-boned, light-skinned fellow. Leroy Carr was slender and brown-skinned with a long face—and soft spoken.

Did you see a lot of drinking going on?

Edward Lamont "Guitar Pete" Franklin. Photo courtesy Lester Johnson Family Archive.

Louise: Well—our parents didn't drink—if there was a lot of drinking going on, it must have gone on somewhere else before they got to our house. Our parents didn't swear or curse—they didn't drink; my father would smoke a cigar occasionally—when he could afford one—or his old pipe. They didn't smoke or curse or drink. Now I think their background—having parents who were in the ministry had an influence—they would not allow anybody to curse in front of us. When I was young, I can remember that anytime anybody would curse in our home, our parents—both of them—would say "I'm sorry, but you can't curse in here—you have to respect our children." They always said that. Now we know that Leroy drank, but I never saw him drunk—never. I can tell you how I knew the difference. When he died—which I believe was in 1935—my mother was shocked. She didn't know what nephritis was, but he died of nephritis—an inflammation of the kidneys caused by drinking. He died of nephritis, yet we never saw him drinking. He must have done his drinking before he got to our house. I believe that he died in a hospital, and I believe that he's buried in Floral Park Cemetery here in Indianapolis.

Did you lose track of Scrapper after Leroy's death?

Louise: More or less. They were friends of our parents—and we were children.

Dorothy: If anybody saw him after that, it would have been our brother Pete (Guitar Pete Franklin), but he didn't stay in close contact with him.

Louise: They both played guitar and played blues, but there was a huge age difference there. Scrapper was our parents' age.

Did Scrapper have any hand in teaching your brother guitar?

Louise: Not to my knowledge—Pete was already playing.

Dorothy: Pete learned to play mostly on his own. I don't know anybody that taught him. He started playing when he was very young.

Franklin family (left to right, front): Dorothy, Edward (Pete), Flossie, Mattie; (back) Unknown, Sylvester. Photo courtesy Lester Johnson Family Archive.

Is the house where you used to live—where much of the action took place—still standing?

Louise: Well—yes and no. You see, one house has been demolished for an expressway—down there where there's an underpass; another house may yet be standing at Twenty-Fifth and Harding, and another house on Eudell—one street over—is still standing: 642 Eudell.

Those are the only places we lived where Leroy Carr would have visited.

Were there any other musicians who came by your house?

Dorothy: Champion Jack Dupree. He came often.

Louise: Oh yeah—very often. And tell it all—you know what we did. Oh, I hope Champion Jack Dupree never hears this. We were young and ignorant, and we didn't know about the Louisiana style of blues. We were accustomed to that smooth, creamy, urban sound of Leroy Carr and people like that. So when Jack Dupree played the piano—in our first exposure—we thought the man just had fists without any fingers! [*Laughs.*] We didn't know about the Louisiana style. But now we know what the Louisiana style sounds like. We hid in the back of another room and just chuckled and laughed—and we said, "This man surely cannot play a piano." And at that time he was riding high on his record "Cabbage Greens." That was a big hit—among blacks anyhow. Even teenagers liked "Cabbage Greens"—but that piano. We thought it was atrocious the way his fists just seemed to be hitting any old keys—just any old where! And we laughed at that man—and we still chuckle when we think about our first exposure to Champion Jack Dupree.

Dick LaPalm Talks about **Nat King Cole**

I met Dick LaPalm through veteran jazz host Dick Buckley. Buck and I worked together at public radio in Chicago for twenty-five years. The earliest of Buck's Chicago radio gigs was at WAAF, and he's been on the air somewhere on the Chicago radio dial ever since. LaPalm spent his entire career as a record-promotion man, at first working "in shop" for a series of record labels and then later ran his own promotion business, where he did promotion-for-hire by specific jazz record labels or by their jazz artists. He billed himself as the Jazz Lobbyist and worked a list of selected radio stations and radio hosts that specialized in jazz. Buck and LaPalm had shared a bachelor apartment in Chicago during the 1950s and had remained friends over the ensuing years. LaPalm didn't really handle much that I could play on my program, but we shared a fondness for Nat King Cole and his music. LaPalm would often tell me stories about Nat during our conversations and had actually broken into the business by working for Nat, promoting his records and as a part of his management team. I asked if he would tell me some of his Nat King Cole stories that I might play on the air, and we got together for the following interview, recorded March 3, 2005. Dick LaPalm died in October 2013.

Nat King Cole and Dick LaPalm shopping at Marshall Fields. Photo courtesy Dick LaPalm Archive.

■ ■ ■

Well, first of all, Steve, I think it's important to go on record by telling you that I'm really the self-appointed head of the Worldwide and Intergalactic Nat Cole Fan Club. It's a position I've held for over fifty years; and I have to confess that I'm intensely prejudicial and completely inflexible about it. I love Joe Williams and Tony Bennett, Ray Charles and Mel Tormé, but I've got a Nat Cole shrine in my home. The very first thing of his that I heard was a record called "I'm an Errand Boy for Rhythm." It completely turned me around. I was on Roosevelt Road when I heard it—coming out of a store as a matter of fact—and I just could not stop listening to it. I saw him for the first time in a place in Chicago called the Rag Doll, a club on Western Avenue near Devon, and I was determined that at some point I would meet the man and I would go to work for him; and that's exactly what I did. This would have been 1950, I guess. I was a student. I attended University of Illinois at Navy Pier, and I actually went to the Regal Theater in Chicago with a small Zenith radio under my arm, one of those shelf radios. I went in and said I was delivering the radio to King Cole and they showed me up to his dressing room. I pitched to him the fact that I was a big fan, how much I loved his music, and how I would like to go to disc jockeys all over the country—especially in Chicago, which was his home, and constantly get his records played on air. It was all part of my plan; a couple of days earlier I had lobbied some disc jockeys in Chicago and said I would deeply appreciate it if they would play a Nat Cole record and asked the time they would play the record on this particular day. So on that day, when I went to the dressing room and plugged in the radio, I just kept playing with the radio dial. I'd tune the radio to a particular station and say, "OK—in about ten minutes we should hear your record right here." And after the record played I'd tune to another station and it would play over there, then in another ten minutes we tuned to another station and it played there. That was the period, Steve, when the right hand side of the radio dial was what they called "the Race Stations," and he was getting airplay galore on those stations but very, very little—very little—on the "Pop" stations. So I prearranged to get his records played; I knew where on the dial and when it would play. I knew that so-and-so on WIND was going to be on the air and would play one of Nat's records at such-and-such a time. So I tuned to WIND and we heard the record, and I knew that a few minutes later, say, Marty Hogan would play one of Nat's records on WCFL, so we tuned over there and heard the record again. And I kept doing that. There was a guy named Jim Gray at WAIT—I don't even know if the station still exists—but I knew that he would be playing a couple of Nat King Cole records and so I tuned to the 820 spot of the radio dial—where we heard the records. And I just kept doing that! So I went into the guy's room, told him up front I had arranged to have disc jockeys play his record, where and when they would play it—and it actually happened. Well, that was kind of impressive. Nat, on the spot, called his manager in Los Angeles and said, "Listen I met this guy and this is what he can do. I think we should hire him on a temporary basis and see exactly what he can do." And that's how I started. I got the account. I was paid $20 a week, Steve—$20 a week! And Carlos, the manager, was so impressed with the job I was doing generating airplay, that he gave me a few other clients to do. He gave me Charlie Barnett, Nellie Lutcher, Mel Tormé and Peggy Lee—that was five—so I was getting a hundred bucks a week from the management company. And that's how I started my business. I went to cities like Detroit, Minneapolis, St. Louis, and Cleveland and lobbied disc jockeys to play Nat Cole's records. That's exactly what I did—I was a lobbyist for Nat Cole—and for other clients, but primarily for Nat Cole. The very first record I worked was "Mona Lisa." That record was released during the period when record companies determined which side was the "A" side and which was the "B" side. And they determined initially that the "A" side of the record was "The Greatest Inventor of Them All." That was the song we were working. Well, as it turned out, a disc jockey on KRNT in Des Moines Iowa started playing the flip side, which was "Mona Lisa." When we called he said, "Look, every time I play this I get a wonderful telephone response. Perhaps you guys should be working the flip side." If I remember correctly, this was May of 1950—just when I first started. So we just started playing the "Mona Lisa" side and it took off from there.

Were the records on 78 at this point?
Absolutely!

How did you get the records that you supplied to disc jockeys?
We got the records from the management office. They would call the local distributor in Chicago and say, "Listen, give this guy whatever number of records he wants." And I would take them around. Or in many cases we would give the folks at the Capital Record label a list of names and they would mail them from Hollywood. I would say, "OK, mail these records to so and so in Detroit and so and so in St. Louis and this guy in Minneapolis and this guy in Cleveland," and they'd do it. I would follow up with phone calls and in most cases with a road trip. I would go out on the road to make sure the jocks were getting the records—and playing the records. Gosh, Steve, there must have been at least twenty hit records, "Walking My Baby Back Home," "Nature Boy," "Somewhere along the Way," "Unforgettable." Let's not forget "A Blossom Fell," "If I May," "Night Lights," and on and on and on. During that period I was accused of being the first guy to start what they called an independent record

promotions—and I was doing it back in 1950. Now there are lots of other people that do it; but I started doing it back in 1950.

When you first went to work for Nat, did the King Cole Trio still exist?

No. They dropped the trio billing—I believe it was in 1953. He had the trio with him but the billing was "Nat King Cole—With the Trio." But it was a period that featured Nat as a single. He did have the trio with him; he always had the trio, but he made his appearances with a full orchestra behind him because there were arrangements, and the orchestra was there when he worked the Chez Paree and the Copacabana—or anywhere around the world, for that matter. But he still did material that he had recorded originally with the trio and always took time somewhere over the course of the performance to do something with the trio. He always went to the piano and would say, "It's time for a little piano." And he would go over and would play some with the trio only.

Who was in the trio when you worked for Nat?

It kept changing. After Oscar Moore left, Irving Ashby played guitar. When Irving Ashby left, John Collins came in. On bass, Wesley Prince was the original bass man, then Johnny Miller for many years, then Red Callender, then Charley Harris, then Joe Comfort. Nat always had a trio.

After performing for so many years in the trio format, was it Nat's wife, Marie, who urged him to step up front as a single?

No—I've heard the same story, Steve, but it is absolutely not true—not even close to true. Management made the decision. I happened to be in the club—the very first club when this man stood up and said, "Let me step away from the piano and stand up and sing." His management felt that as long as he sat behind the piano with a trio—and didn't stand up to sing—he was a cocktail lounge act; and there was no way he would get into the big time and be able to compete with the Sinatras and Comos. It was management who said, "Nat you've got to stand up and sing." His answer was "What will I do with my hands?" "Well, I don't know. Put them in your pocket." But no, his wife had nothing to do with that decision. It was strictly a management decision. And the very first place he did that was in a club out here called the Tiffanee. I happened to be out here at the time; and he got up and sang and it was fine. He was able to do it accompanied by guitarist Irving Ashby. The credit belongs to Carlos Castel and his management company—and his booking agency, who just felt he should get away from the piano and be a stand-up singer. What happened, Steve, particularly during the period when he had all these hit records, people didn't realize—just simply didn't realize what an absolutely marvelous pianist he was. When they heard him, they'd say, "Oh Gee, he can play too!" To old fans, that certainly was not a surprise, and often it's difficult for me, personally, not to regret his exile from active playing because he was a very key influence in the development of modern jazz piano. The people he influenced are just unbelievable. Oscar Peterson once said to me, "Every time one of his releases would come out I felt like I was taking a correspondence course." He influenced people like Oscar and Bill Evans, Herbie Hancock and McCoy Tyner and Chick Corea, and you could go on and on. Talk to any of these guys and they'd look you dead in the eye and tell you Nat was a major influence on their playing and a major contributor to the development of bebop—when you consider the number of things he did: the openness, the balance, and the really unorthodox combination of the trio—the piano, guitar, and bass. It opened up some wonderful harmonic possibilities that people like Dizzy Gillespie picked up on immediately. And he influenced other people, like Art Tatum, who put a trio together immediately, and Oscar Peterson, and the Softwinds and hundreds of emulators—in cocktail lounges and jazz clubs all over the world. It was really the most influential trio of all time, without question. People don't realize that America's first number 1 album, literally America's first number 1 album—from the first *Billboard* chart was Nat Cole: *Nat Cole—The King Cole Trio*. That was the album that included "Sweet Lorraine," "I'm Through with Love," "This Is My Night to Dream," "Paper Moon," "Little Girl," and "Too Marvelous for Words." That was America's first number 1 album: *The King Cole Trio*.

Earl Hines is always cited as the major influence on Nat's piano style. Were there other pianists who influenced Nat's style or he liked in particular?

He admired Oscar Peterson immensely, also Phineas Newborn. He loved Newborn's playing, which he pulled my coat to. He also liked Horace Silver a lot . . .

What about Nat's singing? Was there any particular influence on Nat's vocal style?

No, but I can tell who his favorite singer was. I kind of chuckled when he told me this—until I really started to listen to him. One of his very favorite singers was a guy called Perry Como. Now that may sound odd to you—it sounded odd to me when we talked about it, but he said, "Wait a minute—just listen to what this guy can do." And I did. He was some singer—some singer. Because he was so popular, of course, you're not supposed to be, you know, "that good." But Como was one of his very favorite singers. And he had a lot of favorite songs that touched him deeply. He loved a thing called "Funny." He also loved a thing called "I Keep Coming Back to Joe's." He loved "This Is All I Ask"—"When I Fall in Love."

Perhaps you can shed some light on Nat's management team. What kind of people did he keep around him—and how were bookings handled?

He had an absolutely marvelous crew of people, Steve. His crew—every member of his crew, including his musicians, during their off periods, listened to Nat Cole records. In other words, not only were they members of the band but they really were devoted fans. Sparky Tavares, who was his road manager for many, many years—I don't think that Sparky listened to anything other than Nat Cole; the same thing with his management, the same thing with his press office. He had those kind of people around him—people who were just totally devoted to him. He had a wonderful crew—from management to the booking agencies to his promotion people—they were very devoted to him, and he in turn was devoted to them. The thing that we all really admired was that he really stood for all that was clean and decent and yet he never built for himself a righteous pedestal on which to pose—he just did not do that. He always appreciated everything that came his way. There was nothing phony about him—he was real. Also, he had a great sense of humor. He was very quick with jokes, always ready for a laugh. He could find a chuckle in the least likely situation.

How many months out of the year would Nat work? And how did bookings come down the line from management to Nat?

I would say that Nat worked approximately eight months out of the year. This was not a straight eight months working and then four months off. He might work three months, then a month off, then back to work for a few months, et cetera. But in total I would say he averaged eight months out of the year. And as for bookings—well, let's say the booking agency was a company called General Artists Corporation, GAC. They would get an offer and bring that offer to his manager, Carlos Castel. And Carlos would decide "Yes, this is a good move" or "No, this is not a very good offer—we don't want to do this."

Where was Nat working? Where were the clubs during this period? Was there a Las Vegas? Was there a "Chitlin' Circuit" at this point?

The Howard Theater in Washington, D.C., the Earl in Philadelphia, the Regal in Chicago, the Apollo in New York. He absolutely worked that circuit. Yeah—he worked it initially, but, just as an example, we worked a week at the Howard in Washington but then two years later we were at one of the big hotels—I've forgotten the name—in their big room, their main room. Ironically, he was outpricing himself with the money he was getting for those engagements. Theaters like the Howard, the Earl, and the Regal could not afford to bring him in for a week—and their bookings were for a week. . . . There were venues like the Sands in Las Vegas, the Chez Paree in Chicago, the Copacabana in New York, the Gelatin Casino in Philadelphia, Lindstrom's in Boston, the Rio in Argentina and Brazil, the Tropicana in Cuba—this was while Batista was still in office, as a matter of fact. Batista came to his opening show in Havana, the very first time we worked Havana. Batista came to the opening with twenty-five guards [*laughs*]. Nat worked all over the world—all over.

Can you tell me what you remember about Nat Cole and his television show?

It started in November of 1956—on a Monday. The very first show was fifteen minutes long. Then it became quite popular, and after the first six shows NBC decided to extend it to a half hour, but they just simply could not find a sponsor. The last show was on the seventeenth of December 1957. So it lasted just a little over a year. And everyone—I mean everyone—tried to get a sponsor. Everyone was in his corner. People like Sammy Davis and Dean Martin, Peggy Lee and Ella Fitzgerald, Sarah Vaughan and Oscar Peterson, Stan Getz and some of the great jazz musicians—all made appearances on the show for scale(!). He just could not find a sponsor. When he finally decided to just walk away from it, Nat came up with a great quote—"Madison Avenue is afraid of the dark."—and it was the truth . . .

Was Nat bitter about this?

Absolutely not—Nat was not a bitter man. "Well, that's the way it is. . . ." In fact, his very first national exposure was in 1950 on the Ed Sullivan Show, which was huge. And it was because of the many appearances he made on the Sullivan show and the ratings those appearances generated that NBC said, "We better hire this guy." Yet they still couldn't find any sponsor.

Hadn't Nat hosted and starred on his own national radio program a few years earlier—sponsored by Wildroot hair creme?

Indeed there was. In fact, adding to his legend, his was the first American black jazz combo to have its own sponsored radio series; Wildroot was the sponsor in 1948/49.

Nat Cole was not an angry person—it took a lot to make him angry. In my sixteen years with him I'll bet I saw him get angry no more than a half-dozen times. You had to do a lot. For example, it was the opening game of the World Series in Chicago. The White Sox were playing the Los Angeles Dodgers. That was a game Chicago won 11 to 1. Nat was an enormous sports fan, and especially baseball. He was in town appearing at the Chez Paree and he was asked to come out and sing the national anthem to open the game. We got to the park and we sat up in the owner Bill Veeck's little dining room. Kiddingly, I said to him, "You do know the lyrics to the national anthem, don't you?" "Yeah—of course I know the lyrics to 'The Star-Spangled Banner.'" So he gets out to center field to do the anthem, but instead of singing " . . . the land of the free and the home of the brave," he sings " . . . over land and over sea, and the home of the brave." We came back to our seats and somebody came over and said, "Hey, you know you blew the lyric, right?" "No, I didn't." Of course we learned later that he actually did [*laughs*]—because it was televised! It just happened that way. But because it was the World Series, reporters were there from all over the world. And some guy from a Canadian newspaper came over and said to Nat, "Well, I suppose with all that's going on (in terms of civil rights) you probably did that intentionally. You didn't want to sing 'land of the free.'" Nat hit the ceiling— "Out of my room—Get out of here!" So, you could get him angry—but it took an awful lot. I remember at the opening of the Tropicana, in 1956 in Havana, Cuba. It was alright with him when Batista came to his opening with twenty guards. It didn't matter to Nat—Batista could have come with one hundred guards and Nat wouldn't have minded. What he did get angry about was that the guards kept their rifles on their laps. That offended him and got him angry because, as he said, "Here I am singing about love and in the audience are twenty guys with guns in their laps."—that did get him angry—and I don't blame him. We were doing an engagement at a club in Boston, a place called Winstrup's; at the time it was the Copacabana/Chez Paree of Boston—a prestigious club. People like Sinatra and Peggy Lee worked there. This particular night was Nat's opening night, and Capital Records had invited all of the radio people and the press, et cetera. And Nat gave a spectacular performance—an incredible performance—and he got three or four standing ovations. The show is over and I go backstage to let him know that there were several people who want to say hello to him. I walk into the dressing room and his road manager, Sparky, says, "Not now, Dick." And I look and Nat's in the corner of the dressing room with Lee Young, the drummer. Lee Young was Lester Young's brother, and he was working as Nat's drummer. And they're really into it—Nat is carrying on and carrying on. I turned to Sparky and said, "What's going on?" And Sparky simply says, "Later!" So I'm watching and waiting—I got people outside waiting to come in and say hello. So finally Nat finishes the discussion with Lee. Lee goes on his way. I walked up to Nat and asked him what happened. And he's talking about the tempo on a particular song—THE TEMPO—and he was really upset about it. I turned to him and said, "Wait a minute—you got three standing ovations!" He said, "It might have been four." [*Laughs.*] That'll give you an idea of what it meant to him to entertain the people.

We were working Detroit in concert for three or four days, and Henry Ford and his wife, who were big fans, came backstage. Ford loved the tune "Straighten Up and Fly Right," and he just wanted to make sure it was going to be included in the show. He related to Nat that his wife's favorite tune was Nat's "Christmas Song," and Ford's wife just rolled her eyes and said, "Oh for heaven's sake, leave the man alone—it's April." Well, at some point in the show Nat says, "Hey, I've got a special request for a very special lady. I know it's not the season but—" and he did the "Christmas Song." He got a standing ovation in April [*laughs*].

Nat Cole absolutely adored Joe Williams. We're working the Chez Paree, and Joe wants to come to the show. He gets in touch and Nat's manager, Sparky, makes the reservation for Joe Williams.

Nat opens the show and Joe Williams is ringside—I mean ringside. The show is over. I go backstage with Sparky; Nat turns to Sparky, and he said, "How could you do that!?!" "Do what—what did I do?" "You put Joe Williams in my face—*right in my face!*" [*Laughs.*] Of course, Joe Williams came backstage, and they hugged and they carried on, and he went on to compliment Nat. And Nat said, "Yeah—but I sure wish you'd have been sitting a few feet further away. It's very difficult to perform with Joe Williams sitting in my face!" And they both laughed about it. He had that much respect for Joe's work—Nat Cole absolutely adored Joe Williams.

Nat King Cole and Dick LaPalm crossing Wacker Street Bridge, Chicago. Photo courtesy Dick LaPalm Archive.

You know when Nat woke up in the morning, he didn't really wake up. He'd get up whenever the alarm went off but he wasn't really awake until maybe a half hour after the eyes were open. He could be talking but he wasn't completely totally awake. We were working in Washington, D.C., in 1960; President Kennedy had just been elected, and Nat had performed at the inaugural in 1960. I had gotten up and gone to Nat's suite. The phone rings and I pick it up. "Mr. Cole?" "Who's calling Mr. Cole?" "It's President Kennedy." Whoa, whoa whoa

whoa whoa—wait a minute! So I go to the bedroom and he's sound asleep. So I shake him. "Nat—it's President Kennedy calling!" I'd never seen someone wake up so fast in all my life! [*Laughs.*]

Nat passed away on the fifteenth of February, 1965. He was losing weight. He was appearing in San Francisco, and Sparky called me and said, "He won't see a doctor. He's losing weight. I had to punch another hole in his belt—will you come on out?" I said, "Absolutely"—and I did. I flew out from Chicago and went up to the suite. We hugged, and I said, "The first thing, I want to see your belt." "What?" "I want to see your belt—I want to see your belt." And he wouldn't show it to me, so I went in the closet and went to the belt rack and pulled the top one off, and I said, "Look at this—this is a brand new hole. You're losing weight. Go see a doctor." Well, to make a long story short—he went into the hospital on the fifth of December and was there seventy-three days. He got out of the hospital just long enough to have his wife drive him to the ocean about a week before he died. I saw him about nine days before he passed away. I had come home, and my wife said that Marie had been trying to reach me. So I called her, and she said, "Dick, he's been asking about you again. Will you come out?" I was out there the next morning—the very next morning—and we lost him on the fifteenth of February.

Nat Cole was really a very special person. He was warm. He was loving. He was generous. He was very respected—and gifted. He was disciplined. He was professional. He was real—and he was my dear friend. He was Nat Cole . . .

Grady **Freeman**

In all the years I spent on the blues scene here in Chicago, I had never seen, heard, or heard of Grady Freeman. Grady was a minor-league harmonica player who had grown up as a childhood friend of Junior Wells. An additional claim to fame was that Grady was a cousin to the Myers brothers. Mike Flynn sent me an email telling me about Grady Freeman, listing Grady's credentials, included Grady's phone number, and told me that Grady was battling cancer and if I was interested, I should act before it was too late. By this time I had moved from Chicago, so we did this interview by phone on October 23, 2014.

Grady Freeman. Photo courtesy Michael Flynn.

■ ■ ■

I was born in a place called Byhalia, Mississippi, March 31, 1935. Most people have never heard of Byhalia, but they've heard of Holly Springs, Mississippi. The reason more people knew about Holly Springs was because they had two black colleges there—M.I. (Mississippi Industrial College) and Rust College. It was the only town in Mississippi that had two black colleges—so most of the people remembered Holly Springs from that. My father had a sister in Chicago that was managing a building. It was at 3948 Indiana. My father came up here and stayed with her. He told me he slept on a couch and the chinches were so bad he couldn't sleep [*laughs*]. But he came up to Chicago first. Then other people came up and stayed with her, because the first time I came here I was four years old and my brother was six. That was the first time I came to Chicago because I stayed with my auntie at that same address when I was four. I can't even remember her name, it's been that long ago—but I'll tell you this, she was an ordained minister, and women in those days didn't even think about being ministers. She had this certificate on the wall that she was so proud of and she was always showing to people. That's how I remember her.

Now, if you're talking about Louis and Dave Myers, my father was their uncle. Now, Louis and Dave were born in Byhalia, too—and they had an older sister that was born there. She passed a couple of years ago. We really were first cousins. I don't remember when Louis and Dave came here. I didn't know about them being here until they hooked up with Junior Wells. I didn't deal with them too much until they started in the music business. As a matter of fact, my father got Dave and Louis and Junior Wells their first gig. It was at a hotel, and a woman named Tilford had a club in the basement. My father knew her because we lived in one of her buildings at 2323 South Calumet. My father told me he learned how to do banking because this lady would write checks and then have my father take money to the bank so they could cash their checks. That's how he learned banking, because he never had any money of his own to put in a bank.

My father and I used to see Louis and Dave at little parties, so my father got Ms. Tilford to hire them to play in her tavern. It's been so long, I've forgotten the name of the club. Louis had forgotten all about it until I reminded him in his later years, but my father got them their first club job. That's Louis and Dave Myers, Junior Wells and Fred Below (Bee-low). They called themselves the Aces. Junior told me he would rather play with Louis on guitar than anybody else, but they just couldn't get along. Now, I found by being in a group why most of the time people don't get along—and Little Walter was like that.... See, Louis and Dave played with Walter in the 1950s: when he put out "Juke" and "Can't Hold Out Much Longer," they were playing with Walter. I found out that most of the guys want to be the leader of the band because that's who controls all the money. And still today everybody wants to be the leader. When Walter was popular, Louis and Dave and Below were playing for him—and Walter told me this himself: they were traveling and Walter would get $800 a night and was paying his sidemen $25 apiece [*laughs*]. That's why most of the guys wanted to be the leader. Muddy, Wolf—they were all handling the money. The sidemen only got what the leader offered them—that's why everybody wanted to lead the band. Louis and Dave were brothers but they never could get along because both of them wanted to be the leader. Dave wanted to be the leader and Louis wanted to be the leader, and I think that's why Junior and Louis could never get along—Junior was the leader of the band, but Louis wanted to be the leader.

It would seem to me that the front man would be the guy doing the singing.

That's the way it's always been. When I was in bands, I wasn't leading the band, but they always came to me because I was singing, so they came to me about the gigs. They always think the singer is the leader—and mostly he is.

You don't remember the name of the club where they played their first gig, but what was that location again?

Junior lived at Twenty-Second and Prairie, and I lived at Twenty-Third and Calumet, so we were right around the corner. It was at Twenty-Second and Prairie, but I don't know what the exact address was. It was on Prairie in the twenty-two-hundred block. It was at a hotel with a tavern in the basement.

I know you were related to Louis and Dave. Were you better friends with them than you were with Junior?

No! Me and Junior were real close. Junior and I grew up in the same neighborhood. He lived on Prairie right around the corner from me. I went to the same school as Junior—Drake Elementary School. So we lived in the same neighborhood and went to the same school. Junior would always have his harp and would be blowing for us. We thought he was making a lot of noise, and we'd all say, "Man, that's a lot of noise . . ." and Junior would say "One day you're all going to pay a lot to see me!" Well, we never believed it [*laughs*]. And I'll tell you something else: when we were kids, Dick Tracy was in a comic strip in the newspaper. There was a villain in Dick Tracy who was bald-headed. They called him "Cueball." Most people don't know this, but when we were kids, Junior's mother used to cut off all of his hair. We didn't go to the barber, she just clipped all his hair off and made him bald-headed, so we called him "Cueball." [*Laughs.*] Junior and I and my wife, and all her brothers and sisters, we all grew up in the same neighborhood. Every time we would go and see Junior play—and Junior would be up on the stage playing—my wife would walk in and say, "Hey, Cueball!" [*Laughs.*] He never got angry about that because my wife's childhood nick name was "Pig" and he would just say "Hey, Pig!" [*Laughs.*] I probably remember more about Junior. As a kid I would go around his house. He lived at 2220 or 2221, and I would go around his house because I wanted to learn how to play the harp. I would ask Junior to help me. Nobody could show you anything about how to play harp back then. If they showed you anything, by the time you got it to your mouth you was lost. And I asked Junior to teach me. I'll tell you exactly what he told me: "Put it in your mouth and blow your ass off!" That's what he told me. . . .

Junior would always call me. I don't care if he was in Europe and just came home or wherever he had been, when he came to the city, he would always call me. He never got too big; he would always call me and say "Grady, I'm going to be at such and such a place—do you want to come?" And I didn't care where he was, I would always go. He would call because he didn't want me to have to pay to get in. He would always leave my name at the door so I could get in free.

If you paid any attention, Junior always dressed well. When we were kids, Junior didn't have no clothes. I believe that's why he dressed like he did when he began to make money, because when we were kids he didn't go to school dressed too good—and the teachers at school could tell when children weren't dressed well, which meant that the parents weren't doing well. Later he spent quite a bit of money on his clothes—and that was why.

Did he have a father in the house?

Not that I know of . . . I never met his father. I met his mother and his sisters but I never met his father. In fact, as many times as I went around there I never saw a man in that house. I remember his sisters—he had a sister named Irmagene and he had a sister that was sort of tall—a little dark girl—real tall, I don't remember her name—and then he had a sister that was sort of fat. I saw her at their mother's funeral and we spoke, but I don't remember him having a father.

I'm told that when Junior lived down home, he and Junior Parker were good friends. Did he ever mention Junior Parker to you?

No. But I believe Junior patterned himself after Rice Miller, Sonny Boy II. When we were young, he would try to blow the harp like Sonny Boy II. I saw Rice Miller. He came to my school when I was a kid [living] in Byhalia, Mississippi. He came to our school, and he didn't have no amplifier or nothing—just his harps. We had a little stage, and he sat on the side of that stage and blew his harp. I always tell people that I believe he walked to our school—because I never did see that he had a car. B. B. King came to my hometown. B. B. used to come to our town and stand out there on the streets and play his guitar and sing. I remember he had a blue '48 or '49 Chevy with his name on it. I don't believe he got more than $10 or $15, but that was all he could get at that time. Those were the only two musicians I saw in person when I was a kid.

Me and Junior were always pretty close. I wasn't like that with my cousins—just Junior. I was closer to him than I was Louis and Dave. They were my relatives, but I really wasn't close to them. I just have to tell the truth. They had an older sister named Louise Porter. She was the only one that accepted my father as her uncle. Louis and Dave had other brothers—and they had another sister, too—but they never accepted my father as their uncle. Louise always visited my father and was always at the house. When he got older, she would bring him food. The older sister was always at the house looking after my father. My father always told me, "Whatever happens, you stick with Louise." And she told me that the reason she stuck with him was that her mother always told her that my father was her uncle—her mother's brother. She accepted that, but the other kids didn't. Louis and Dave and the others never associated with us that much. I'll tell you something else that happened to us—and this happened years ago, and I don't even remember where the place was: it was somewhere on the northwest side. Junior was playing there with Louis, Dave, and Below, and Junior asked me if I would come up there. I was trying to learn how to play the harp. I told him I'd come up there. So I drove up, and when I got there, Junior asked me if I wanted to try and play a number. Now, I had never played with any band—but I wanted to try. I'd never been on the stage before, but he was trying to help me. He said, "I'll ask Louis." So Junior asked him to play with me, and Louis said yes. Then he asked Dave and—I never will forget—Dave refused. He said, "Let him go home and learn." You know, I probably wasn't going to do too well, but I wanted to try. That really hurt me. Well, it probably helped me in the long run because I said to myself, "I'm going to learn to play this harp and they're going to want to play with me someday—and it wound up that way!' [*Laughs.*] I went home and scuffled with that harp until I learned how to play it. I believe that helped me. I'm just trying to tell you the truth about them. It looks like they had fits or something. People used to ask me, "Are you sure you're a relation to the Myers brothers?" [*laughs*] because I acted so much different than them. I don't know what was wrong with them guys. I knew drummers that would play with them one time and then refused to play with them anymore. When he was young Louis was real good on the guitar, but Dave was a bass player. He tried to tell me he taught Louis all he knew on guitar—and he was lying, because Dave never really could play the guitar: he was a bass man. Louis and I were playing at a place called Biddy Mulligan's and we had Dave with us. We were playing a number called "The River's Invitation." I asked Dave if he knew the song and he said yes. We started to play it, and we had to stop because Dave didn't know the bass pattern. When we came down, he told me it was Louis's fault. But I knew he was lying because I had rehearsed the song with Louis—and I had it on tape. He was just the type of guy that would never admit that he was wrong or didn't know.

Did you know their older brother Bob?

Yeah, I knew Bob—and they had another brother named James. Bob used to try to play the harp himself. And they had another brother—he was a little odd, he didn't associate with rest of them too much.

Didn't you tell me that they still have a sister who's alive in Chicago?

Yeah—but I never associated with her that much. The one I associated with was the older sister. We traveled together and would go to my mother's house together. She really loved my mother. They were my relatives, but I don't know what was wrong with them. I just have to tell the truth.

Junior and I were pretty close, so I don't have anything but good to say about him; but I was with Louis one day [and he] said to me "Man, you know, Junior won't try and help anybody." I'm listening to this, but this don't sound like the Junior that I know. And it just so happened that Louis said, "Let's drop by the Checkerboard [Lounge]." We walked in the Checkerboard and there was Junior, tending bar. I said, "Hey Junior—how are you doing?" Louis said, "Hi." And Junior said, "Hey Louis—where's my motherfuckin' amp?" That's the way Junior talked—I don't know if you knew that, but it was. So Junior said, "Where's my motherfuckin' amp?" Louis says, "It's in the shop." Junior says, "Well you done had it three years motherfucker—get it out." [*Laughs.*] And he just got through saying Junior wouldn't help anybody. So Junior went in his pocket and he gave Louis a hundred-dollar bill and said, "Get my amp out of the motherfuckin' shop." The next day I took Louis to get the amp. We found out that Junior had the amp insured—so it didn't cost anything to get it out of the shop. I've forgotten where it was we went to get the amp, but they had a microphone on sale for $99. I always kept quite a few mics. I bet I've got five or six mics right now. So I told Louis, "I'm going to buy myself another new mic." And Louis said, "I'm gonna buy one too!" And he took that $100 Junior gave him to pay for the amp and bought himself a microphone! This is the guy who said, "Junior won't help nobody." [*Laughs.*]

In 1952 Little Walter made "Juke," and it was a big hit for him. After he made that hit, he left Muddy Waters and took Junior's band. Now, I liked Junior, but comparing Junior to Little Walter—there just wasn't any comparison when it comes to the harmonica. All of Little Walter's notes were clear as a bell. He never played bad notes. Junior had his own style, but he couldn't be compared to Little Walter. Nobody else could be, either. I really didn't know Walter personally.

I had a three-year contract with the Chess recording company in the 1960s, and I was coming from the studio one day. There was a club at Twenty-Fourth Street and Cottage Grove, and I stopped by there. Even when I was a teenager

I would go there and buy stuff, so I stopped by that club. Little Walter was sitting in an old Cadillac—I think it was a 1963 Cadillac—with a drummer that I knew from the neighborhood. The drummer called me over to the car—I didn't know Walter was in there [when] he called me over to the car. He told Walter that I was coming from Chess Studios and that I was trying to record down there. Walter told me about his career. He told me how much money he made a night, and he told me they would always pay him in cash. He said he had a shopping bag in the trunk of his car and when they paid him, he would just put the money in the shopping bag [*laughs*]. When he needed money in his pocket he would just reach in the shopping bag and put the money in his pocket. He told me sometimes he would send somebody else to get the money and they would put some in their pockets too. [Laughs.] He said, "I made $800 a night—that was a lot of money for 1952—I made $800 a night and I couldn't go home. I couldn't go home because I was dealing with so many women. Now I make $75 a night—and I go straight home." He came from nothing, and he got the clothes and the car—he was popular! Louis told me Walter used to say, "I'm burning up, boy, I'm burning up!" Walter's records weren't like Muddy's—you could bop off Walter's records. That's what the youngsters were doing. With Muddy's records all you could do was slow drag or two-step—something like that. Most of his records were sort of slow. But Walter's records were swinging! Junior didn't have a car at the time. One time he asked me to drop him off at the 708 Club. Everybody played at the 708 Club. On our way he said, "Let's stop by the Hollywood Rendezvous." That was a little place at Thirty-Eighth and Indiana. That's where Walter played all the time. If he wasn't out on the road, he played at the Hollywood Rendezvous. Walter used to play there with Robert Jr. Lockwood and Luther Tucker. This was at a time when Walter and Junior were the two main guys playing harp in Chicago—Cotton hadn't arrived in Chicago yet. Well, Walter had put out a new record, and he wasn't blowing too much harp on it—just mostly singing. Junior said, "Man, Walter got so that he can't even blow his nose." So when we got to the Hollywood Rendezvous, Little Walter looked up and saw Junior, and Walter broke out with some instrumental—and all Junior and I could do was look at each other. Walter tore that harp up!

Theautry **Jones**

The name is pronounced Thee-Autry F. Jones, but he was known to fellow musicians as T-Jones. This tip came from Studebaker John Grimaldi, who ran across him one day when they were both in a hockshop looking for amps and guitars. They starting talking and realized they both played blues. When listing his credentials to John, T-Jones mentioned the fact that he had played with harmonica genius Little Walter. John came away with his name, Theautry Jones, but no working telephone number or address. He also mentioned that T and his wife operated a church, Sacred Heart of Jesus, on Chicago's Westside. This tip put me on the trail, and I spent the next six months trying to make contact with him. It turned out that he had an adopted son with the same name and that both had moved several times.

Theautry "T" Jones. Photo courtesy Steve Cushing.

This generated multiple listings in the Chicago area—again, none with working phone numbers. So I sent letters to the listed addresses and finally made contact. Theautry and I met at his house and drove over to the church, where we held the interview. His wife, Mahalia S. Jones, was the minister of their storefront church, while he served as music director. Before we began the interview T-Jones played a few songs for me on guitar and then we sat in the front row of chairs used to seat the congregation to do the interview.

This interview was recorded November 14, 2016. As of this writing, Theautry Jones is still alive in the Chicago area.

■ ■ ▪

This was during the time when blacks had a separate musician's union. We were in the 208 union. Blacks couldn't get in the 210 union at that particular time. So we had our own union. I can't say whether he got us from the union or whether we were on another gig or just word of mouth—but Little Walter needed a band. He needed a band, and we needed to play some music. We didn't ask him what kind of place it was. At that time you only wanted to know two things about a gig. If it was a jazz gig, you grabbed your fake book, your guitar, and amplifier. If it was a blues gig, you grabbed your guitar, your amplifier, and went on it. This is what we did back in those days. If a musician was in trouble, somebody would always help them out. I can't remember everybody who was on the gigs. At that time the city of Chicago wouldn't let us have more than three musicians on the stand at one time. I remember playing in this place—it was a small place somewhere around Thirty-Ninth Street on the East Side—but this is where Little Walter played all the time. I don't know what had happened, whether his musicians had gone on another gig or left him stranded or what—but he needed some help. So we just went on in and pitched in and started playing behind him. He was well-known—just like Little Jr. Wells was known at that time, and Muddy Waters—we all went down by the old Pepper's Lounge. After you got through with your gig you went down on Forty-Third Street to Pepper's Lounge. We all talked to each other, and if you say, "Well, I need a bass man," and I'd say "Well, I got one and he's not working right now." Or whatever you need. This is how we met Little Walter—by him needing a band. We were hustling gigs, and I only remember two times we worked with Walter. The first was at his regular spot there on Thirty-Ninth Street. And then the next time when we played, he said, "Get ready early. We're going to Elgin." That was a big gig for us, to go out of town! We just thought we were going to go back to his regular place, but instead we went on out to Elgin and played. It was a black club. I don't remember who all was on that gig. I remember Richard, who was my drummer was on the gig. I don't remember if Scotty—Ken Scott of the Scott brothers—was with me or not on that gig because he was my regular guitar man and my bass man. I recall it was Richard on drums because it wasn't Bobby Davis. Bobby Davis was our regular drummer, but we would often switch up musicians in those days. It was one guitar and a bass plus the drummer. So we did this nice gig in Elgin, and after the gig we came to Thirty-Ninth Street. This was two or three o'clock in the morning. All of our instruments were in Little Walter's car, that Cadillac of his. His wife was driving. When we got back, we needed to call the club where Walter played all the time so we could drop off our instruments. They were closed up and the doors were locked, so we needed to call the owner to let us in. So we stopped at a place on the East Side somewhere near Thirty-Ninth Street. We wanted to use a pay phone, but it was a red-light district, and when we went in to use the telephone, two policemen came by. They said, "You can't stop here. This is a red-light district, and you're going to have to move on." The guys that went in to make the call came back and got in the car. Little Walter and his wife were having an argument and were talking with each other. One of the policemen said, "What did you say lady?" She said, "I wasn't talking to you—I was talking to my husband." He said, "Well, you better move on or I'll lock you up." And Little Walter, who was sitting in the backseat, said, "And I'll get her out." And at that moment the policeman said, "Everybody out of the car!" All of us began to get out of the car and stood up, including Walter, and we didn't say another word. But when Walter got out, one of the policemen—we called him "Lock 'Em Up Jones"—he stepped behind Walter with his billy club. The other policemen stepped in front of Walter and they took him across his hands and hit him in the back of his neck. Little Walter went out like a light, fell in front of me on the concrete and couldn't even brace himself up. The cop said, "Everybody get back in the car. What I remember was that Walter wasn't able to get back in, and I think they put him in the squad car. They told us to drive to the nearest police station out there. When we got there—any time you go in this station, you're locked in—you're not locked up but you're locked in. We didn't see Walter. I think they took him on to the hospital. The way he fell, he had to have a concussion or something. But it was uncalled for. He never said anything else to the policeman. It was brutal—I'd never seen anything like that. They charged all of us with disorderly conduct. Later on, the club owner we were trying to call came and bailed us all out, and we went home. This was a Saturday night, and we had to go to court early on Monday morning. When we were in court, Walter didn't show up there. We didn't know why. We didn't know if he was in the hospital—nobody told us anything. They probably put out a warrant on him, and that's why he didn't show up. But later that week, Walter and I went down, and Walter talked to Leonard Chess. Leonard Chess should have helped him because Walter was violated. He only said one word and nothing else. Leonard Chess said, "Well, you're always getting in trouble. I'm not going to help you." I thought that was wrong. He should have helped the man. I think Walter wanted Chess to get him a lawyer and fight the case against him. But Leonard Chess didn't do that. He turned him down flat because, he said, "You're always getting in trouble." All this was about two years before Walter died.

Part Two **Amen Corner**

Clarence **Small**

Very early on in my blues record collecting I realized that I enjoyed black religious recordings almost as much as the blues. I loved the close vocal harmony and the way the singers, unrestricted by musical accompaniment, would bend time. And in the later records I loved the vocal intensity, once hard "shouting" was in vogue. There were scores of groups and hundreds of records to hear and buy. Because I enjoyed the religious recordings so much, I added a regular feature to my *Blues Before Sunrise* program. I called it the "Vintage Gospel Set," and most weeks it was only three records: a prewar gospel tune, a recorded sermon—starting in 1926 there were many black clergy who made their way into the recording studios—and then a postwar gospel tune to wrap things up. Among the many groups I came to love was a twenty-five-voice choir that took vocal harmony to its tasteful extreme, Wings Over Jordan. WOJ was founded in Cleveland, Ohio, during the mid-1930s by the Rev. Glenn Settle. After a couple of years doing mostly local recitals, the choir was in such demand that they spent the next fifteen years touring from coast to coast, spending as much as ten months out of each year on the road. In addition to the many concerts they did, they were contracted each and every week to the CBS radio network to do a fifteen-minute national broadcast from wherever in the nation they were on that particular Sunday morning.

Clarence Small, 2016. Photo courtesy Steve Cushing.

Wings Over Jordan recordings were a regular part of the "Vintage Gospel Set." I would play the records and praise the sound they created and, on more than one occasion, lament the fact that there seemed to be little or no information available about the choir. This went on for several years until one night I received a phone call from a white couple, Todd Zimmerman and Cherie Burton, who lived in Kalamazoo, Michigan. They had seen a performance by a fellow who claimed to be a former member of Wings Over Jordan. His name was Clarence Small, and he was based in Kalamazoo. They were impressed enough to get his name and telephone number. On that particular night, they heard me play a WOJ record (and my latest lament) and decided to see if they couldn't put the two of us together. So I called Clarence, introduced myself, and we got together to do an extended phone interview. Clarence gave me a wonderful interview and later made available copies of the vintage photos he had saved from his years with the choir. The interview presents a fascinating look at the inner workings of an African American group of entertainers, touring and performing in the era of segregation. We both hoped to draw the attention of anyone who might put Clarence or Clarence and myself out on the lecture circuit and make some money, but it never worked out that way. Many years later I decided to include the interview in this book, so I contacted Clarence. It turned out that we were both curious to meet each other in person, as the original interview was by phone. So he and I got together in Kalamazoo to sign a permission slip. Our meeting gave me a chance to ask a few follow-up questions and for Clarence to talk about his time in the military during World War II. Ironically, we got together at the house of Todd and Cherie, who had originally put us

Clarence Small (r) outside tour bus. Photo courtesy Clarence Small.

48 AMEN CORNER

in touch. At age ninety-one, Clarence drove us over in his silver Lincoln, a trip that might have been mistaken for the pace lap at the Indianapolis 500.

This interview was recorded October 16, 2003, and October 31, 2016. Clarence Small died in September 2017 in Kalamazoo, Michigan.

■ ■ ■

Let's go back to the very beginning. Where were you born? When?

I was born in 1924 in Grand Rapids, Michigan. My twin sister and I came down to Kalamazoo on a train. That's an interesting story. We were shipped on the train in separate baskets under the care of the conductor. Once we got here to Kalamazoo, we were met by our prospective parents, who subsequently adopted us at the age of six months. So that makes me almost a native of Kalamazoo, and I've been in and out of here ever since. Well, my mother was a piano teacher. She taught both my sister and me piano. Later I got interested in the violin. They gave me lessons in the violin and then percussion for high school. I played drums as well and any other percussion instrument. Then I taught myself organ. I played in a church and then decided I would teach myself organ. So I've been doing that too. I always sang as well as played instruments. My mother was the organist of our church, and of course she took the twins to every service. In fact, during those days she sometimes made the fire in the church—an old furnace that she would bank and put coal on and so forth. So we were in church all the time. I was singing in the junior choir, and I just loved it and took it in high school, and this fellow Barnes, his father had a quartet, and he would take the two of us out on the road with him to get our feet wet, so to speak, in quartet singing. That's how we really got interested in a professional type approach to singing.

When you say you were singing with a quartet, was this a religious singing like a gospel quartet?

No—in those days they frowned on that kind of music. They wanted to sing classical music as a quartet and spirituals. That's quite a while ago; there was not the emphasis on gospel music that there is today. We were grounded, we read music. Gospel people rarely read music except the very talented musician who may play—even a lot of them don't read music. They do it by ear. We were reading music that was written expressly for quartets. They liked nice harmonies and that sort of thing with emphasis on more classical training and more classical singing, and that's what we did until we went to "Wings Over Jordan"—of course, those were spirituals that we did.

What would be some of the songs? Would there be any that we might know today?

I don't know. We did a *fantastic* quartet piece called "The Lost Chord." Yes, that was the title of the piece. "Seated one day at the organ, I was weary and ill at ease." *Gorgeous* piece for a quartet—I can't find it—I tried to find it a few months ago and it's probably out of print. But "The Lost Chord," that's an old, old piece; probably older folks would know about it. But the rest were spirituals that were arranged. Ordinary spirituals. "Swing Low," whatever. One of the other members of the quartet was the baritone, Emery Barnes, who came from Kalamazoo too. He preceded me in Wings Over Jordan. He was instrumental in calling me up when they needed a replacement for one of the tenors. Well, it happened right out of high school: I graduated in January of 1942; the call came about June of that year. There was a fellow by the name of Al Meadows, who was with the original group of Wings Over Jordan. I think he probably started in the thirties, '35, somewhere in there with that original group. He decided to quit singing—quit going on the road anyway. They wanted a replacement for him. He did solo work, and they wanted a voice—that was the format of Wings Over Jordan. Every time a person would drop out, they tried to get a voice that approximated the same voice, and that's how they could continue to carry on the tradition. So I was that person after having gone by recommendation to Cleveland and they had decided to hear me—although I was hired before I even got there. So that's how I got there. I was the youngest person in the group: right out of high school. I was seventeen, and then in February I had a birthday and turned eighteen—so I was actually eighteen when I went to Cleveland.

When you made the move from Kalamazoo to Cleveland, how did that happen? What kind of arrangement did you make?

Well I just went and got on the bus or train—I don't know which—and just went to headquarters where they were stationed there in Cleveland. They were just off the road and staying in town, and they found a place for me to stay with some of the other fellows; I went to rehearse with the group every day until we went back out on the road. They would do a tour and come back after maybe six months or maybe a year out on the road. They'd come back and rest a little bit and go back out again in another direction. Say we went east: they would tour a lot of states east and then come back and then go west, or south or north whichever—which would be the best way to tour the country. So that's what I did. I went there and joined them, and our first concert was at the Cleveland Stadium—for me it was. It was Cleveland Stadium, and I think there were ninety thousand people in the stands. It was Fourth of July, and I just knew that every one of those people could tell that I didn't know half of the words to those songs [*laughs*]. That was a scare. We marched out onto the platform, which was right at home plate, and faced the stands and sang on Fourth of July. There were other people who were on the program, of course. But I think the group was so popular that we were probably, as you call them, "headliners" for the whole celebration. So that was quite a first concert for me as a kid joining this very famous organization. We turned out to be a national treasure.

When was the group Wings Over Jordan originally founded?

It was 1936 or thereabouts, '36, '35. Well, it started in a church, as a church choir, and they were so good—and the owner, who was the minister of that church, was so adept at speaking, and he made narrations for each song. They were heard over the local CBS station there in Cleveland, and there was such great interest in the choir that somebody decided that he would try to get those people heard on the radio as a sustained feature and also some trips across the country for everyone to hear.

Do you recall the name of the fellow who started the choir?

Of course—the Reverend Glenn T. Settle was the owner and started the whole thing, but the fellow who really put the choir on a map and really did the conducting and the fine-tuning was a man by the name of Worth Kramer. I think he was affiliated with the radio station as well . . . I did not tour with him. By the time I'd got there he had decided to not direct the group anymore, so I came under a lady by the name of Gladys O. Jones, and subsequently there were three or four other conductors that I was under before we disbanded.

Wings Over Jordan in concert. Photo courtesy Clarence Small.

Do you recall the call letters of the station? Which station were you heard over in Cleveland?

That's WGAR.

What about the makeup of the choir? How many members were there, and what was the breakdown in terms of gender?

We had about twenty-five voices, and it was about half and half—probably one more woman than men. So that meant we had first and second tenors and first and second basses and then sopranos and altos.

And what about music accompaniment?

No accompaniment—we were all a cappella, and we baffled the public with our pitches. You couldn't hear the pitch. After several of the conductors, it fell my lot to give the pitches. Now, I had this little pitch pipe that I would conceal and I knew all of the pitches of each of the songs we were going to do. I had a list of what we were going to do, and I would give the pitch and no one heard it. It was so very, very soft that no one even in the first row could hear it, and we would start the next song and they would wonder how in the world did they all start on the same pitch. But that's how we did it. No accompaniment.

Now, when you did live concert performances, was the Reverend Settle up front doing the narrations for these tunes?

Yes—yes, he did—and they were very unique. He would write out some of the nicest and most profound narrations for all of the songs that we sang and he had a marvelous voice—stentorian tones. What a guy. He was self-educated and he just had a very, very, very strong presence and very intimidating presence about him. He was quite a self-made man.

What about soloists?

Yes, we had soloists who were unique and were the mainstay of the choir. I did some solo work myself for a time. Until I went to the army and I came back—and a very strong contralto had taken over my solo. Which was fine with me.

Which part did you sing?

I was first tenor. First tenor sings the highest tenor notes that the tenors do. I didn't do any falsetto work.

Can you—going back to the soloist—can you recall any of the outstanding soloists that passed on through the years. And were there any people who actually just were in for the long run as opposed to changing personnel on a consistent basis?

Emelda Herring (l), Ester Overstreet (r). Photo courtesy Clarence Small.

52 AMEN CORNER

Well, yes—the tenor soloist was a fellow by the name of Paul Breckinridge. And he sang a very high falsetto and became very famous across the country with his brand of soloing. And I toured—the first year that I toured, he was still in the group. Then he dropped out. He was replaced by a fellow named Cecil Dandee, who could do exactly the same falsetto that Breckinridge did, and then he wound up as our lead tenor in our quartet. And as I say, I replaced a fellow tenor—Al Meadows. He had a solo that he did, and so they thought that my voice approximated his; so I did his solo. And then there was Esther Overstreet, who replaced Martha Spearman, and she was on tour for quite a while. But she, being one of the senior members of the choir, decided she no longer wished to travel, so Ester Overstreet became her replacement. So that's how the integrity of the group was maintained: by bringing in a soloist who very much sounded like the preceding soloist. Let me see . . . we had Haddie Easley who was a soloist . . .

—Did the Reverend Settle do any singing at all?
Not at all. He couldn't carry a tune in a basket [*laughs*]. Nah, he did no singing.

How often did you rehearse?
Well, we would—when we were off tour, we rehearsed every day. But it would seem like we were always rehearsing, in a sense. When we got on a bus to go from one town or one state to the other, we would be singing half the night. We'd leave a concert after having sung maybe two concerts—there were so many people going into the hall that it could not hold everyone, and we would have to do two concerts. And we would invariably—if we traveled—get on the bus and sing for part of the trip going to the next town. So we were always sort of rehearsing or tuning up, but it was not a formal rehearsal; but the conductor usually tried, if we had time, to give us some tune-up rehearsals at least two or three times a week.

In the course of all that work did members of the choirs ever get into bad habits in terms of their singing?
I would say that the singing perhaps brought about laryngitis, and that was the only bad habit: singing too much and too long. But all we ever did was perfect our singing and sing so much that we became very immersed in the production of voice and sound, and that was the uniqueness of this group. It sang for the love, the pure joy and love of it, that it perfected itself as it went—almost without any prompting or any training. There were lots of people who had absolutely no training whatever. Only a few people had formal training in the group, but we sang so much together that the sound became—we became as one.

Did you ever rehearse as sections?

No, no—only once in a while the guys would get together and do whatever they were going to do. If there was one or two songs that the men came out and started the piece, and we would all get together off on the side and do what we were going to do, and the ladies come in with a couple of voices, and then we would all come together where all voices were singing together. Only in those instances would we separate. The rest of the rehearsals were always, *always* with everyone—the whole group rehearsing at the same time.

Where did the repertoire come from? Were there things that were added? Were there things that were of a secular nature? Did the material stay consistent, or did it cycle?

It stayed consistent, and these were—with the exception of the quartet, I don't think we did secular songs. These were all old, old spirituals that we knew about. Some of us who knew a spiritual that the rest didn't know would bring it and start singing the melody to the rest of the group. And we just right on the spot would make up the harmonies and sometimes aided and abetted by—well, we had one lady who came to us as an arranger and she helped to forge some of the arrangements. But we were so used to singing whatever part we had, we all knew where our part ought to go. So that was easy. Once we had the sound. You know you develop through the years a particular sound, just as Count Basie or Ellington. They have a sound, and so they strive toward that and they just go with that sound and produce it, and all of the arrangements go in that vein.

Here's another question: You mentioned before you brought up the notion of laryngitis—do the folks in a world-famous vocal choir have any secret tips on how to soothe a ruffled voice?

Well we did all the old things, you know, the lemon in the hot water, gargling with various things, Sucrets and whatever we could take that would soothe our throats. But, you know, if you're hired to go out and sing every night, you somehow sing over the top of that ailment and it was very infrequent that someone could not sing no matter if they could hardly even speak. In Florida—we would be in Florida and sometimes we would be so hoarse; there was a difference in climate there, and people who could hardly speak would go on stage and sing, which was very remarkable. But I think the adrenalin flows and the necessity of having to come up with a concert—when you go out there on that stage and it's already been programmed for an appearance—in Orlando, say—they looked forward to it and booked us six months ahead, and we got to go out on stage and deliver. People did it. As opposed to people in a single performance having the same malady today perhaps would not sing, perhaps would cancel the concert. We never canceled. If we had a solo to sing, whatever it was—we sang it. We did it. It was just a must. You overcome it somehow.

Let's talk about attire, the wardrobe. What was it that the choir would wear when you performed?

We all wore robes. The fellows had white shirts and a bow tie and black robes. The ladies had robes, black robes with white collars and that was our attire. When the quartet went out, we wore tuxedos. That was what we wore year after year. Well, there was a group that went overseas, and they had a different attire—sort of patterned after a World War II uniform.

Who took care of the robes? Was there one person in charge? Did everyone take care of their own?

No. No we took care of our own, and we had to have it laundered; and we did our own pressing, perhaps. We just carried irons, and we just would make sure that we were presentable. If it was wrinkled, we would have to iron it somewhere: in a dressing room, at home or at the hotel—wherever we were. There was no extra personnel, no wardrobe people, no people who did those things. It was a pared-down organization. We were all responsible for our own uniforms and our own attire, decorum, and that sort of thing.

With the travel arrangements—you had a bus. Did you have one specific person who was the bus driver, or was that a member of the choir who drove?

No, we hired a fellow who drove for us. Year in and year-round, and we had a very marvelous bus driver. This guy was really skilled—I remember—he's probably the only man, if he's still alive, who can say that he successfully negotiated the Grapevine; that's a very dangerous mountain [road] in California that claimed lives if vehicles got out of control going down that mountain going into Bakersfield. They never lived to tell about it. We got to the top of that mountain going into Bakersfield for a concert and the brakes gave out and everything was by air on this bus and we couldn't get it into gear to gear it down so we rode that bus down. We were late for the concert and someone called along the road and said, "Have you seen a bus with the name 'Wings Over Jordan' on it go by?" and they said, "Yes, we sure did—down the mountain and you'll find them somewhere out in the ravine because they went by us about a hundred and twenty miles an hour going down that mountain." Well, this guy steered that bus all the way to the bottom. He went around trucks and everything along that mountain. How we got by them I'll never know. What an experience! I think we were the only ones that for years and years who ever made it from the top of the mountain wide-open down that mountain safely.

> On the bus it seems to me, I guess, you would have your own personal luggage and you would have your wardrobe [and] your robe. Was there any specific place where everything was stored?

Yes. Well, you know, we started out with an old bus that the engine was up under the hood way out in front. You see these old buses with a double tire on the back and a luggage rack on top. They were buses with, I think, the vintage was the '30s. Great big old monstrous buses. Very picturesque. Well that was the first bus that we had, and that old bus would wheeze up and down mountains and get hot, and we would have to rest it and then go on. And then all our luggage was stored inside and outside. The very large baggage was in a rack on top of the bus. We would tie that luggage down on top and put a tarp over it in case of rain. Then we got a more modern bus with a storage underneath as you've seen the Greyhounds do. So that's how we transported ourselves across country.

> Tell me about the pay system for Wings Over Jordan.

There was a flat pay rate for performing in the choir. We had very little or no negotiation for pay. You just came in and you took the regular chorus member's pay—whatever that was. And if you were a soloist, they gave you a few bucks more—not very, very much more. Our pay came as cash in an envelope—because we wouldn't have been able to cash checks—which was given to us every two weeks. I don't remember if that envelope included any record of the cash you were to receive, but I do remember you received an envelope with your name on it, and that was the end of that. The Reverend Settle wasn't involved in any hands-on way, other than to approve it. His secretary was the paymaster. She ran all the disbursement—it was just the two of them. There was no board or committee involved. I did earn a little extra for handling the luggage—which was considerable among the members. Each of us had all kinds of clothing and items that we acquired on our travels through the country. The girls especially could not handle their luggage, which was located on top of the bus, at least on the old bus. There was also

Members of WOJ eat watermelon. Photo courtesy Clarence Small.

56 AMEN CORNER

space inside for very small bags. The large luggage was on top, and I would climb up there and get it and then take it to their abode, wherever we were being housed. So I earned a little extra money. Looking back on my salary, there was not much difference—in fact, very little difference between the little porter job I had here in Kalamazoo before I went to sing. I would have thought our professionalism and the notoriety that the group got singing around the country would have garnered more in salary than it did—but he just didn't want to pay big salaries—and he didn't! Of course, we had no unions to help us along those lines. The members were very unhappy about those conditions, and that was one of the reasons they ultimately disbanded.

I've always wondered what sexual conduct was like in the choir. You had twenty-five people, men and women, who were out on the road together for eight or ten months at a time. Did Reverend Settle have a code of conduct for choir members?

If he did, it was a tacit code. He wisely neglected to express it out loud to the group, perhaps to avoid disappointment, but he never lectured, and tacitly there seemed to be an understanding that everything must be on the up and up. Of course, you couldn't cohabitate—and when we would come to a town we were assigned lodging with a roommate—guys and gals separately. There were two married couples, and they were sent to homes as a married couple. When we were in the big cities and had hotel rooms, it was with the same roommates. But what happened between consenting individuals in this hotel is left to the imagination. There were no hard-and-fast rules. People did have romantic relationships within the group, and a relationship might sour along the way—but therein lies the professionalism I first encountered within the group. Your personal life had absolutely nothing to do with what happened onstage. When we went onstage, we were paid AND prideful of the product. We supported one another whether or not we were angry or had been in a soured relationship. We backed each other fervently, regardless. That's professionalism—and that's what we had. It's remarkable when you consider that none of us had studied psychology or behavioral science that people use to enhance their ability to get along. We just seemed to know that professionally we must maintain integrity in performing—and that's what that group did. I'm amazed as I think about it now—all those years ago and many of us were very unsophisticated. And Reverend Settle never lectured or took individuals aside.

Were choir members discouraged from associating romantically with the individuals in the audience? And with the choir maintaining such an active performance schedule, was there even any opportunity to romance an audience member?

It seems that there was always at every concert a party or reception afterward. Naturally, women in the audience wanted to meet the fellows in the choir—and the fellows definitely wanted to meet them. That was always going on. Keep in mind that as a performing group, we had to maintain some semblance of dignity and propriety, but we just had the greatest time. Of course, we always had to be back on time when the choir bus departed. None of us earned enough to miss the bus and find alternative transportation—"I'll catch up. I'll meet you in the next town!"—no! [*laughs*]. None of us had that kind of money, so we were back when our bus headed out and took our own seat—each of us had a seat that we sat in. We never swapped seats. You were always in your same seat on tour. It was a great experience. I was eighteen—wow! [*Laughs.*]

How was the name of the choir displayed?

Big letters: "Wings Over Jordan" "Radio." I forget some of the logo on the bus—"Recording Artists" and our manager from the people who managed us out of New York as far as the records and that sort of thing.

Did you find that people knew who you were?

Oh, my—yes! Oh, yes. We were known from coast to coast. Every, *everybody*, you know, we were a sustained feature every Sunday morning. We were probably the oldest sustained feature on CBS beside the Mormon Tabernacle Choir—in fact, we were longer running than the Mormon Tabernacle Choir. Everyone listened to us in this country from coast to coast. Every Sunday morning. The broadcast was a half hour.

Now how was that done when you were on the road?

Well, we always made certain that our tour would take us to a city that had a CBS station for Sunday because wherever we were on Sunday, we must be where we could go into a studio, a CBS studio and broadcast which went from coast to coast and some of it went over into Europe as well. Broadcast there. So everyone around the country knew who we were. People today don't know anything about the group, but some of the older people do. But young people have never heard of it. But it used to be that everybody had to listen to *Wings Over Jordan* every Sunday morning across the country.

Did those broadcasts have a specific sponsor?

Gee!—That's a good question. I don't know—I don't know.

Another question about the broadcast, in addition to the sponsor: I know that the choir's job is to essentially show up and perform. Is there anybody or was there anybody who specifically coordinated the repertoire for every week's broadcast who was in touch with the network themselves; you know—obviously, it would seem to me, you wouldn't want to go on and sing the same songs every week.

No.

Who took care of that?

The Reverend Settle, the owner of the group, took care of that. He knew and certainly would apprise, work with the directory of the group with the songs that had been done and that must be cleared. Everything had to be cleared every week because of its origin and copyrights and all that sort of thing. The owner knew what he wanted to write—the narrations—and he did them every Sunday. He would call upon the directors to produce those songs, and the directors gave them to the choir.

There was one time that I can remember, and I'm very proud of this time. We went into a studio, and it just didn't sound right; the song that we were going to do just didn't sound good to either Reverend Settle or the director. They went into the control room, and we sang the thing several times and it just didn't click, it didn't work. So they said, well, knowing the quartet and their prowess in doing songs, putting together songs, [they] sent us into studio B and said, "OK, fellows, see what you can come up with." And so we went in there for a short time and came back out and did the broadcast with the quartet singing the song in place of the twenty-five-piece choir. So we thought, "Hey—boy, we're good." We were able to do our own arrangement right on the spot and fill that void.

Another question that occurs to me with the Reverend Settle and his narration: When we hear the recording with his narration preceding the actual choir—obviously, they are the same because you went in and you preserved them one time. When he would sing the same song, would the narrations change?

No, they would always be the same narration. He had those narrations on cards, and he would just produce those cards and read them. Sometimes he would know them from memory, but if the song was on the program, that's what the narration would be; and it would be that this time next year. It would be the same narration. Because they were all set. Then, if we went into a new song, he would produce a new narration, which would endure. Well, we were singing to USO groups and servicemen throughout the country. We even went to Tuskegee and saw the famous Tuskegee fliers and got in their planes and they flew their planes for us in a demonstration. We also saw George Washington Carver and sang privately for him.

He must have been fairly old at that point.

Yes, he was and quite ill, and he saw us from his balcony of his abode; he was in one of the dormitories there on the Tuskegee campus, and we stood outside, out in the open, and sang a private concert, just a mini-concert, for him—alone. Those were things that we did. We would sing in a cow pasture if we need be.

Any other notable black celebrities of the day that you folks performed for?

Oh, let's see. Well, Mary McLeod Bethune, who founded the school in Florida [and was] a famous person at that time. She got on the bus with us and rode around with us. Marian Anderson—we were in joint receptions with her. We met all of the people of the day. Joe Louis and Lionel Hampton and Duke Ellington; we took pictures with them along the way. If we were in a hotel, they might be in the hotel, too; if it was a large city back east, we would all be in the same place and fraternize with one another and go to one another's concerts if we could. So we met all of the people of that day who were famous black performers and personages of the time. Which is a marvelous time, and as a youngster—you know what callow youth is: we don't really understand history in the making, and if I had really understood how important all of that history was, I would have taken pictures and had more pictures. I have a few. I would have taken a picture everywhere I went of everybody. But when you're young, you just take it all in and you're marveling at the experience and going along but have no real, no real clear understanding of the importance of the history that's being made.

Let's talk about the records. You did record while you were with the group?

Yes. Oh, we recorded three or four times, and those records were sold on the road. Everybody wanted a record. Oh, my goodness—they sold like hotcakes.

When were the records made, to the best of your memory? What years were the sessions?

Oh, my goodness. Oh, golly.

After the war or before the war?

Just before the war. I think in '40s—between '42 and '43 we made some recordings, if I remember, and then afterwards we did so in '46, I know—I think. I'm pretty sure.

What labels were these for?

Oh, my gosh! One was with a crown.

I've got records on the King label.

King, yes. Yes, King. Yes.

Can you shed any light on the sessions? Where were they recorded?

Major studios. I think one of them was cut in Philadelphia. I think, but I'm not sure where the other one—

Well, King was based in Cincinnati.

Okay, all right, well, so that could be. I would not remember what cities—I just go, you know, and record those things. As I say, being a young person, you don't care. You just go to the recording studio and do it. You don't know—it could be in Fairbanks, Alaska. No—you would know that! But callow youth, as I say, we don't care where we do things. We just don't think it's important to remember or record any of that stuff, but if I had one in front of me, I certainly would be able to see on the jacket where it was—where it was originated. But I don't have a *one* of those recordings.

What format were these recordings at that point?

We did seventy-eights—they would be seventy-eights.

You say you sold the records at appearances. How was that done?

They would have them sitting out in the entry of the hall. They would be there for sale by personnel. The secretary would be out there and someone else assisting to sell those records. Those would go into the coffers of the owner. We never saw those monies at all.

Did you ever autograph records?

Not so much records. I've autographed programs. I don't remember autographing any of the records. You received a program with the ticket. You were automatically given a program. If you bought a songbook—now, those were sold. I have one of those now.

Explain this to me. What are you talking about when you say "songbook"?

The songbook is a yellow book, and it says "Wings Over Jordan" on the cover and a picture of the choir. "The famous choir of radio and concert stage. Favorite spirituals of 1939." And it says "arranged by Worth Kramer." It was Rodeheaver Hall-Mack Company, North Fifteenth Street, Philadelphia. And at the bottom: WGAR, Cleveland, Ohio, originating station, coast to coast every Sunday. So, I have that book of songs.

Is this sheet music, or is it just lyrics—or both?

It's sheet music, lyrics in there and regular arrangements that we did—and certainly not the way we used to do them. Close—close enough, you know?

What did they sell for? Does it have a price there?

One dollar, heh, heh, heh.

It sounds as though this is a group that had a great deal of discipline and a great deal of pride in the work they did. Were there ever any kind of disciplinary problems within the ranks, and was there any kind of discipline enforcement?

This guy struck such fear and trembling in the hearts of all he hired. He was very imperialistic in his demeanor, his stature, everything. I'm talking about Reverend Settle—we called him the deacon—behind his back, of course—but boy, we used to say "Uh-oh, here comes the deacon. Don't let him see. No, no straighten up!"—you know? But there was a pride, if you will, in who we were and what we did so that if somebody did something—didn't show up on time—he was reprimanded. [A person] didn't do that very often, and if he did, he was summarily dismissed. That just doesn't work in an outfit like that. In a group which had such—you realize in the '30s and '40s there was a great deal of struggling racially to be accepted. When one has a group of such stature, there is this need among all who belong to shape up and do what's right and to not disgrace either him or herself or the group by doing things that are unseemly. So there was very little, very little need for discipline. We got more flak from the conductor, who might have been, on any given night, a little temperamental and not getting what he wanted out of the group. We might have to deal with that kind of a personality. There always are personalities when you have conductors. Some of them are a little more persnickety or a little more emotional than others, and you have difficulty with them. But the discipline—we had very little that we had to impose upon its members.

Ever see anybody crash and burn out of the group? For that kind of problem?

Maybe one or two. We usually didn't know about it; they were gone. Almost like disappearing. We didn't know what happened. All of a sudden overnight they're gone. Something happened. They were dismissed. We don't know what they did or what happened. But very, very, very few of those—as I say, when you join Wings Over Jordan, you better know that you're in for the long haul if your voice will certainly be accepted. Because people were trying to join that group from all over the country: wherever we went, people were clamoring for auditions.

How was that handled?

That was handled by the director, and maybe you would have one or two people listen in. Some of us out of each section would maybe listen to see what kind of voice the person had. But it was by the director of the group.

Was there anybody who was such a towering talent that they were just added, or was it only in the need of replacement?

They were added as a person auditioned and they said, "My goodness, that's a very fine voice." Let's just add them where there's room. But there usually, you know, if you're carrying twenty-five voices, there's very rarely any room for anyone to come additionally. For the most part [he or she would] have to be a replacement for someone who dropped out. But I think, as I remember, while we had to replace people, I was replaced when I went to service; several people went. While I was in the group, there were very, very few people that we heard that we just had to add to the group. In fact, I can think of only perhaps one person; the rest were replacements.

What were the accommodations like for a traveling black choir in a segregated world?

For the most part the sponsoring aggregation would provide—say, for instance, it was a church—they would provide homes for us to stay in from the congregation. Of course, that would be very easily done because everybody was clamoring to have these famous people in their homes as guests. And then other times we would stay in hotels if that was not provided. These would be black hotels, during those days. There was no staying in white establishments—or eating, or any such thing. We ran into a lot of difficulties traveling on the road. Very, very tough traveling.

It would seem to me that when you—and this is something else we'll talk about later—a lot of your audiences were integrated, weren't they? I mean, you had a great white following as well as black listeners.

Yes. Yes.

So when you went and did these tours, this wasn't strictly a matter of going to a black church or something. You were playing white venues in places probably where there were not great black populations.

Yes. Sometimes we would, but if black people came to that auditorium—a large auditorium in a city—they were still segregated. We didn't do a lot of those. There came a time when we declined to go to a segregated auditorium, but I remember when we did, and we might sing for an all-white audience. But a lot of our concerts were for black audiences sponsored by churches.

If you went to what was essentially a white venue for a white audience, where would you find accommodations to eat?

In black establishments or for wherever they suggested. The white people who got us to come would certainly understand where we might find places to eat or maybe put us in a banquet hall somewhere and have it done there. But of course that would be black cooks and the like. Those who served us would certainly be black. They knew what black restaurants there were, accommodations as well.

It sounds as though there was a system—that segregation bred its own system of accommodation.

Yes. There's always a way to travel about. You find a way. You find through the underground, almost, ways to circumvent that which is troubling. You find, if you're going to go here or there in the South, ways to get around the problems of segregation—where you can sleep, where you can eat. That was done even before the tour was started. So we knew where we were going. The experiences that you meet while on the road are memorable and they're exasperating.

I was going to say that's a pretty polite word. [Both laugh.]

Very exasperating, and they make you angry. There were times, because we were so famous, there were exceptions made for us; for instance, if we stopped and got gasoline. They looked out and saw this great big bus with all these black people. This is down in the hills of Kentucky or Tennessee or somewhere, and they look out and saw black people on a bus. This is a huge bus, and it stopped and it needed gasoline. They say, "Come here! Look here—out here! Look at all these here people!"

I assume that "people" was not the word they would use?

No, [*laughs*] it certainly wasn't. Well they were just aghast at what they saw—but the dollar signs would be turning in their eyes. If they could sell one hundred gallons of gasoline, that's more gasoline than they would probably sell for a month. We would buy the gasoline *if* we could find something to eat there. We would still have to go to the back of the place to get it, but otherwise they would not even serve it in the back. But we could get something to eat or maybe even restroom facilities. We might be able to use them—with the power of the dollar that was going to be spent there—at that little roadside station. So we saw some weird things. We would get on the bus and laugh about it and how these country hicks would behave looking at us, never seeing anything like us before in their lives. Here are some people, obviously cosmopolitans, civilized people who didn't have farm attire on—no overalls for these people. Speaking in a language that sounded like it was from the North—a different brogue and, well—just a different attitude. People who were self-assured and knew who they were and not used to taking any guff from people. They were awed by this and they had a different look on their faces.

Plus, we ran into ugliness as well. We ran into ugliness. Very, very ugly things. That I—gosh, I tried to forget. Because one must go forward regardless of the things you experience in life and not harbor anger and all of the things that make for prejudice and ill will and all that sort of thing. We must go forward and think of ourselves as one human race of people who must get along. So I have chosen *not* to remember some of those ugly, ugly things, but as we talk I can remember that some of them were just horrendous.

I would think that with white folks who were uneducated and backwards, that you could probably deal with that a lot easier than you could when you met white folks who were educated and accomplished, who—though probably not giving voice as openly as what you experienced down home—would basically have the same attitude.

Exactly. Exactly: you've hit it right on the head. Exactly. There was a difference—and there still is a difference. Very polite people here in the North would say if you were to apply for a job or you want to buy a house or you want to rent some property, "Oh, I'm sorry—it was just filled." And of course it wasn't—but they were polite and smiled. But they said, "Get out of here" and used the "N" word down South. They let you know right away. "No you ain't—get out of here and don't let the sun catch you here." "Don't let the sun come down on you here in this town"—or wherever you were. And you knew. You could deal with that, but the disingenuous stuff you ran across in the North is very hard to deal with—disconcerting and hard to deal with.

Was there a general personality profile for members of the choir? Were there people who were uneducated and spoke backwards who were members of Wings Over Jordan?

Some—one or two. We had a lady who was one of our soloists who had absolutely no musical training; she was from Kentucky. And back in those days she spoke as a Kentuckian would. Splitting verbs, sometimes, but she learned to elevate her speech. But she was very uneducated and sounded very much like an old-time slave would sound in singing the spirituals and therein would lie the quaintness and the appeal of her for that spiritual. I found that to be so here in Kalamazoo. Just last year a group sang that spiritual. This was a white group with one or two black people in the group. There was a white lady who managed to capture that way of singing that took me back to this lady I'm talking about in our group who had that very primitive sound, that primitive way of pronouncing and singing words that took you clear back to slavery days—very, very unique and very appealing. She was recruited for her ability to sing in that manner. Her vocabulary and elocution had absolutely nothing to do with what she was hired for. Wings Over Jordan was expounding the spiritual. The spiritual is by definition a music that is indigenous of a group of people who were enslaved. Therein lies the appeal for her to sound as though she was back in those days. She did so very well.

You joined in '42 and then, you said, you went off to the war. Well, how long were you with the group before you went away?

Until the end of '43. I think I went in September or October. September perhaps of '43. Seemed like a long time, but that's because we went everywhere. We were just on the road all the time. Seemed like a long time before I went to the service, but it was not. That's a very short time; '42 to '43 is just one year on the road. We were deferred, some of us; were deferred by Mrs. Roosevelt, who saw to it that we had tires and gasoline, [which] was rationed during the war. Well, the deferment ran out for me. The war escalated. Kay Kaiser and his band was doing the same thing that we were doing, and Eleanor Roosevelt saw to it that those guys were deferred too, because they were entertaining troops.

So the war escalated, and then my deferment ran out. They had to have every available man who was fit for service to go, and so I had to show up there in Cleveland for duty. Cleveland, Ohio, which is where the choir headquarters were located. I had no other address other than the Wings Over Jordan offices. My notice came to the choir offices; I don't recall specifically, but I may have been on the road when the notice arrived. I was subsequently shipped out for indoctrination into the service.

When you went into the service, as I understand it black men were not allowed to see combat. What type of duty did you see?

I went to Texas and went into the Air Force. I went to basic training in Texas and then was shipped to Kearney, Nebraska, where we arose every morning and got into formation and marched briskly and at attention over to the barracks of the fliers—the white fliers—who were shipping out overseas and cleaned their barracks. We were incensed with that. Some of us had high scores. Some of the men in our outfit had as high an IQ as the fliers who were shipping out. There we were, cleaning their barracks. We were highly incensed for that, and some of us marched over to the adjutant general office and demanded to be transferred. We got that transfer. This is before Harry Truman integrated the service.

So I was in the signal corps and assigned to Okinawa. My company would put up telephone poles and then string telephone cable along those poles. And wherever those the cable ran out, there was a splice on that last pole. I went to school to be a cable splicer, and I had a jeep and a cable cart with supplies that I towed behind the jeep. I would go to where the cable ran out, and with my helper I would raise a platform on the pole, climb up to that platform. I would put on gaffs [climbing spurs] and climb up the pole. It wasn't just one wire, it was a bundle. We used fifty-pair cable. They were color-coded, and you matched same color ends. We had instruments to do that. You splice it, twist the wires' ends together, hammer it down, put a plastic sleeve on it, and then you boil it out with paraffin to seal it. If you've done your job right, the splice will last and there will be no trouble inside that sheath. Most of this work was done behind our lines. By that time the Japanese had fled to and were still holding the north end of the island. We were putting the poles and lines up on the south end. I understand that some of that stuff is still there after all these years. But we would go out on our own. We had no one along for protection—we'd had combat training, so it was just us. The only times we ever saw combat was when the stray Japanese who had been stranded on the south end of the island would attempt to slip through our bivouac area, our camp, in an effort to make their way to the main body of Japanese on the north end of the island. There might be shooting then—but nothing terribly dangerous—except for one incident. At our camp I was sergeant of the guard. Company A was on one side of the river and Company B was on the other side. I had a man stationed down at the bend of the river way over on the Company B side. I was asleep in a tent. There were twelve or fifteen people altogether in one big tent. The first sergeant was on one side of the tent sleeping as well. I was awakened by shooting and heard the guard I had stationed at the bend of the river shouting, "Sergeant of the guard! Sergeant of the guard!" That's what they're trained to do when there's trouble. I slept in the tent with my rifle down beside me and a belt with cartridges and bare-chested from the waist up. When I heard the guard shouting I jumped right up.

I slept with my boots on. I jumped up and ran to the front of the tent and shook the first sergeant, "Do you hear that?' And he said, "Yeah—but I ain't goin'. I ain't got nothin' to do with that out there. Go ahead!" So he stayed on his cot—a first sergeant. So away I went, and some other guys followed behind me, but I was very fast in those days and I left them behind—way behind me! By that time I had crossed the bridge to the other side of the river that divided our camp. On the other side in the first tent there was a guy who had a fifty-caliber machine gun set up right in the front of his tent. When the commotion started he looked and saw me running in front of the other guys and thought I was a Japanese being chased by those guys. He was ready to pull the trigger on that fifty-caliber machine gun but just as I passed by one of those guys behind me yelled, "Small—where are you?" I said, "Over here!" He later told me that the only thing that saved me was my yelling back in English as I passed by. That guy on the machine gun would have cut me in two. That was the closest I came. Another time I came close to danger—the captain took my jeep and got it stolen one night—and I never got the jeep back. So they gave me a driver with a recon—a bigger conveyance to pull my cable cart. So I had this driver, and they had coral roads over there that, when wet, were worse than ice. It was raining, and I told that fool driver to slow down—and he wouldn't. I could tell that he couldn't handle it, he didn't know how to drive on slippery roads in the first place. It was a very narrow road to start with, and there were vehicles parked on both sides of this road. One big vehicle with its tailgate down was stuck on the right. The driver started sliding and hit a vehicle over here. I saw what he was going to do and I bailed out. Just as soon as I bailed out, he swerved over to the right—and where I was sitting in the passenger seat, he impaled that seat on the tailgate. Well, we got him off of that, and I didn't ride back with him. I said, "You go back and turn in this vehicle and you tell them I sent you." He never drove again, but I never did get a jeep back. That was the second time I almost got killed. We went to a movie there on Okinawa, shown

CLARENCE SMALL 67

by another company. The people in our own company were just as skittish as they could be—and they saw people there off in the distance walking and they started shooting at them. It was us. They were just scared. If a grasshopper jumped up, they'd shoot at it. They were just scared to death of anything that moved—and they saw us walking in the distance and started shooting at us. You know what I did? I hit the dirt and came up shooting back at them. I did! I hollered back at them, "Stop you fools! It's us—it's us!" And when I started shooting back at them—then they quit shooting. You know, this was very late in the war—the war was really over but the Japanese were very stubborn. They continued to fight. They wouldn't believe they had lost the war. I was in an all-black platoon, and I had a Japanese prisoner of war in my tent and showed him my rifle. They didn't have any quarrel with black soldiers. They said, "Our fight is not with you." Isn't that interesting? They knew our history. Everybody in the world knows our history in the United States, from the Indians on down, slavery, everything. Everybody knows our history. So I didn't fear our prisoners of war—they weren't fighting us. So that was my job in the service. I applied for warrant officer junior grade as a musician. I couldn't get that. I had a very high score, and I wanted to be a radio operator in a bomber; and I couldn't get that, of course. I remained in the signal corps and then came back to Wings Over Jordan in 1946 and rejoined them in Houston, Texas.

In the years that had passed while you were away, what differences did you find when you came back to the choir?

Just in personnel and also director. I came back to a lady directing—one of the ladies who was a soloist in the choir. She was directing in the interim between some of the fellows. The last director before we disbanded was a fellow by the name of James Lewis Elkinson. I was talking with Ellison White—the bass of the quartet—and he and I both agreed: that guy—man, he was just the essence of a director. He knew his stuff and was a very fine director on stage. He had it together. So I came back to him. But the personnel had changed somewhat. But how it sounded remained the same and did quite well in the interim. It maintained its integrity, and, of course, when I got back we started our quartet, the Wingmen, and that augmented the group.

When our quartet went to California, we had been thinking for some time that we were good enough to be on our own. We made contact with a person who would represent us—act as our booking agent. This was a manager who knew his way around California. We tried to keep it quiet that we were going to leave the group. We didn't want to scuttle Wings Over Jordan. We wanted the choir to continue. We just wanted to be on our own, but as they said during World War II, "Loose lips sink ships." Somehow, they discovered we were going to leave the choir and didn't want to go on without us. We were the nucleus of the choir. Emory Barnes, our baritone, was the personnel manager—highly skilled in keeping the choir together and organizing the choir's bookings—where, when, and how we went—where we ate, where we stayed. He was integral to the day-by-day operation of Wings Over Jordan. The guy was brilliant. Well, you know he went on to manage Nat King Cole, so you know he had the wherewithal to manage a group. Then the first tenor, Cecil Dandy, was a soloist. I had done some solo work, and the bass singer was a soloist as well. So the rest of the choir didn't want to do the tour without us. But money was also a factor. We never received any royalties for the recordings. Back in those days very few artists received any royalties unless they were represented by a union. So they said, "We'll quit too." The rest of the choir was in San Diego when they decided they were going to leave. When the bus came around in San Diego for the Sunday broadcast, no one got on the bus to do the broadcast—and they refused to board the bus. So Reverend Settle was all done as far as the group was concerned. The bus actually had to return to Cleveland without the choir. The choir members decided to continue to perform, and our quartet stayed with them for a short while to get them up and going. They found a minister in Pasadena who helped them reorganize and get some performance dates—and get some vehicles. I think they bought two Suburbans—which held nine people—so about eighteen voices went back across the country. The group did concerts, recorded, and managed to make some money. Reverend Settle held the patent on the name Wings Over Jordan, but as long as they paid a certain percentage of the profits to Reverend Settle, he allowed the group to use the name Wings Over Jordan. They billed themselves as Formerly Wings Over Jordan, and it worked for a short time, but without any experienced management eventually the group failed. This was in 1948. Reverend Settle returned to Cleveland, Ohio—which was the headquarters. Then he put out the call for new members. That's what happened.

So that would be the reconstituted version of the choir that he founded when he went back to Cleveland?

Yes—and they never really sounded like the old group—they just couldn't. There's no way—I guess they were somewhat successful because if you take a group out on the road and you manage to imitate a former group, you can get by, somewhat, but it never, never sounded like the old group. Of course, it couldn't—it didn't have its personnel. The people, the new group, just didn't have the knowledge of the harmonies—it wasn't written down. We didn't have anything written down. I wrote and someone else wrote some arrangements in a book that we sold around the country, but it was not written as we sang it;

we deliberately *did not* do that—why give away what your trademark is? You certainly don't write arrangements so that people can sing it the way you do it. So no one really actually knew exactly note for note how we sang, and of course they didn't have the voices. That's what happened with that second group.

Tell me the story of the Wingmen.

We always like to—fellows when they get together always start singing, you know, and we found that Emery Barnes, who is a baritone, was from Kalamazoo. He joined Wings Over Jordan before I did and sent for me. He told them about me because I had sung with him in his father's quartet. He and I had both had experience in a quartet. Cecil Dandy, who was the lead and second tenor, and Ellison White, who was the bass, sang together in Florida. They knew one another in school, and they sang together before they got to Wings. Now you got four people who, in a sense, sang together. All we had to do—two people each singing together. Just put those two together and now you've got the makings of a beautiful blend. We started singing on the bus and decided "WOW!"—we sound great together. We had a terrific blend. The bass, he could sing; he sounded like a Russian bass. He could really go down there. The baritone—I was a pretty fair first tenor: I could get up there where first tenors belong. It just made a fine blend. Every time we would sing a song, everybody just marveled at how we sounded. So they just decided they had to have us sing on the program every night wherever we went. That's how the quartet got together, and we called ourselves the Wingmen as an addendum to Wings Over Jordan. We got out to California and then we decided to make our own break from the group as a quartet doing pop things in California. We let the group know that we were going to leave—after we got ourselves an arranger from RKO—the movie studio RKO—and a manager who had properties out in Los Angeles and who knew his way around. We began to sing around in the various venues there. Some were discovery rooms, and we became quite popular there. We were very unique in that we sang close harmony, unlike the Mills Brothers—who had a very fine group. Their harmony was straight. Ours was beginning to be modern and closer. Ink Spots were different. I think we were closer to a white group. What's that group that came along? We preceded them and they were very, very, *very* popular. They did pop things—the Modernaires!—stuff like that. Our harmonies were so good and so close and the blend was so good that we could have done that. But they weren't ready for us. Every time they looked at us, they either wanted to—when we come on the scene, they either wanted us to sound like the Mills Brothers or the Ink Spots, and we weren't any of that. Hey—we're not doing any of that stuff—[*laughs*] that's not up to par—that's not modern enough for us. In fact, we were supposed to make a movie in place of the Ink Spots, who were in England and couldn't make a movie. We had been heard at Friar's Club—I don't know which place—but somebody's producer heard us and said we were the group to make a movie. Well, we couldn't find the lead singer in the quartet, and the window of opportunity closed on us. So we could not make that movie.

Were you singing secular material? Pop material?
Yes. Yes.

Were you singing that when you were with the choir?
Oh, no—oh, no. *Oh no*, we dare not do that. We might sing some humorous things but nothing of a secular nature, especially pop tunes. We only did that when we were on our own. We did some spirituals, too, when we were on our own because we would sing in churches. We sang in cathedrals—wherever they would have us sing. There was a Foursquare Church, which was very popular during those days, heard around the country. They would have us come—the Aimee Semple McPherson Temple there in Los Angeles. We sang there. They had us come every so often to sing there, and we sang spirituals. The other venues would be places like the Friar's Club. We sang with Frankie Laine one night, and we were a smash hit—much to the chagrin of Frankie Laine, who was the headliner. They shouted, "More, more and more," as opposed to being polite for his offerings. I remember that very vividly because George Burns was sitting down in front with that trademark cigar and invited us to come to his table to talk. "Fellows, very good fellows. What are you going to do next? Where are you going?" He was very, very enthused about our group. So we did pretty well. A couple of us didn't want to travel. We'd won on Horace Heidt's, who had a talent show around the country. We had won one of his talent shows. He wanted us to headline a group to travel around the country. And he wanted us to record, which we did do. We didn't sign a contract for five years with him; he kept our recordings on the shelf—never did put them out. Then, Amos and Andy had a radio program—I know you've heard of the *Amos 'n' Andy* show. Well they had heard us, and we are on the classic Christmas show—our quartet is. They have a classic show that comes on every year somewhere in the country on radio.

You mean some real black folks actually made it to the Amos 'n' Andy *radio show?*

[*Laughs.*] Yeah! And you know we don't have any residuals for that show. They said the credits at the end of the show—they said Jeff Alexander and his singers and his musical aggregation or whatever they say of any orchestra. We'll see you next broadcast and te da, te da, te da. Well, it was the Wingmen who did this "Oh, Mary, What You Going to Name That Pretty Little Baby?" at the end of the program. It's a marvelous program; you know, we as black folks were very, very angry about the *Amos 'n' Andy* program. But that was a very fine program, though—that particular program where Amos tells the meaning of Christmas to little Arbadella, who wants to go to sleep to await the presence of Santa Claus the next day. He tells the meaning of Christmas in a very, very lovely way. So I really liked that show no matter what people say about it—and of course our part in it. She wanted to hear some Christmas carols, and so a group of white singers started to singing "Silent Night." I believe it was "Silent Night." Then they faded out, and we came in over the top of them singing "Oh Mary What You Going to Name That Pretty Little Baby." That's a spiritual. And it had to be done by a black group. They didn't know how to sing a spiritual in those days—even if they tried.

What happened to the Wingmen?

Fame is fleeting and depends on so many variables. You've got to be in the right place at the right time. We did have the stuff to make it, but a lot of things just conspired against us at various times. We formed ourselves a full group of four singers and the arranger and the manager, and we each had a vote. They voted not to accept certain contracts because there wasn't enough money. But two of us wanted to sign some contracts—Ellison White and myself—but we weren't enough to swing it. Also, it appeared to me that the quartet was just not going to travel. Two of the members didn't want to travel—Emery didn't want to travel. He and Cecil wanted to do some things in the Sacramento area. To me, it became evident that we weren't going to get off and running the way that we wanted to. So I came back home for my mother's funeral and I never went back to California. I just never went back. Those other guys did other things, though, remaining out there. Emery Barnes was the personnel manager for Nat King Cole. And Ellison White sang with other groups and did other things. He and I sang with Jester Harrison, who was on the *Amen* show on television. He was the old man who had a very funny part on the *Amen* show, and he was quite a musician. He had us in his quartet singing for various segments in the area. Friar's Club and you name it. So they stayed out there and did other things, but I came back home and stayed.

Is there anything we haven't discussed that you feel we need to talk about?

I don't think I've told you about what happened in Houston, Texas, when I rejoined the choir. I went into the service and wound up on Okinawa. I couldn't join the members of Wings Over Jordan that had gone to Europe to sing for the servicemen. I had to serve my entire time. So when I got out of the service, then I rejoined the choir in Houston, Texas, in 1946. I rejoined around Christmastime. I immediately got a girlfriend—that happened very quickly. We were housed in the Fifth Ward there in Houston, which was amazing for those days—brick homes, which were just lovely to look at—very nice neighborhoods with well-kept, manicured lawns.

All black people living in this Fifth Ward. We lived there, and it was almost Christmas, so we decided to go to town to look for Christmas presents. We boarded the bus there and sat in the first seats behind the sign that said Colored. As we proceeded into town, the black section of the bus filled up. As we got closer to downtown the white section began to fill up and within three blocks of the center of town it was filled as well, and two white men got on. The bus driver turned around to us—my girlfriend and I, who were seated in the section legally allotted us—and told us we would have to move. I was highly incensed. I had just returned from a very dangerous situation in the service—I could have been killed serving the country—taking time out from my avocation in a dangerous situation: and I'm told I have to get up for two white men and give them my seat? I said "No!" At this early date, 1946, neither Martin Luther King, Rosa Parks, nor the civil rights movement had ever been heard of—and we were in Houston, Texas! All the people in the black section listening to this, their eyes got big as doughnuts. They were frightened to death—they'd never seen anything like it. They'd never heard anything like this. This young black man—sound like he's from up north and he's going to get us all killed. So they all said, "Here's a seat, here's a seat!" and they all started to get up. I said, "Sit down!" I was as angry at them as I was the bus driver. I said, "Sit down—I've got a seat!" They didn't know what to do. Now, my girlfriend had begun to see how bold I was, and how angry I was, and she was emboldened as well. She spoke up then: "Well—I don't want to ride this bus anyway! Just let me out!" We were about three blocks from the center of town. So she got up and walked down the aisle and stood beside the bus driver, who was turning all kinds of colors. He knew that something was highly unusual about this couple. He didn't know why I would object. They were so used to telling people what they must do and what they must not do and having people be frightened and abiding. He had a billy club about this long [*demonstrates*] and this thick by his side. He'd have been in for a surprise if he'd brought it out, but he didn't. He turned every color there was, and she put her finger in his face—just like Jan Brewer did our black president—wagging her finger in his face. My girlfriend did that to this bus driver—and I've forgotten what she said, but she just let him have it. She went off the bus first—usually guys get off first and help the lady off, but she went first because I wasn't going to have him do anything to her after I stepped off.

So she stepped off and then I backed off the bus. We walked the three blocks to the center of town and shopped. Her present to me was a Bulova watch, which I still have. One of these days I'm going to have it repaired. They say it cost more to fix it than to buy a new one, but as a keepsake I want the thing to run. The incident was surprising. It was probably a good thing we got off the bus. I probably would've been dead if there was any further confrontation—but nothing happened. I just knew that the gendarmes would come and get us, but there was no recrimination for our activity—whatever. We were unmolested, and I survived and have had things to do. I've discovered after all these years that there are no accidents in life. We experience things that are in store for us. History sometimes takes note when it's time—and sometimes does not. It was not time for the [civil rights] movement to start at that particular time and place—so it started instead at a later date with Rosa Parks.

Reverend F. W. **McGee Jr.**

One of my favorite listeners was Robert Little. Robert was a black senior and blind. He was a regular caller—in fact, there were very few weeks when he didn't call, and his calls were always welcome. He would call while I was on the air, and we'd talk for ten or fifteen minutes, sometimes longer. When he found out that I drank Coca-Cola while doing the program, he started sending me a case of Coke each month, delivered to the studio by his brother Milton. During one phone call Robert surprised me, telling me that he attended the church where the Reverend F.W. McGee Sr. had pastored. Reverend McGee was a pastor in the COGIC [Church of God in Christ] who gained some recognition for a series of recorded sermons done for the Victor label during the 1920s, when COGIC was working to establish itself as a major denomination. I would include records by Rev. McGee on my program's Vintage Gospel feature. McGee had passed away in the 1970s, and his son, Rev. F. W. McGee Jr., had taken his father's place, pastoring his church in Chicago. Robert asked if I would be interested in talking with McGee Jr. if he could arrange it, and the three of us got to-

Rev. F. W. McGee Sr. Photo courtesy Robert G. Koester Collection.

gether at the radio station's production studios located at 310 W. Pershing Road (Thirty-Ninth Street), which at the time served as headquarters for Chicago Public Schools.

This interview was recorded April 11, 1985. Rev. F. W. McGee Jr. died in March 1991.

■ ■ ■

Please tell me about your father.

Ford Washington McGee Sr. was born in Winchester, Tennessee, on October 5, 1890. There were fourteen children in his family—his mother was the mother of fourteen children—they had a lot of children in those days. He was the third child—the two previous to him were boys, and he was the third child. His family moved from Winchester, Tennessee, to Hillsboro, Texas, when he was a young lad. After finishing grade school in Hillsboro he attended higher education in Waco, Texas; the name of the school was Paul Quinn College—which was an African Methodist Episcopal Church–affiliated [college], supported by the church—the church supported the college—it yet exists. That same school—Paul Quinn College—is still there in Waco. Most of the male children that went there at that time were, more or less, candidates for the ministry—since it was a religious school. In those days—just like now—most faiths were looking for prospects to perpetuate their work. And so he was a good candidate. I can tell you that he was very bright. Then he met my mother, and they got married in 1910. My mother's father was a professor there in Paul Quinn. Then they moved from Texas to Oklahoma about 1912. He taught school—he was a rural schoolteacher, and he was also pastoring an AME church. He was converted to this faith in 1918; he went to San Antonio, and they were having a Church of God in Christ meeting. He attended that meeting, and he was converted; after that, he left the AME religion and started with this new faith—the Holiness Church, Church of God in Christ.

What was the difference in the two different faiths?

The difference between the two church organizations was that this church here—the Church of God in Christ—believed in the interpretation of the scriptures as it was written in the days of the Apostles. They believed in the speaking of tongues, the baptism of the Holy Ghost, and the actual practice of the laying on of hands and the sick being healed and all of the signs that went with the Holy Ghost—that was the difference. The AME said that they believed that, but they didn't practice it in the same manner. They didn't have the demonstrations. The Church of God in Christ had actual demonstrations of the spirit taking place, just like it did in the days of the Apostles. And if you know the Bible—the Apostles laid hands on blind people and they restored their sight—they healed crippled folks and all that—and they did all of that in that day: they did every bit of that.

What was the reaction of the African Methodist Episcopal Church to a religion that was so demonstrative? Did they regard them as hucksters?

They labeled them as being deluded! There were all sorts of derogatory things being said about them—that didn't stop them! They had similar experiences as the first church had.

Now, if you know the history of the first church—the Christian church—the first church had similar persecutions—all in the New Testament—from the acts of the Apostles all the way through.

So there wasn't much credence given to acts of healing?

No—not even in the day of the original church! The established church—churches everywhere—opposed the new doctrine. They opposed Jesus because he came with a new commandment—and so it was the same thing repeated, more or less.

How did your father's conversion set with your mother? They were both originally from the AME faith.

Well—she didn't take to it too well—not to start with [*laughs*]. Later, she became adjusted—but she didn't take to it too well. That was a good question.

And I assume that would have caused problems with his in-laws as well?

It caused a lot of problems—but he was so dedicated. He was convinced he was on the right track: he didn't allow any of that to stop him—and they all got in line sooner or later. It was a brand-new faith at that time. The founder of the church was the Bishop Charles Harrison Mason, and the headquarters of this church was in Memphis, Tennessee. Charles Harrison Mason was the founder—and he sent all the ministers that showed a special talent and zeal for the work to different places. So my father was sent, first to Kansas City to help the minister there, Reverend B. M. Parker, run a revival in Kansas City, Missouri—and from there Reverend Parker recommended him to go to Iowa and establish a work there—in other words, they were evangelizing. That was in 1921 when he got a really good foothold—which was just three years after he was converted into the church. But he already had some background in the church because he'd been in the AME Church. The church was young then and he was one of the pioneers—he had a lot of talent and ability—and was very full of the spirit. He established the Church of God in Christ in Des Moines,

Iowa—and also in other cities in Iowa. In that day they called the chief priest of the church the "overseer." He became the first overseer for the state of Iowa for the Churches of God in Christ. And that's when he first became known nationwide—not just there in Iowa, but in other parts of the United States, because he traveled all over, running revivals. It was still the year 1921 while he was based in Des Moines, Iowa, that he came to Chicago to run a revival at Fortieth and State Street for the Reverend William Roberts, who was the head of the Church of God in Christ for Illinois. That church is still at that original location, and his son, Bishop Roberts, succeeded him as pastor. After that, my father was invited to come back here and run revivals. In 1926 he moved his family here to Chicago. He also pitched a large tent at Thirty-Third Street and Prairie Avenue. He held nightly meetings with thousands of people coming around. This faith was very new at that time, and many miracles were being wrought through him. He also sang and played the piano along with his preaching. He had a great gift of healing as well. Many people were drawn to him by his singing and playing—he was quite an attraction at that time. Everybody who heard him was very much impressed—he was quite a character.

Since this was—as you say—a very new religion, were most of their meetings in churches, or was the majority of their work done in tents?

In most places that was the way they got started—in tents—at least during the time of the year you could use tents. After the tent season was up they would rent halls. He rented a hall at 3140 Indiana Avenue—that's where he would winter up. Then, in May or June, they'd pitch a tent again. Finally, he built a church, which still stands today, at 4946 Vincennes—they built that in 1929. In other places they would start in homes—until they finally could build places. He was known all over the Brotherhood. Even today they refer to it as the Brotherhood because they all preach the same doctrine—they all believe in the same thing, and they all practice the same thing. That's the church right now! If you'd see it in Memphis now during the time we call Annual Convocation, you'd get your eye full—because we have twenty-five [thousand] or thirty thousand people there in one session on the official day—more than the place will hold, more than the largest place in Memphis will hold—Cook Center. The present presiding bishop of the church is Bishop J. O. Patterson—the son-in-law of the founder of the church—Bishop Charles Harrison Mason.

When did you come on the scene?

I started out with my daddy as a little boy—and I'd go wherever he went, because I was the only boy at that time, when we first started out. I was born January 19, 1916. I was just two years old when he started out, but by the time I got to be four or five years old, I was pretty much aware of what he was preaching and teaching about. As I got older and older, I wasn't always in the church—but I always had that church background. As he got older—and I got older—I got very active in the church. I became a convert myself in the mid-1940s. After that I became a minister, and I was ordained by my father; I became his helper and when he got to the place that he wasn't able to carry out his duties like he had been—he put more and more on my shoulders. I was co-pastor with him for several years. When he passed away in April of 1971, I succeeded him as pastor.

I don't know how they got in touch with him, but the Victor record company contacted him to make recordings. One of his first recordings was "The Lion [of] the Tribe of Judah" and "By His Strength We Are Healed"—and some of the others you have here.

Who were the composers of the sides you mentioned?

"Lion [of] the Tribe of Judah"—he composed that. He also composed "Jesus the Lord Is a Savior." I couldn't say who was responsible for several of the titles you have here, but Lion [of] the Tribe of Judah" and "Jesus the Lord Is a Savior"—I know he composed those. Some of the other songs recorded by him were composed by other writers.

If you were born in 1916, you would have been ten or eleven when these sides were recorded. Were you aware of the recordings?

Very much aware! [*Laughs.*] I was so much aware of them that I'd try to imitate him by preaching and singing some [*laughs*].

Were you ever able to go to the studio when he was recording?

I think I went once or twice. The Victor studios were down on north Michigan Avenue. The setup there was similar to this—they had a room with several singers and a piano. They didn't have organs like they do now. But they had that piano, and several of his main helpers would come along with him—I'd say seven, eight, or ten to help background him.

You wouldn't have any knowledge of what session payment was for the records?

No—I didn't have any knowledge of that, but percentage-wise it was a great help—particularly if you compared the day, the time, and the money—and how far a dollar would go then compared to how far it will go now; the additional income certainly aided him in providing for his family—and in helping him to travel. At all times travel is an expense, and in some of the places he would go the smaller churches weren't able to even approximate what the expense was getting there. It wasn't done with the notion of how much you could gain materially. They were primarily concerned with the saving of souls and converting people—which I think should be the motive at all times, for religious purposes anyway. He went all over the country, and the records made a great big difference. It was a great boost to his ministry

Did he regard the recordings as an accomplishment in terms of his church work?

Very much so—it was a great help! It was a great aid—naturally the records went before him, and that made it even better. They weren't thinking so much in terms of profit. The records were a help to a lot of people—people that never saw him or heard him in person.

A lot of people were healed by hearing the records also converted by hearing them. Practically everybody who was a member of this faith had the records! Yes, sir! The records were available through the church—even the national church at the headquarters in Memphis—they were available there. Naturally, Bishop Mason was an agent for it, [as were] and all his members throughout the United States. So there was practically no one in the Church of God in Christ who wasn't aware of his records. He was a great preacher!

So your father had no problem with the church higher-ups receiving all the attention and travel opportunities that the records provided?

No—none. Bishop Mason excelled him. Bishop Mason was one of the greatest persons that ever lived on this Earth; my father's accomplishment was no threat to him in any way—because he had the whole church. He was the one sending people out—he wanted them to do well. Any accomplishment by a member of their faith was a boon to the entire church. There was plenty of room for everyone. My father loved him—he just adored him! All of us did. We still revere his memory to this day. Bishop Mason lived to be ninety-five years old.

Can you talk about the end of the road for your father?

He died April 8, 1971. He was eighty years old. But he had slowed down for fifteen or twenty years before that. His age began to show—he fathered nine children.

He had worked pretty hard—traveling around, that's pretty difficult. He died from a heart condition brought on by arterial sclerosis—that was the listed cause of death—but arterial sclerosis is a long process, and sometimes it takes years. My father was very influential in helping a lot of people—including his own family. Not only was he, in my opinion—naturally I may be prejudiced—but I thought he was one of the greatest ministers that ever mounted a rostrum. Also, he was very aware of what was going on around him. His mother passed when some of the other children were at an early age, and he took one of the children, whose name was Henry McGee, into his home and after he finished high school he kept him right there in his home and assisted him in going to college. Later Henry became the first black postmaster in the city of Chicago. Henry Wadsworth McGee—he's yet living but he became the first black postmaster of Chicago.

He has three daughters that were schoolteachers—two have passed away. He has a son who's now the principal of a school in Chicago Heights.

For most interviews done in the production studios it was common practice to have an engineer on duty who would set and monitor recordings levels as well as start and stop the tape recorder—typical production work. On this particular interview no engineer was available—so I did the engineering myself, which meant I would start the recorder, then walk into the studio, sit at the microphone and conduct the interview. When it was over, I would leave the interview room to stop the tape recorder. A curious thing happened, though. Once the interview was concluded, in the short time it took me to reach and stop the recorder, Reverend McGee Jr. confided to my friend Robert Little that despite his earlier denials during the interview, his father, Reverend McGee Sr. had indeed encountered great jealousy and resentment from other COGIC leaders over the recognition and acclaim his recordings had generated for the church and for him personally. But despite this negative backlash within the church, Bishop Mason, leader of COGIC, both condoned and encouraged the continued recordings. This admission by McGee Jr. was captured unintentionally and directly contradicts his response during the interview.

Pastor Donald **Gay**

I first met Pastor Donald Gay when we both appeared on an engagement at the Old Town School in Chicago. Pastor Gay was the much younger brother of Evelyn, Mildred, and Geraldine—the famed gospel group the Gay Sisters. It was a piano evening at the Old Town School. I played drums behind Henry Gray, while Pastor Gay sang with his sister Geraldine Gay on piano; the final act on the bill was Erwin Helfer and his blues band. During our downtime in the green room Pastor Gay sought me out and started talking to me about artists and records he had heard me play on the radio program. It was a fascinating conversation for me because the pastor apparently had firsthand contact with many artists I knew only through their recordings. Our conversation continued behind the scene through most of the evening. I didn't hear from him directly for a while, but I continued to hear secondhand conversations from a friend who met with him regularly for meals at the Valois Cafeteria in Chicago's Hyde Park. After hearing a number of those secondhand accounts, I decided I would get in touch. I called him and made arrangements to do an interview at his church at 526 East Sixty-Seventh Street in Chicago.

Pastor Donald Gay. Photo courtesy Gay Family Archive.

This interview was recorded March 8, 2008. As of this writing Reverend Gay is still living and pastoring in Chicago.

■ ■ ■

I was born right here in Chicago. My family consisted of my father and mother; my oldest sister was Evelyn. Next came the middle sister, Mildred; between Mildred and Geraldine was my brother, Robert. He was a trumpet player who played in Dizzy Gillespie's band. The last sister was Geraldine. The three sisters sang—Evelyn, Mildred, and Geraldine. I came along much later. As a matter of fact, Geraldine is closest in age to me, and she's fourteen years older than me. I'm sixty-two this year. If you take a quick look at this picture, that's the three of them right there—and that little kid sitting on the piano, that's me. My father was born January 1, 1898, and came to Chicago from a little town in Georgia called Alma. My mother was born February 22, 1907, in Atlanta. Her father first came to Chicago and worked in a place called Daniel Boone Woolen Mills. He sent for his children one by one—and that's how they got to Chicago. My mother was brought up in the Methodist Church, but there was a little lady that lived in their community who was part of a Pentecostal organization called the Church of God in Christ. The church celebrated its one-hundredth year just this past year, but it was just getting off the ground back then. My mother was brought up Methodist, but she got saved and the Lord touched her. So my parents got married and started their family over on the West Side. They lived in an integrated community where Jews and blacks all lived together. As a matter of fact, there was a rabbi who lived upstairs from us, and the rabbi's daughter was named Evelyn. My mother thought it was such a unique name, she named my oldest sister Evelyn. My mother was the choir director at Elder P. R. Favor's church. As my sisters were coming along, they sang, and at that time she noticed that the girls had a talent to sing. So she had Evelyn take piano lessons and made sure that Evelyn could play the piano. Then one day when my sister Geraldine was about three years old, she asked my father to lift her up to the piano. She said, "I think I can play what Evelyn plays." So my father lifted Geraldine up to the piano and Geraldine could play the same thing Evelyn could play—and never had a lesson! How this happened was that Mother Bell, who was Sister Rosetta Tharpe's mother—Bell was Rosetta's maiden name— Mother Bell was running a revival in Chicago, and she stayed at our house. And my mother, who was pregnant with my sister Geraldine at the time, said, "Mother Bell, I want you to pray for my unborn child. Put your hands on me and pray for my unborn child so that my baby will have the gift—the same gift as your daughter Rosetta"—because Rosetta Tharpe never had any music lessons. Mother Bell prayed for my mother, and Geraldine could play as a three-year-old—that was the phenomenon. Geraldine could play everything that Evelyn could play—and without taking a lesson! And it still to this day has made her such an unusual musician. Evelyn played a much bluesier style, while Geraldine played a more jazzy style with chord progressions and all. And Mildred was the singer, with the high soprano voice, and they were a trio. They went out to California in 1948 and made their first record for John Dolphin—a song called "Have a Little Talk With Jesus," which was arranged by Evelyn. But they were the first musical group from the Church of God in Christ, because prior to that everybody who came from the COGIC were looked upon as un-educated, uncouth, didn't know how to conduct themselves. And here were my sisters—they were polished, and my sister knew how to arrange and knew about style. In addition, the music my sisters made had range. They could sing sweet songs and they could sing house-rockers. That's one of the things that made them so unique. Another unique thing about the group: one sister would introduce the group, another would be playing piano—and then when she

The Gay Sisters. Photo courtesy Gay Family Archive.

got through playing, my other sister would come over and play, and they'd both play for Mildred. Those are among the things that made them a unique group.

As they went along they traveled the width and breadth of the country. They went to New York City and recorded for Savoy Records—Herman Lubinsky. Herman Lubinsky was a wonderful man—I think you can say that [*laughs*]. The Gay Sisters recorded a song for him called "God Will Take Care of You." That song was the bestselling record he had ever had on the label. My sister Evelyn said it sold over one-hundred-thousand copies. That song, that record carried them for many, many years. That was the thing about gospel music back in those days—you could have a hit record and travel on the strength of that one record for the next ten years. And what happened was they had that hit record, "God Will Take Care of You"; it was such a phenomenon that Herman Lubinsky said, "You're great, I love you. You're just like my own children . . ." but they never got any money! [*Laughs.*] He gave all three of them mezuzahs, you know. He said, "You're wonderful." My sister Evelyn thought he was such a great person that she told other people about the label. She brought the Davis Sisters to the label and James Cleveland. She said, "Come on out. Lubinsky will take care of you." Apparently, at that time he was taking care of some of the people, they had a guy that was working with the label named Lee Magid. Magid was an A&R-man-turned-talent-manager, and Lee tried to tell Evelyn at the time, "Let me manage you." He pointed out to them that they weren't making any money, but they were happy just going along. But what did they know? I'm told that he went on to manage Della Reese.

How many sides did they make for Lubinsky?

They put out at least twelve sides. They had an album called *God Will Take Care of You.*

What was the musical accompaniment for those recordings?

Mostly just Evelyn on piano. On some of the sides you can hear Geraldine on the organ and someone would play tambourine. They had a song called "We're Gonna Have a Good Time." Mildred would sing this repeating chorus, "We're gonna have a good time, good time, good time, we're gonna have a good time," and then Mildred put in the lyrics, "We're gonna rock and roll." And at that time nobody had heard about rock 'n' roll—this was the early 1950s. Then a few years later it became the popular term, you know, "rock 'n' roll." Evelyn wrote a lot of the songs. She was a member of BMI [Broadcast Music Inc.] and AFTRA [American Federation of Television and Radio Artists]. She was way ahead of her time. The girls kept traveling, and I traveled with them at an early age. I remember a lot of the other singers and acts had cars, but neither Evelyn nor Mildred drove, so if Evelyn and Mildred had an engagement, they'd travel by train. One time they were sponsored in Picayune, Mississippi. The sponsors had posted a picture of the two of them to promote the event, but the picture had faded. So the sheriff sees the picture and says, "We're not gonna let these white folks sing for these niggers down here." In some of these places you could take the Illinois Central just so far and then you'd have to ride the bus the rest of the way, so when they came into town, the sheriff met them at the station. Then, in later years, we would travel by car. Geraldine had a car, and I bought my first car in 1967, and sometimes we'd travel in that.

Were all the engagements done for the Church of God in Christ?

Oh, no! The COGIC didn't bring my sisters in very much. In its early stages, COGIC stressed revivals. The girls would do more jobs outside the church— Baptists churches, Methodist churches. They sang for a lot of Baptist churches. For example, they had a guy, Herman Nash, who would book them in Atlanta, Georgia—into different halls and theaters. They traveled around. They appeared at the Howard Theater in Washington, D.C., and at the Apollo when gospel first went to the Apollo. Back then my sisters were being paid tidy little sums, but at the COGIC you could sing their ears off and they'd walk out and say, "God will bless you." And that's why they lost so many acts.

How long did your sisters stay out on the road?

I'd say from 1947 to 1976, which was the Bicentennial Festival; I traveled with them for over a year. I remember my parents called and told my sisters it was time for them to send me home because it was time for me to start school. But my sisters would make money because they knew the promoters. In Georgia there was Herman Nash; in New Orleans was a guy by the name of August Jackson. My sisters knew the promoters around the country. Evelyn was such a caring and legitimately nice person that she shared her book of promoters with other singers. Subsequently, they ended up blackballing her because that's the kind of people they were. They didn't believe in helping each other. For example, one very prominent singer active today, when asked, "Where are the Gays?" answered, "Oh—they're dead." But my sisters were the first to actually come out with their style of singing—and it was from COGIC! COGIC had *no* other singers that reached the level my sisters did. And to this very day the church has never really honored my sisters for the contribution they made. They made a great contribution. They were great ambassadors for the church. They had an appearance, they had presence. Evelyn was aware and worked public relations when no one else did. Evelyn always taught us [that] when we sang, our diction was important. Evelyn reminded me that the reason she liked Sam Cooke was Sam was very precise on diction. When he sang a song, you could understand the words. When they recorded for Decca, the studio was located right across from Lawry's Restaurant in Chicago. They were in the studio doing a song called "Oh Lord, Won't You Have Mercy?" The verse goes, "Lord, I'm weak—Please make me strong." Mildred sang the verse, and Evelyn stopped: "Ooopp—wait a minute. Mildred, the words are "Lord, I'm weak—Please make me strong—Direct my steps—All the day long. Where I have faltered. . . ." Evelyn was right on the money. That's the type of person Evelyn was. Your appearance counted and your presence when you gave an interview—you had to speak with a certain decorum. You're a gospel singer—exemplify what you talk about. A lot of the gospel singers were, when the show was over, let's go back to their hotel rooms and let's have a fifth. Evelyn—uh-uh! We're from the Holiness Church, and if you're going to sing for the glory of God—DO IT! Don't go out and drink or get drunk. Rev. C. L. Franklin—one of the greatest scotch drinkers in the world! [*Laughs.*]

What were the stage arrangements at a Gay Sisters program?

They would announce us: "We have the Gay Sisters." Or, if I was fortunate enough to be on the program, "We have the Gay Sisters—with their little brother, Preacher Gay." When we came out, Mildred would come out first, Evelyn would come out second, then Geraldine—and I'd come out last. The microphone would be here for Mildred; I'd stand behind Mildred because I was the third singer. If they needed harmony and needed the alto, I became the alto voice. Evelyn would always be at the piano—with a microphone at the piano. She was the one that would talk you through the song. She would say, "We're going to sing a song that everybody needs to know. In this time when we're going through troubles and trials, it's good to know that 'God Will Take Care of You.'" And, of course, the audience would recognize the tune—and that's how it would be set up. And then if Geraldine was with us, we'd come out—Evelyn first, then Mildred, Geraldine, and I'm after Geraldine. Geraldine would go to the piano and Evelyn was the director. One problematic situation, Geraldine didn't like it when Evelyn would say, "It's got to be played this way—staccato—quick! This is the way it's supposed to go." If Geraldine played it choppy, Evelyn would step back from the microphone and go over to the piano and say, "Okay—you go over and sing with Mildred and I'll play it." Evelyn was precise—Evelyn wanted it THAT WAY. Now, Geraldine tried to imitate that, and there's no other singer there but me, so I have to catch it.

One of the great things about them was that Evelyn had these songs—I didn't know what they were. She had this song that I always hated. We went to Gary and recorded this song, "I Cried and God Heard Me." It went, "When I couldn't see the raindrops for the trees," and the background voices sang, "I cried and God heard me." And I'd be saying to myself, "Is he really listening to this song?" [*Laughs.*] If he was listening, I didn't know why! Then there was "Tell It to Jesus"; that was a song that Evelyn wrote. She'd sing, "Are you burdened—Are you heavy laden," and the others would sing, "Are you . . ." No—no! Stop! It's got to be quick (finger snap).

"Tell it—tell it—to Jeee-sus" [*sung in waltz time*]. That was Evelyn's style—precise! She could read, she could write, she could arrange. She wasn't bogus. Evelyn was the great one—and she got that from our mother. Our mother started out as choir director in the Reverend P. R. Favors's church. For example—they would have in the COGIC what they call revivals. A preacher would come in and preach, everybody would be singing and shouting, and my sisters in their early years would come in and play these revivals. At our particular church was a lady pianist, Sister Lee, who couldn't play a lick. The revivals would be swinging along and Sister Lee would go up to Rev. Favors and say she wanted to play. She'd get up and play, and the revivalists would say, "We don't need nobody to stoke the fire—we need somebody to keep the fire going. Where are those little girls at?" [*Laughs.*] This went on for some time, and finally my mother got tired of it and took my sisters over to All Nations Pentecostal Church, run by Lucy Smith over at 3900 Oakwood Boulevard. She was one of the first black ministers heard on WCFL radio in Chicago. This was the late 1940s—early 1950s. So that's where my sisters played. I traveled with them as a very young kid. And when I got older, my parents made me leave the road and go to school. When I was in school, I met a woman by the name of Mrs. Laurenson. She thought I was an exceptional child, and she introduced me to Joe Kelly. I was on television, on *Joe Kelly's Quiz Kids* that emanated out of the old Garrett Theater down on Randolph, on CBS television. I was on the program with a handful of other kids and they paid us with a $100 war bond, which I kept until I bought my first car. Evelyn was the thing that kept the Gay Sisters going. She was a songwriter. Geraldine developed over the years. She's a good arranger. And she wrote—but not as good as Evelyn. Geraldine's strong suit is reworking vintage tunes and modernizing them. She's like a furrier that takes an old fur coat and revitalizes it. She takes vintage tunes and reworks them to sound contemporary.

How many records did the family make?

There were twelve good sides issued on the Savoy label—plus the unissued sides Lubinsky had on the shelf. Then two sides for John Dolphin plus another two for an unknown label, including "On My Way to Heaven." Another two sides for Decca. Evelyn had her own label for a while and had over a dozen sides there. "I Must Tell Jesus"—that was me and Evelyn, and "While I Run This Race"—me and Evelyn again. And then "New World in My View"—that was my mother. I was there on the session when she did that. Then we recorded for the Chess brothers; in 1967 Geraldine got a record deal with Chess. We went down and recorded a song that my brother wrote called "Let Me Alone—Let Me Be" . . ."for my savior's face I see. If you won't go brother please don't hinder me, let me alone—let me be." Then we recorded a song called "It Is Finished"—that was a song we were going to release at Easter time. Also, we recorded "Take Care"—that was Geraldine—and "I Want to Walk Out," which was unissued. We also did "Without a Song" for Chess. At the session there was Geraldine at the piano, Jesse Dixon on organ, Louis Satterfield played bass, and Al Duncan on drums. For background singers we had Imogene Greene and Lee Charles Neeley.

So Geraldine got the session with Chess. I remember, she got paid and I didn't. [*Laughs.*]

The very same day, we were sitting in the studio and Willie Dixon was standing outside in the hallway with a young woman. He introduced us to her—Koko Taylor. Willie always told everybody about all the tunes he had written—but I always kind of doubted Willie with his music. I believe he borrowed a lot of stuff. He did—he stole people's music. My sister Evelyn told me that Willie stole people's music. Evelyn was a prolific songwriter. Al Benson had a church down just south of Thirty-Ninth Street. It was an old theater. Evelyn said she went down and played there, and Willie Dixon came down and played bass. Willie said to her "You know, Sister Gay, I'm going to take your song and help you with it." She gave him the song and never heard from him. He was a song thief. I've heard Thomas Dorsey was another great song thief. Dorsey wrote "Precious Lord"—but the rumor is that a woman gave him the song.

I'm trying to remember what gospel groups were on Chess . . .

There were the Violinaires, the Soul Stirrers, with Martin Jaycox doing the old Paul Foster stuff and Willie Rogers singing the parts Sam Cooke did. Sam Cooke had died. Chess also had Reverend C. L. Franklin. Chess had Leroy Crune, who was pushing this young woman, Jackie Ross. The first time we were there, we were introduced and were told we were going to talk with Leonard. We were there, and Gene Barge was setting us up in the studio and he was talking with Geraldine and going over the ideas she had with her. And in came Jackie Ross with Leroy Crune. We were in there recording, and Jackie came walking through there to see Leonard. I would've thought they'd go to the office, but they sat down right there in the studio. Chess said, "What's up babe?" And Jackie said "I need a car—a road car." "Okay. You know what you want to get?" Crune whispers to her, "Get a Cadillac." So she gets a Cadillac convertible—and that's the road car. Then she comes back in a few months later, and she'd had this hit called "Selfish One." She comes in and she's cussing—everybody at Chess studios is cussing—all the time. [*Laughs.*] Jackie says to Leonard, "I want to see Phil (Chess). Where's my money?" "Don't worry, it's going to be all right." They sit her down and she starts talking—"Look, I just had a big hit here, and I should be entitled to some money." And Chess says, "I gave you a car, babe—and a mink coat. That was your money—that's it." And that was the end of it. The artists didn't know any better. And Phil comes in and tells Geraldine and I about what Ramsey Lewis has done. Ramsey has this big hit, "Wade in the Water," and we're sitting there listening to the playback of the record. He's also dumped his long-time band members L. D. Young and Red Holt from his group—and they didn't even know it. And while we're sitting there listening, all of a sudden here comes L. D. Young carrying his bass and his doesn't even know he's been bounced from the group. They didn't tell him anything! He was totally in the dark—he didn't even know he'd been fired. But he was gone—BAM—now you've got no job, you're unemployed. You've got nothing. So long! Bye! The Chess brothers didn't care. But the funny thing about it was, if you couldn't get on the Chess label, you'd go across the street to Sonny Thompson, who was in the old Al Capone hotel there. Sonny was the A&R rep for the King label. The first time I met Sonny Thompson, I went over there with Evelyn; I sang a little audition for him and he told Evelyn, "Yeah—your brother's got a great voice. We could put him together with our writers and do something with him." But when you sang for Sonny, he'd have a little guy there with a microphone and tape recorder recording you—and you didn't even know you were being recorded. That was the kind of guy he was. And just down the street from Sonny was Vivian Carter and Jimmy Bracken of the VeeJay label. And then there was Jerry Butler, who had been in the Impressions with Curtis Mayfield. Curtis Mayfield was the real creative spark for their group [the Impressions] and once Curtis split, Jerry struggled. He started the Musicians Forum—where he was helping the young musicians. All he was doing was stealing their songs. He had Leroy Hudson and Donny Hathaway, who would write stuff. Jerry's career might have ended, but he had the young guys there writing stuff for him, and it kept his career going.

The Gay Sisters with young Donald Gay. Photo courtesy Gay Family Archive.

Getting back to my sisters—Evelyn was the catalyst behind the group. She wrote and arranged the songs. Evelyn had an idea for a television show, and she got together with a guy named Ozzie Vincent. They came up with the idea of a variety/gospel program, showcasing black gospel singers—here in Chicago. Ozzie came up with the idea because he had a gospel radio show over at a place they call the Packing House. Every Sunday morning Ozzie Vincent had this gospel radio program. Every Sunday he would bring in a group that was appearing in Chicago. If they needed to be heard, they would come on his radio show and let everybody know that they were appearing in town. They would perform on the radio and promote their live appearance. One of my favorite groups were the Swan Silvertones. They had Claude Jeeter in the lead, and Claude was the guy Al Green styled himself after—Claude could sing that type of falsetto better than anybody and wrote a song called "Oh, Mary, Don't You Weep." The Swan Silvertones did it first, and then the Caravans did a popular version as well, but they did it after the Swan Silvertones. Sunday after Sunday, groups would perform on the radio program, and they'd all stop by and pick up Evelyn. She became their staff musician and [would] play for those that would come on. So Evelyn and Ozzie Vincent came up with this idea—Ozzie's going to merge his radio program with Sherman Abrams. Abrams had a radio program that emanated from an automobile showroom on Forty-Seventh Street—between Lake Park and Woodlawn Avenues. The showroom was for Al Abrams Pontiac. Everybody would gravitate down there. The program was already going and the guy who would MC was Bud Reiley. Well—they didn't think Bud Reiley was the ideal MC, so Abrams made a deal with Ozzie Vincent—and Ozzie was very smooth in his MC delivery. But what happened was Ozzie got killed in a domestic dispute—his wife shot him to death. So Sherman had to find another guy who knew something about gospel music. And they brought in Sidney Ordower. Sid had run for congress and failed. He ran for alderman—and failed. Then Sherm brought him on to host the radio program. When he began, Sid didn't know anything about gospel music or the musicians, but he was smart enough to realize that if you want to be in the gospel business, you have to go to the programs, you have to go to the churches. You have to meet the singers and their managers. And that's how Sid developed the rapport to become the resident expert on gospel music. Sid became the host and the resident expert, and the program snowballed. It went from radio to television, and *Jubilee Showcase* became a great success. Meanwhile, Evelyn is saying, "Wait—this was originally my idea." Sid insisted he wasn't trying to cut her out and that she could stay on as the staff musician. So even though she helped to originate the entire idea, ultimately she was reduced to simply playing piano accompaniment—and Sid Ordower became the face of *Jubilee Showcase*. Evelyn stayed with the program—for a while. If you go back and watch some of the early programs, you can see her accompanying, and Sid would even mention her name in the opening credits, but eventually she was gone.

Perhaps you can shed some light on the history of the Church of God in Christ . . .

It started in 1907. The late Bishop Charles Harrison Mason was the founder of the church. He was a charismatic leader. The headquarters of the church is located in Memphis, Tennessee. He started out in the Baptist Church as a minister. He went out to California and had an experience—they call it the Azusa Street Experience. He came back to Mississippi, went back to his Baptist church and told them of his experience and that he had received the baptism of the Holy Ghost.

Part of this experience involved the speaking in tongues. But the Baptist Church rejected his experience and put him out of the Church. That led Bishop Mason and those that followed him to organize the Church of God in Christ. This new church took off and spread wildly. It was a demonstrative religion. The music was up-tempo, while the music of the Baptist Church was mournful— what we used to call as kids "the Baahh songs." They were chant-and-response songs. [*Laughs.*] But the Holiness folks would sing "Jesus brought me out—all right, all right, all right!" The music was spirited and lively and infectious. In the Holiness Church the music was so contagious that folks would come from everywhere to hear the music. So Bishop Mason started this church, and it just caught on. It spread in every direction and came north on the train when the brothers left the delta—it came right along with them, right up the Illinois Central and got off in Chicago.

In Chicago they were located at 4021 South State Street—a one-story building that was classified as the mother church. Mother Marion Davis held the church together until they were able to send somebody to pastor the church. When Bishop Roberts came, he brought his whole family from Mississippi. They started that church, and he became the bishop of Illinois, from Chicago to Cairo—over four hundred churches under his auspices in a black organization! Then Bishop Mason built a five-thousand-seat auditorium in Memphis on Mason Street, and whites were included in the organization. But back then some states wouldn't allow blacks and whites to worship together, and as a result the Assemblies of God were developed. That came out of the Church of God in Christ. Among those that came out of the Assemblies of God were Oral Roberts, Jimmy Swaggart, as well as Jimmy and Tammy Bakker. The Assemblies of God is a thriving organization. Sometime back in the 1990s they all came together in the COGIC and said, "Thank you—for being the catalyst to bring us all together." It's been a great church—it's still a great church! If music was among the defining experiences of COGIC, it's caused a metamorphosis in the Baptist Church; everybody is singing the same style. Years ago you would never hear a guitar in the Baptist Church—or a drum or tambourine or somebody shouting in church! Now they shout, they sing. There's drums and guitars. These were things that were only heard originally in COGIC. But the music, along with the message, has always been the charisma of the COGIC. That's the thing that made it such a great church. For example—the tune "Yes, Lord"—that was the theme of Bishop Mason, that was his song. But now you go in the Baptist Church and hear people singing that same tune [*sings*] "Yes Lord—put your hands up!"—is this the Baptist church? [*Laughs.*] Even in the Methodist Church you'd be awake at least a little bit, but in the Baptist Church—they were known for their kind of starchy services. If you wanted to go into a church where you could get a good nap, go to the Baptist Church!

So there was no conflict between Bishop Roberts and Reverend McGee?

Wellll . . . the conflict came when he started traveling and making records. It was like when I was a kid. I was born August 28, 1945. And television had been around, but it didn't come to fruition until around 1949. So here we are in our church, and our pastor was the late Elder P. R. Favors. In our church and our community the pastor's word was law. My mother lived and breathed by whatever the pastor said. If Favors said, "Don't do this," we didn't do it. If Elder Favors said, "Don't go to the show," we didn't go to the show. I think I was ten years old before I went to a movie theater for the first time. And they preached it so hard—my sister Geraldine took me to the show when I was ten years old and I was frightened to death because I thought they were going to eventually turn the lights on and say "There's Donald Gay!" [*Laughs.*] But they preached it so hard. That was frightening. So here we are—television comes along and they told us "Don't buy a television—no television." So one day, one of the members went by the pastor's house, and there he was sitting up in his living room, eating peanuts and watching television! [*Laughs.*] But hey—then everybody else started buying televisions. I remember the first one we bought was an old round-screen Zenith. And we started watching television. I remember back then they'd have Mahalia Jackson on the Dinah Shore program—church members would get on the phone and call—the phones would be ringing all around the neighborhood: "Mahalia's on television!" And we'd have so many people come over to watch television that I didn't know who half the people were . . . [*laughs*].

Utah Smith—one of the great talents of the church! He had a song called "Two Wings" to veil my face. I first saw him in Memphis, Tennessee. He would run what they called the old Midnight Musicals. After all the business of the church was over, he'd have a revival. The guy had a strong voice and he could play. You'd recognize his voice anywhere. After the main service was over we'd all stay up past midnight, and he'd get up and sing "Two Wings." He was just one man, solo guitar. The Midnight Musicals were held in Mason Temple in Memphis, and he'd have the place half packed.

We never followed up on what happened to your brother, Robert. What happened to Robert?

In the late 1940s Robert went to New York City and joined the Dizzy Gillespie band. Robert got a lot of fanfare coming up, and people thought that he might be able to play as well as Diz. Everybody would call Robert "Little Diz." But somehow Robert got hooked on heroin. In those days the government had a place in Lexington, Kentucky, where you could go for the cure. So he and a friend went down there for the cure. When Robert was finished, he called my parents and said he was clean and he wanted to come home. So when he came home to Chicago he brought his friend with him. And he and his friend stayed with us for almost six years. His friend was Sonny Rollins. Sonny's whole family all had careers. He had a brother who was a doctor, but he stayed with us all those years because he wasn't welcome at home—he had gotten involved with drugs. So he stayed with us. He'd take Geraldine to the movies, and he and Robert would go down in the basement at 6544—and practice. They were down there with the washing machine and the old coal furnace keeping their chops in shape. Every time Dizzy would come to town and see my mother, he'd say, "Ms. Gay—how do you feel Ms. Gay? I didn't put Robert on drugs. Ms. Gay, I never did! I never put Little Diz on drugs!" But Diz was a funny fellow—if he thought that you might excel, he'd have a little something he'd introduce you to—"Hey man, here's something for you.—though he never got on it himself. But he led others down that path. Sonny got back on his feet and eventually

Mother Fannie Parthenia Gay. Photo courtesy Gay Family Archive.

went back to New York and established himself. His family understood that he'd cleaned himself up, and they opened the door again—and it was all good. Robert, on the other hand, floundered. The music he wanted to play was passé, and he started drinking and died in 1966.

Tell me about your mother ...

My mother was singer in her own right. She had a unique style, particularly when singing up-tempo tunes. But she had a gift. She was a missionary—she was a great speaker. As a matter of fact, she was the founder of this church. If women had been accepted in the COGIC as preachers, she would have been the pastor of this church. But due to the fact that it wasn't politically correct for women to be the pastor of a church, she turned the reins of this church over to me when I was only fifteen years old. I did what they called OJT ("on the job"). I learned from my mother, and my mother taught me what the responsibilities of being a pastor were about, about working with people and understanding. My mother started a food pantry here in the neighborhood. She gave out food—she gave out clothes. She had a reputation, certainly citywide and even on a national scale, if anybody needed help and needed prayer, she was the one who could get a prayer through. My mother was known for that! She had a great reputation for that. I remember any time Mahalia Jackson would get sick, she would always call for my mother. Mahalia was over at Billings Hospital, and we drove up in front of Billings. On the West Side there was this woman that had a great church—her name was Mattie B. Poole—she had a church called Bethlehem Healing Temple. Mother Poole was coming out after seeing Mahalia and my mother was going in. Mahalia had a lot of faith in my mother, and the Lord touched Mahalia's body and healed her—and she was able to take her European tour. But—she never gave my mother any credit—never! The only time my mother ever got her deserved credit was in a book by Laurraine Goreau. She wrote a book called *Just Mahalia, Baby*. Laurraine Goreau wrote extensively about my mother, her influence on Mahalia and the things she did for Mahalia. My mother prayed for a lot of singers, that was her reputation—because she could pray. Gloria Griffin of the old Roberta Martin Singers had cancer. My mother prayed for her—the Lord delivered her! That was the type of person my mother was. She was a singer, she was the impetus, she had a great calming effect. She was a great counselor. We even named the street here after her.

What has happened with your sisters? Have they passed away?

Evelyn died in 1984. Mildred died in 2001. After Mildred and Geraldine stopped singing, Evelyn went on. She had a song called "I Shall Not Be Moved."

Evelyn had a knack for the business and she kept on going. She became a solo act. She started her own label. She kept her own publishing and her own copyrights. Evelyn was a dynamo—she was really the spark behind the Gay Sisters group. Evelyn wrote tunes constantly, and not only that, Evelyn wrote to people in the business. She always had her hand out there trying to get in the business—trying to open up a door. When gospel music had a down period, Evelyn got with other people and started going into the colleges. The classic is my sister, Evelyn, who was the writer, arranger, and had a heart of gold. We had a record contract with Decca records in the 1950s. Evelyn was a member of Local 10-208. In Chicago we had two unions—one was black, one was white. The president of the black union was a guy named Harry Gray. The other, head of the white union, was Caesar Petrillo. So Evelyn got a contract with Decca, and the guy who came out was a fellow named Leonard Joy. Leonard came out, and they recorded a song called "Oh, Lord, Won't You Have Mercy?" On the session, Evelyn played, Mildred sang, and they had a harpist who was on the staff of WGN, Peter Eagle. She also had a violinist by the name of William Petty. It was a great combination—but the stinger was William Petty wasn't a union musician. At that time the union had a guy by the name of Youngblood who would go around and check for scabs, and he found out that William Petty wasn't a union musician. There was another lady in the gospel business who recorded for the Columbia label, who had the distinction of being the queen of gospel singers and had heard through the grapevine that my sisters did a record on Decca. So the record is released and it's doing well—and all of sudden the record is stopped. My sister and my mother go over to see Harry Gray and they plead ". . . whatever we have to do. We'll even pay to get William Petty in the union." And Gray says "There's nothing I can do." They didn't know that Mahalia Jackson called Harry Gray to put a stop on my sisters' record. Leonard Joy called from New York and said they were stopping the record and that he didn't want any problems. Well there were only six months left on the contract and that was it. They stopped the record and the contract ran out—and the record has never been heard of since that time. When people talk about the Queen of Gospel being magnanimous—not in my book! I know what she did. I saw her up close and personal. Ironically, she made a lot of money, but the guy she married, Sigmund Galloway, took every dime she had. My mother went to help her every time Mahalia got sick. I don't know why she went—Mahalia didn't do anything for anybody. She didn't want to help anybody. She told me one time that she was going to give me a scholarship. If I got the scholarship, you're singing in church with us every Sunday on the front row—I haven't seen you there, but maybe you've been coming! [*Laughs.*] That's the kind of stuff she did. I'm probably the only one left who remembers when gospel first went to Carnegie Hall. Joe Bostic was the sponsor. Joe Bostic put us all together and we, all my sisters, were there to sing in Carnegie Hall. My sisters went on, Evelyn and Mildred, and they had a tambourine—unheard of at that time to sing with a tambourine at Carnegie Hall. I remember the scene backstage: they called Mahalia and went to her and told her she was on next. She got nervous, and my sisters had to go in and have prayer with her. Finally, she regained her composure, and she went out and sang her song. Oh, boy—that was a time! Here's a Mahalia Jackson story: she's traveling through Alabama and she gets pulled over by a policeman. The officer says, "What are you doing with all these men in the car?" "Officer—these ain't men—these is sissies." And the guys who were sitting in the car said they could've gone up under the seat, they were so humiliated. [*Laughs.*] The cop let her go—Yeah, that's my Mahalia Jackson story. But that was her!

Part Three **Bronzeville**

Andrew **Tibbs**

I had just played a record by Andrew Tibbs on my radio program when a listener called in and told me that Andrew Tibbs was still alive, living in Chicago, and that she worked with him on her job. She said, "If you'd like, I'll have him give you a call"—and a couple of minutes later he called. He said that he was listed in the Chicago phone book, but most people didn't know to look under his real name, which was Melvyn Grayson. During his call we made arrangements to do an interview for the program, and he came down to the studio a few days later.

This interview was recorded November 10, 1989. Melvyn Grayson died May 5, 1991.

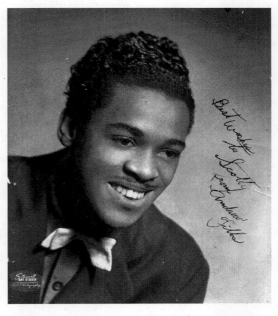

Andrew Tibbs. Photo courtesy Scotty Piper Collection, Chicago History Museum.

■ ■ ■

When were you born?

1929.

How many brothers and sisters?

There were four boys and one girl. My sister was the oldest. They were in New York when she was born. My father had a church there. Then they moved to Pittsburgh, Pennsylvania, and two other brothers were born, which was my oldest brother, Paul Grayson—at that time it was Grayson—and Bobby Grayson, and they moved from there and come to Columbus, and two other boys were born—my brother Kenneth and me. I'm the youngest one.

So the family name is not Tibbs?

Not Tibbs—Melvyn Andrew Grayson is my real name. Andrew is my middle name—and then Tibbs is my grandmother's maiden name on my father's side. And I have taken that name by being out in show business and my father being a minister. It conflicted me at the time—you know, a long time ago, things were a little more foggy then. My brother Paul used the name Tibbs first. He played bass with Cecil Gant on the record of "I Wonder"—and the bass fiddle he was playing was a tub.

But other than that nobody played an instrument in the family?

Nobody played an instrument. We always had a piano around house. We all picked the piano a little bit. I have a lovely organ at home. If I had to play for myself, I would have to fire me. [*Laughs.*] I was about six or seven years old when I came to Chicago. My father was a minister, and he was called to preach here in Chicago in 1937. So we all packed up and moved here—with a truck—and we moved to 5723 South Michigan. And I went to Carter School. The church was the St. Luke's Baptist Church, which was at 3663 South Indiana Avenue. He was the pastor there for many years until he retired. I had been singing for a long time, even back in Columbus, once I turned three. Church numbers and whatnot—"Give Me That Old Time Religion"—things like that. And when we got to Chicago, at the St. Luke's Baptist Church, I got a little closer to the singing. While we were at the St. Luke's Baptist Church, I was coached by a Ruth Jones; Dinah Washington—she was the director of the choir there. She was a very wonderful pianist. Mrs. Jones, her mother, was there first. She was a pianist. She taught music, and I guess she taught her daughter—who was Dinah Washington. Mrs. Jones was the director there with the junior choir. So was Mahalia Jackson. You know, they wanted Mahalia Jackson to wander off into nightclub life, but she stuck with the church—which is good. I think it's good—it's according to the individual. Because the way I was raised coming up, I was taught not to do two things at once. You got to do gospel songs—and then you do the blues. Now days you bring it together because it helps. I notice now that they are bringing a lot of the blues into the church. Different flairs the way they use it. Because a long time ago they didn't put those flairs from the church into the blues. Dinah Washington did—she used those flairs. That's soul. My brother went to school with Dinah Washington—at Wendell Phillips. Finally, they got married and they had a son. I have a nephew by the name of Bobby Grayson. He's here in Chicago. Well, my brother Paul—he's passed now—wanted me out into it. As he wanted me out into it, I found people liked me as a blues singer. I took the first blues song that I knew, "Did You Ever Love a Woman?"—that was by Gatemouth Moore because I liked his style, and I went from there. I treasure some of the musicians and entertainers who were out there before me. There was Jojo Adams, Gatemouth Moore, Ivory Joe Hunter, Wynonie Harris. All of them were big brothers to me. I went away from my brother Paul because his type of music was little more into vaudeville, and I wanted to go a little bit into the jazz. It was a little more up to date, I guess, in the way of speaking. I used to see Jojo Adams—I used to peek in the place to see Jojo Adams. They used to hand me the mike out the window because I couldn't go in at Du Sable. The Du Sable Lounge and the Du Sable Hotel before they tore it down. They took the mike—it was in the basement. They would play in the basement—it was Lefty Bates. They would hand the mike out into the window—just playing—and I would sing. They would say, "Who's that kid singing out there?" Then I was about fifteen.

Would you hold a day job at this time? You were sort of young, but were you still in school?

No. No. I was all out for show business. I should have gone back to school. It was like my father told me, "Son, what are you going to do if you'll lose your voice?" See, my family took me back to Columbus on vacation to try to get me away from show business—before I made the record. And while I was there, there was a club there on Mount Vernon that wanted me to take someone's place because they got sick in Huntington, West Virginia. So they ask me if I could go. I said, "I don't know, I'll have to ask my father." They went and saw my father. My father said, "Well—how long is he going to be there?" "Two weeks," the agency said. So he said, "Well are you going to have him back in time for us to go back to Chicago?" He said, "Yes." So I went to Huntington, West Virginia. That's the first time I really had been out of town to enjoy and be around show people. It was just like brothers and sisters around you. When it got time to leave they had some "white lightning" or something, and I got to crying because I didn't want to leave. So when the man give me my money, I went to the station, and he said, "Where do you want to go?" I said "Charleston, West Virginia." I was supposed to go back to Columbus, Ohio, so we could come back to Chicago. I went to Charleston, West Virginia. I ran into a fellow named Sir Charles—he had a group there. I won a prize there—that's what it was. I stayed there in Charleston, West Virginia, for six months. They were leaving that club there in Charleston. This was before I made records. They were going to Pittsburgh, Pennsylvania. So when they getting ready to go to Pittsburgh, I didn't have any money, so I called home and told my mother: "Mama, I got to get me some money to get home. I done lost my money." She sent some money to Pittsburgh. I stayed in Pittsburgh two years. Two years. I got sort of tired of it, living in Pittsburgh. Sometimes I had a place—sometimes I didn't, you know? I'm by myself and I'm learning. And while I was there, I wandered into a group called the Camp Meeting Choir—like the Wings Over Jordan. I went with the Camp Meeting Choir. It was beautiful. They went all the way to New Orleans [and] Tampa, Florida, and I enjoyed that—because it gave me a chance to branch out a little bit. After they made all those trips they came back this way. When I came back to Gary, the bus was there. My brothers came up to see me and try to get me home. So I came on back to Chicago. That goes back to 1945.

Let's talk about some of the clubs that you played. Name some of the places.

Ritz Lounge was at Fortieth and Oakwood Boulevard at the Ritz Hotel. Joe Williams, before he got in with Count, we worked together. He was a wonderful person. We worked together there at the Ritz before he went with Count Basie. He'd been singing for a long time, way before I had got started. He was always quiet—always kept to himself. We would talk. The first set he would start, the second set I would start, just like that; we would just start together, you know? And then they had a group there called Top & Bob—they were a dance team. They were good. Oh there was another singer that was beautiful—[Little Miss] Cornshucks. That's way back. I don't know where she is today. I would be at the [Club] DeLisa from Tuesday straight through Sunday. Off on Monday—yeah. Now, in between Saturday night I would run down to the Indiana Theater. We had a schedule to run in there and do two numbers; we'd get a pay envelope and run back to the DeLisa. Then at the DeLisa at four o'clock in the morning, say like it would be Sunday night into Monday morning, we would go down to the Grand Terrace. All the musicians and all the entertainers would meet down there, and we would just have a ball down there—Monday morning. We would be down there from five o'clock that morning till almost noon.

So you would be out every night?

Somewhere singing—sometimes I held down two jobs. I was at Jimmy's Palm Garden—right across the street from the El Morocco Hotel. In between shows you would go around to another club, and they would call you up to sing a number—just call up Andrew Tibbs, you'd get a little applause [*applauds*] and get up and sing. And they liked me there. Then I'd go back to my job because it was time for me to go on.

Do you have any Jojo Adams stories?

Well, yes, I had a dog in my yard. It followed me down to the Ritz. Jojo was working—he was the main man down there, you know? I couldn't take the dog back home, so I put it in the dressing room. Jojo didn't want him in there. "You got to take that dog"—I said, "Look—the manager said I could leave him in here." We fussed about that, but that passed over. But Jojo Adams had a catastrophe at the DeLisa. He had all the younger of blues singers behind him like Gatemouth Moore and Ivory Joe Hunter, and we sung behind them. Jojo—I don't know, we were just buddies, and places he would call me and ask me to share the spotlight with him, which was beautiful. We ran into the same young ladies together sometimes and got mad. [*Laughs.*] We ironed those things out. He was just a showman, and he had personality. He had them tails working [*sings*] "Didn't I tell you women—don't give that lovin' away because you're a hard-headed women—and I don't care what you say." I remember some of those songs. And Gatemouth Moore [*sings again*], "Say, Mr. Jones—turn out all the lights." I mean, he would hold his notes "Sa——y Mr. Jo—nes." That's the way he would start off—I like that, you know?

Then there was a place—after I left the Ritz and then the DeLisa—I worked Jim Martin's Corner for a while. So the agency that was wandering around looking for talent introduced me to Chess; which is at the Mocambo Lounge. They decided they wanted to make a record. They asked me if I wanted to make a record, and I said, "Sure!" First, they had me sign a little contract. They didn't realize that I was not old enough to sign without my father's signature. They had an agent by the name of Sammy Goldberg that brought me around to the Mocambo and introduced me to Chess, and he asked me if I had any lyrics. I said, "Lyrics?"—and I couldn't think of any lyrics. So my mother give me the title of "Union Man Blues." "There's a union for lovers now," you know. I got that, and on the other side I couldn't think of one, and Tom Archia thought of "The Bilbo Blues"—on the way down there. Well, anyway, we got it together and had our rehearsals. They had me stay in a hotel so I wouldn't wander around—and so I could learn my lyrics and things.

Who had you in a hotel?

Sax Mallard. Chess had him to take care of me—to look out for me. So I could learn my lyrics—because I was wild.

How long did they stash you away?

About three days. I ask them, "Could I bring a young lady up there?" They said, "No" [*laughing*]. They wanted me to concentrate on the music, and it came easy to me—but you see, you can't beat rehearsing. You can't beat rehearsing, and I didn't want to rehearse. But I found that I had to, you know?

Did you have any choice about who the bands were, or did Leonard [Chess] assign them to you?

Well, you see, I didn't know too many of the bands by not being on this side of life as far as show business was concerned. But I got lucky because Dave Young's band was at the Ritz. I think that might be on the first record, if I'm correct. Dave Young played sax; I don't know if he was alto or tenor.

How long between the time your mother gave you the title "Union Man" and you actually recorded it?

Within a week.

And you wrote the song and learned it and recorded it.

Along the line we were pressed for time and Leonard Chess was new in it too, I guess. Some of those songs I had to read from the paper. And you can't get the soul that you want until you can get it up here in your mind, you know? Then you can let it all out. Like they say, "Let it all hang out."

How many sides in that session all together?

I'm not sure—because it goes back a long ways. It could have been two or four. But the Civic Opera was where we did the first record—I do remember that. Then a lot of times it was how many tests you had to take. We didn't take but one or two. It went straight down. It went off very good.

Which one was the big hit?

"Bilbo" was the number one, but they couldn't put that on the air at that time. So they used "Union Man." "Union Man" made the hit. And I didn't know that the record was doing that good. Because all I wanted to do was sing. And then I wandered on the West Side to Jim Martin's Corner. There, I picked up a quartet that I wanted to sing with me. Their name was Dozier Boys at that time. I don't know where they're at now. I met them on the West Side—they were in a talent show there on Jim Martin's Corner. It dawned on me at the time that it was a good quartet. So I brought them in and introduced them to Chess, and we recorded. They sung with me on one of the records—"Traveling Man." With the quartet behind me that came out good.

How old were you when that record hit?

Eighteen.

What was your reaction when the record came out? I mean, how did people react to the record, and what was your reaction to success?

I didn't realize what it would be like to have someone recognize who you are all the time. Because I really wasn't prepared for that—I mean, I just loved to sing. I wasn't thinking of that. But as it got into me, I got big headed in a way. We all have our—you know. And then because I was gooood, you know, and

I got to sing, and I didn't have to sing hard because they had heard it on the record. So you don't strain just to make people like it: they had already heard it. But you just get your soul into it. It's all you think of. But when you got your mind on the rent, the babies, telephone, the bills, and things like that. I didn't have that to worry with. A lot of times [when] I was out singing, I would get a room in a hotel where I could enjoy myself. Because I couldn't enjoy myself like I would like to at home because of the respect I had for my people. When I run out of money, I came home. There was always a room there. I enjoyed it. I remember on the West Side—the club, I can't think of the name of it. It was a circle-bar club, and when we got through, this young lady—and we couldn't find a place to go, so she went by her auntie's house. They were playing cards—so we couldn't go there. So we went to another spot where her mother and father lived at, and she said "Shhh—be quiet." So I said, "Okay." We had to go down some steps—it was an old building, and there's an old coal stove in there in the center. They had about four rooms—two bedrooms, a living room, and a kitchen. We went down and we tip-toed. Instead of going to her room, she went to her sister's room—her sister was the oldest. Her father wouldn't come in there. [*Laughs.*] So we got in there. She didn't tell me that her father was there at the time. I just thought it was a dog—she didn't want to wake the dog up. So when I got in there, she said, "Be quiet—I'm scared." I said, "Scared of what?" She said, "My father." And he woke up. I said, "Your father!" So I got behind the bed because it was time for him to get up, "because it's time for him to go on his beat." I said, "Go on his beat?" He's an officer! Oh, Lordy, when it come time about six o'clock in the morning—it wasn't light yet. He called her by name—the door was cracked, you know, and he said—I don't recall what her name was now but anyway it really doesn't matter. He said, "Cherise, I'm gone, has Barbara come in yet?" That was Barbara in the room [*laughs*]. "Mmmhhmm." "Okay—I'm gone." I was scared to death. [*Laughs.*] My knees were bumping up against the back of the headboard—no clothes. But after that she fixed breakfast, and I really enjoyed the stay after that [*laughing*]. But these were little incidents that happened.

Did that do anything in terms of the money that you got from the clubs? Could you get more money from club owners?

Yes. Well, you see, your name is being more recognized. I had trouble staying out of places that I had no business going into. If you go into places they see you [for] free—and then they don't want to go somewhere and pay the fees. But I knew the kids—I went to school with them. They wanted me to stay away from certain areas—which they were right—on the street, you know, I didn't realize. "Aren't you Andrew Tibbs?" I said, "Yes." "Can I get your autograph?" It seemed funny to me to do that.

Did you tour the country on the strength of these records.
Well, yes, I was in quite a few places—St. Louis, Nashville.

Who arranged for you to tour the country?
I can't remember now—it's been so long ago.

Was this through the record company?
No. A booking agency.

Because he heard you had had a hit—
Names. And he contracted with them for a while, something like that. Just like—went to New York with the agent that put me into records. The Baby Grand. First time I had ever been to New York, and the master [of] ceremon[ies] there was Nipsey Russell. I enjoyed him and the Apollo Theater.

How long were you in New York?
Two years. I met my wife there in New York, and I brought her back here to Chicago with me, and we stayed married for twenty-some years before she passed, in '77. I just stayed in Chicago—my home.

Let me ask you about another record. How did you happen to make the record for Peacock? Do you remember that?
That's in Houston, Texas, right? Yes. Don Robey. I was there when Bobby Blue Bland made his first record. He was in the station that night. I was there, drinking like a fish. I wasn't into it. They were giving me $100 or $200 every week, you know, to sit down and rehearse. This night I'm sitting there just having a ball. It wasn't business. As I say—I don't know which records they were. I wish I could hear some of those one of these times.

Do you remember the band on those things you did for Peacock?
There was about seven or eight. It was big band. I do remember it was a house band, so I don't know them by name. Sometimes when you go to different cities, they use their locals, you know?

What about the records with the Tibbs brothers. Who's on the record with the Tibbs brothers?
Kenneth—my brother that's preaching now: when I was out singing, he started wandering out there. He sung too—at that time we all sung. It was an idea they wanted to have a duet. Because he would sing around in areas in Chicago too for a while and he was good. They decided they wanted us to come to New York, and I can't think of the name of the company—Savoy? I think it might have been Savoy—but I can't remember. We stayed there for a while, and I got some letter that states when they were going to release it. It

says, "We hadn't heard from you, so we considered the contract broken." See, that's what I'm saying—I never knew they brought it out on the record you've got. I just took it that they never brought it out.

Who came up with the material? Who was the band? Do you have any of those ideas?

I don't remember that. I really don't. I can't remember—all I remember [is that] we went together with some material they had there. We didn't have any material.

Were you established as a recording star at that point, at the time you did the Tibbs Bothers recording?

Yes.

So your records came before the Tibbs brothers record?

That's right. It came afterwards because he came after me singing as Kenneth Tibbs. I had an idea, just like I had an idea about the quartet.

Do you know when those were specifically?

The late '50s or early '60s.

You recorded that string of records for the Aristocrats or Chess. How did that end?

I went to work for Chess for the simple reason because I had a problem that I had to straighten out.

I understand you had a narcotics problem—was that it?

Yes, I did. Well, you see, that was the problem. In one of the clubs, the kids was going out and enjoying themselves during intermission. So I wanted to be one of the boys, so I went out with them. They were tooting away, it was. I thought they were just smoking. So to keep from being a wet blanket, I went on and acted like I had been doing the same thing. So for a long time I enjoyed it with them until it became a habit. I didn't go into mainline or anything like that but——

Are we talking about heroin or coke?

Heroin. Heroin. Then they come to find out that if you had coke with it that was what they called a speedball. And that hit you right quick, and that's the end of it, you know? But you kept wanting these things, and pretty soon you got to the place where I would wake up in the morning and I was sweating—and I wasn't eating. I told a friend, we were supposed to have a rehearsal, and I told him, "Man, I don't feel good. I feel weak." He asked me, "Are you sweating?" He said, "Have you had any—?" I said, "No, I haven't—no, I haven't." So he come over there and give me some of it. And I rose just like—it's just like a person when you get hungry, you get weak. It's similar. It's all you want to do is get

ANDREW TIBBS 109

yourself back, and you're not. It's a crutch that you're getting on. So finally I got this place; I was working in—while this is going on, I wandered into Walt Keegan, and Fats Cole was piano player there. I was working there, but that night when I came in from the job—I took the train coming back home—I told my Pa, I said, "Dad, I'd like to take a vacation." He said, "When you want to leave?" I said, "Whatcha mean?" Dad said, "I asked you when do you want to leave?" He knew already—but he didn't want to push me out of the house, because he figured I could handle it better while I was here. Well, I did make up my mind. So I could get myself together, see? "When do you want to go?" I say, "Well, as soon as I can finish this engagement in Waukegan. So they said, "Okay, do you mind if your brother and I go with you that night?" They wanted to make sure I would leave that morning—leave for Lexington, Kentucky. And I said, "Sure!" Now I'm sick. I need it to get straightened out, see? But I have to go to work. But I am going to Lexington, Kentucky, in the morning, but I didn't want to go there sick. When I got off from work, my father asked me, he said, "Can Kenneth go upstairs with you to get the radio?" I told a tale. I said, "Yeah." I got up there and got what I wanted and came on home. Straightened myself up so when I got into Lexington, Kentucky—I knew I was going to come down on it. I'd be praying for it then. When I got to Lexington, my father asked me, "Now, there's two way you can go in there. You can either go in there with the key. The key is you can come out when you're ready and they'll let you go. Just like when you got sick just now and said, 'I want to got home'—they'll let you go home. Otherwise you go in and stay for four months and fifteen days and you have to stay. There's no getting out before that time." You had to go on it through the court, and when you decide to go to Lexington, Kentucky, you go to the courthouse and you commit yourself. He said, "Since you made up your mind to go, I'll let you make up your mind how you want to go in there." I said, "Well, if I'm going in there to get myself straightened out, there's no sense in my going knowing that I can come out any time it gets rough. I'm going in there for the full four months and fifteen days." Having said that, I could've kicked myself. But I knew it was right—I knew it was right, you know? So I went there for four months and fifteen days in 1950—and came out on my birthday, February 2nd.

How long were you actually playing with the narcotics before you cleaned up?

I'd say two years. When I got home, my dad picked me up at the train station. On the way back home, just before we got back to the house, I said, "Dad, drop me right there at the Keyhole there by the Ritz." The Keyhole was a local bar right under the el—they call it the Keyhole. I went in there and got me a big shot of alcohol or something. Dad said, "You better watch yourself." He went on home. We lived around the corner on 504 East Oakwood Boulevard. That's right across the street from the Holy Angels Church. Anyway, I served that four months and—I don't know—when I came out I had that drink and came back out and came home—I was scared. But I didn't touch heroin again. But I went to drinking—see. That took the place of it. So I started drinking—and drinking didn't bother me for a long while. And I was the type of person who always liked to be on time—when I was at myself, you know? But when you get like that, I got to the place where I was always late. I had to have a drink in the morning. And I was drinking all day. So that went on for quite a while. But I wasn't doing what I wanted to do—I wanted to do right. In my mind I knew that. That's what was steering me away. Because I wasn't doing my best, you know? And the people knew that. They'd take a chance on me—they wanted to depend on me. So I wandered around for a while. I lost my stature as far as entertaining was concerned. I was known, but I was playing little smaller places because I'm drinking. It's a wonder I didn't get hurt. Because I always traveled by myself and I didn't have a car—I was never interested in a car and I always took the el—it's a wonder I didn't get knocked in the head. Because it was late at night, you know. I didn't have a job. I was too lazy to do any singing because I wasn't right. I wasn't going anywhere—just sitting doing nothing. Finally, my wife asked me, "Why don't you come to Western Electric with me and try to work there?" At first, I didn't want to do that because I didn't have any trade to get in there. But I took her advice and went to work for Western Electric. I worked in there for sixteen years. It took them five years to harness me because I wasn't used to eight hours. You know you can get out of a club when you get ready to. But after a while I enjoyed it. I came home after eight hours. I wouldn't do any overtime [*laughing*]. I didn't want to work any further. Well, I had never worked before, you know what I mean? I'm just talking about on a regular job. So at first while I was there on lunch hour, I wouldn't come back. So my supervisor, he liked me. He called me T's—short for Tears. I was using my real name Melvyn Grayson. So he said, "T's, have you checked yourself out? Have you got a problem or something? Tell the truth." I liked my supervisor; he sort of looked out for his people. I said, "Yeah, I'd like to try to get myself together. I think I'm drinking too much or something like that. I ain't no alcoholic—I just want to drink." He said, "You have to make yourself what you are." But, you see, that's the first thing you got to realize: who and what you are, before you can get help. I don't mind telling nobody because I'm proud of it—because I haven't looked at a drink since 1974. I don't need it. Now I listen—I listen. I had to program my mind. I wasn't born with it. I didn't come here with it. And if it was real poison, you're not going to take it—and I knew it was killing me because the first time I went—he told me if you go home and stay five days and don't take a drink and come back, I'll get you into the hospital. This program—that's beautiful, these programs that they had. So I've heard that they used to put guys into an institution, that was it—a long time ago. When I went to this program, I didn't pay it no mind.

A twelve-step program? Like AA?

Yeah. I got that. I love that. "God, grant me the serenity to accept the things I cannot change and the courage to change the things I can and the wisdom to know the difference." That goes for everybody. You don't have to be an alcoholic for that. That helps, that helps the depression of a person. You got bills, if it's something you can't take care of, no sense in worrying about it. You ain't gonna achieve the answer. So I had to program myself that way. I had to—I was sort of scared. I was doing so good, I was sort of scared to wander back into show business. This is me now—I don't mind telling you that I was scared of the world and I was protecting myself. Now they can say what they want to say—"Why don't you come back, you can handle it. You don't have no reason. . . ." That's not the point. I have to make up *my mind*. So I went back to sing a couple of times but I didn't have that *soul* for a while. But I kept forcing myself until one time I went out there and sang and I felt it—and I hadn't had a drink. Nothing! And from then on, when my wife passed, I didn't drink. Little other problems came up; I didn't drink. My car got totaled; I didn't drink. Just different things, you know, and I found out I felt good. I said, "Hey, I can handle everything now." But I kept reading that scripture. That's a heck of a scripture. Change—changing, I can't change—I can't be tall like you. I have to accept myself like I am. I'm five-seven. And I enjoy to be five-seven. There a lot, a lot of women out there love five-seven [*laughing*]. So I don't—I have to think of it that way. I'm small. I can't be huge, or a football player. But I'm a mellow size this way. I program myself that way. I look at myself and I say, "Man you, you changed." I say, "Man you can't beat that coffee-colored hair man. You can't find that often." That helps you. That's a program I love. So once in a while I go to AA. I stopped going for a while. But just like they say, "Go as many times as you think it will help you." As much as you can. To revive yourself to know where you came from. Sometimes I'd go there, and I forgot that I was drinking. It would make me mad; I'd go home I say, "Damn you of a man." Last man when I got off of work. I stopped at a place, The Other Place they call it, which is at Seventy-Fifth and King Drive. I went in just to sit down to hear some music. Because I'm getting back into it now. Sober! Got me an orange juice, Coca-Cola . . . I get tired of it, though. But I set there and bought one of the fellows what he wanted, you know? And I already come to think of it before I say this. I heard it mentioned sometimes in these meetings that when they go near a liquor store, they go across the street. That don't make sense. If you can't face up to it, there's no sense in hiding—that's not helping you. You got to face it head-on. Not running and buying you some cigarettes or whatever you want. If you wanted half a pint, I'd run in and get it for you. I don't need it. See, I'd pour it for you [*hey hey hey*]. You're shaking, yeah. Okay [*hey hey*]. But I'm not going to preach to you because it's up to *you* to do what you think is best. Because I'm proud of myself, as far as what I did. Just like someone said, "You ought to be a minister like your father." I said, "I'm preaching on the stage." I said, "When I'm on the stage and I see a fellow sitting down there by himself—he's lost or dead or something like that—I start singing along about midnight when you feel the words CHANGING VALUE." I like that coming to me. Then he raise up and help me. "Man," he says, "I appreciate your doing that number" or something like that. Then there's another song he liked. I had a young lady that I couldn't please, so I made up a song "Stone-Hearted Woman." That helps me and maybe it can help them, too!

Bill **Samuels**

Bill Samuels was a pianist/vocalist who led a Chicago-based piano trio, the Cats 'n Jammers. The Cats were based on the style of the then-popular King Cole Trio—piano, guitar, and bass—no drums(!)—with Bill on piano and vocals. The Cats 'n Jammers recorded for the Mercury label and in 1944 had a two-sided hit with their record "Jockey Blues"/"I Cover the Waterfront." The trio followed up with roughly a dozen records before their recording career ended. I had never heard of Billy or the group until I stumbled across a weathered copy on a 78 and played it on the program one night. The Cats 'n Jammers were outside the boundaries of what was regarded as strictly Chicago blues but were fondly remembered by music fans in Chicago's Bronzeville area. I received several calls from black seniors, even as the record was still playing. Among the calls I received was one from Bill Samuels's nephew, Elliot. He filled me in a bit on his uncle and his career and talked about the fact that, though his uncle had passed, there were surviving family members in Chicago who might provide further information. A short time later—that same hour, as a matter of fact—I received a call from two of Bill Samuels's brothers, Art and

Bill Samuels. Photo courtesy The Samuels Family Archive.

Shelly. They were all too willing to fill me in on their brother and his career. And I was fascinated: none of this stuff was included in the books on blues history, but it was impractical to hold an extended conversation while juggling three-minute records on the air, so I made arrangements for the two of them to come down to the studio during the week, and we recorded a lengthy interview on their brother. Bill Samuels in no way fit the profile of a postwar bluesman. He hadn't picked cotton or been a sharecropper or emigrated from the South. He was from a middle-class black family raised on Chicago's South Side, his father was a clergyman, and all the kids held professional jobs. Bill Samuels had been a professional entertainer since high school and played most nights of the week at various clubs in and around Chicago. In the mid-1940s he found limited local success with the Cats 'n Jammers, and when that played out, Bill left Chicago and settled in Minnesota, where he continued to perform until his death in 1964. At the end of our interview, Art and Shelly provided a list of acquaintances and fellow musicians who knew and worked with Bill and might be able to tell me more about his career. I went to work on the list and within six weeks had recorded interviews with most of those listed, including Sylvester Hickman, who had played bass in the trio and was now working as a mail carrier for the U.S. Postal Service; Henderson "Smitty" Smith, who played trumpet on the Chicago scene and worked with Bill off and on; Hillard Brown, who had played drums on a pair of the sessions and who had since managed to make himself one of the most hated men in Chicago, working as a rep for the Chicago musicians union; and Nat Jones, a highly respected alto player in the Chicago area. He recalled highlights from his career, recording with Little Miss Cornshucks and filling in for Johnny Hodges for a short while in the Duke Ellington Orchestra. I contacted Ernest Ashley, a guitarist, who was deep in a battle with cancer and declined to be interviewed; I spoke by phone with Beryl "Berle" Adams, who was one of the partners at the Mercury record label; and, finally, I spoke with Red Maddock. Red was a white drummer who was heard at the time as part of the Butch Thompson Trio and playing each week on public radio's *A Prairie Home Companion* program. Red was the walking definition of everything that fascinates the rest of the world about drummers—class clowns, terminally irreverent, laughing and drumming their ways from good time to good time, right to the end. Red had worked with Bill Samuels in Minnesota near the end of his life and had entertaining stories of their time together. Red and I made arrangements to meet after a Butch Thompson gig on the Illinois/Wisconsin state line. I remember the night vividly—Butch and Chicago blues pianist Little Brother

Montgomery were friends and met as well. Brother was severely debilitated, only weeks away from death, yet he was there to visit an old friend. After the gig Red and I found a deserted dressing room and settled in for a conversation. Butch joined us and sat in on the session, having never heard these particular tales from Red's early career.

Art and Shelly Samuels, Nat Jones, Henderson Smith, and Red Maddock were recorded at separate sessions during September 1984. Sylvester Hickman, Hillard Brown, and Berle Adams were recorded at separate sessions in October 1984. Bill Samuels died March 23, 1964.

■ ■ ■

Art and Shelly (Bill's brothers)

Art: Every now and then, when we slip, and we say Dubb—that's our name for him. You know, Bill is a junior, that's actually what he is. My father was William Burroughs Samuels senior—the Reverend William Burroughs Samuels before he died. Dubb is a junior. William Burroughs junior. Therein lies the tale about the Dubb business, because some people would say WB, you know, just use his initials, and we just shortened it to Dubb—and that's what he's known by affectionately—as Dubb. Everybody knows, in the family, you say Dubb. It's not Bill at all, but close friends all say Dubb. A family of ten. Six boys—two of which are dead now—Bill and the baby boy—and four girls. He was the second born—he had an older sister, she was the first—then Dubb. Half were born in the state of Mississippi and the other half here in Chicago. And my dad came here in Chicago in 1917, I believe it was—and from that point on we all are from here. We can all talk to you about Chicago much better than we can about Mississippi. My dad didn't have much family because he was an only child, but on my mother's side they all sang, and the Wearys—that was her maiden name—they were all into music. In church choirs and things of that nature. We just came up with music, we grew up with music, and there was always a piano at home, and everybody played the piano, including my mother; and you know, we were sitting around banging the piano all day and trying to create things and learn things—doing a lot of fun things together. We talked about having fun together, around home and singing in glee clubs and in churches and stuff like that—but we just had a lot of fun with music. And we all did it—we would be banging on the piano all day. I'd get up, Joe would sit down, Joe would get up, Dubb would play—somebody else would take his place—all day long. My dad worked nights, and the piano in our living room was on the wall—the piano was back to the wall where he was sleeping. Sometimes he would say, "Oh, children—just give me a chance to get to sleep before you start." I don't understand how he slept. Music was going all the time. There was the radio, there was the record player, or the piano was playing all the time.

Shelly: My father wasn't musically inclined—he could sing, but he wasn't really musically inclined—but he would always see that we had the things that were necessary to enhance whatever talents we had. He was the first person I knew that had a recorder—an old Philco recorder—and we used to record on that thing at home. I would like to have some of those records now, but somehow or other the records got away.

Art: Funny thing—when Dubb was a little boy, people used to come by the house and ask my dad to let him come and play for their parties—well, he was just a kid. And they would come and ask him to play for these parties—I guess you would call them house-rent-type parties and that kind of thing.

Shelly: I recall when he was here in Chicago. This was back in the '30s, I guess. Yeah, it was during the Depression years, and he worked at a little joint called the Dee Gee. It was at Thirty-Seventh Street—just off Indiana Avenue. And this was a rather small place, but all the musicians in town used to gather there, and they would have some real swinging sets. There were so many musicians there that there wouldn't be room for the patrons, but it was one of those kinds of places.

Art: He had a trio playing there—Bill on piano and singing, of course; and George Iverson Dozier—he was a drummer, great drummer; and John Mays was on alto. But then these other guys would come by: Henderson Smith on trumpet—a darn good trumpet man—and Nat Jones was a phenomenal alto man. You like Hodges? You'd like Nat. Nat was wonderful—Henderson Smith, too. Both of these guys still live in Chicago—and they still play. But that place was something else. You go in there—well, actually, we weren't supposed to be going in there, we were a little young for that—and then all those musicians would come in and, man, they would just swing. Good jazz!

Shelly: I'm trying to remember some of the other names that came in there. Bill Martin, a trumpet player, used to come in. There were so many guys that were just totally ambitious. We're leaving out one—Abernathy—Marian Abernathy! She didn't work there, but she would come in and sing. She worked out of the Club DeLisa most of the time. And don't forget Dolphus Dean.

Art: All these guys were family men. They didn't travel much. I guess Bill traveled more than most of them.

Henderson Smith

Now, I met Bill . . . I met him in the third grade of grammar school. I met him—and his sister. Geneva was her name, and she was about a year older than Bill. He and his sister and myself were in the same room, in the third grade, and anything that he did that smacked of being wrong his sister would jump up and say, "I'm going to tell papa when we get home"—right in the middle of class. [*Laughs.*] That would quiet him down a little bit, and we would all laugh, you know, and we would get him outside and we would all say, "I'm gonna tell papa when we get home." Now, his sister was the one that was the singer at that time. She had a beautiful voice, and I didn't know that Bill had much of any talent. But I was proven wrong later on, of course, and we had an off-and-on friendship for years—in fact, with his whole family. I knew the whole family. I started to associate again with Bill, oh, about 1936, 1937—when he was working at a little tavern called Dee Gees on Thirty-Seventh Street between Indiana and Prairie Avenues. It was quite a popular little place, and they had three pieces. A three-piece band—a drum, a saxophone, and Bill on the piano. He was the leader of the group. This is where I really came back into contact with him after a number of years. He had gone his way and I'd gone mine, musically. But after I found that's where he was working, I started hanging in there. When I was finished working, I'd come over there—or if I wasn't doing anything I'd come over there and sit in and play. And we had quite a nice time in there, a good time. I never worked with him and his group, the Cats 'n Jammers, but I did jam with him quite a bit on his job. He played good piano. It was more or less a jazz style. It might have been closer to Hines: everybody—so many piano players were influenced by Hines because it was the swing era and most everybody was playing swing piano. You even swung when you were playing the blues, you know? You always played in a swing tempo—even when it was played slow. However, Bill could play the old-time funky blues because we came up in that era. You see when we were children—1919, 1920—there were a lot of old blues players around, there were a lot of old house parties around, and I'm sure Bill picked up a lot of his piano playing from that. You had people like Mr. Freddie and Tampa Red—I think he was a guitar player. These people were around. You had Blind Lemon Jefferson. They were all in the neighborhood, you see? Ma Rainey and her band rehearsed down the street from me. So we were there at a young age and knew all of these people. So Bill could play a good gutbucket blues all right—but his "Jockey Blues" is in a swing style. The very outstanding thing about him was—I don't think Bill could read piano music too well—but he had an ear. I think he had absolute pitch because he could play anything, in any key that you wanted to play. This was what was so remarkable about him. Now, the other remarkable thing about Bill was his charisma, I guess you would call it. Bill could go anywhere—and in three to five minutes he had three to five new friends. He would walk in to a restaurant, knowing he didn't have any money, would order food for himself—and whoever was with him—knew he didn't have any money to pay for it. But somehow when he finished talking to the manager, the manager was about ready to give him another serving [*laughs*]—and anything he wanted to drink—and ask him to come back again! I never could understand this. But this is true. This is absolutely true! Bill could rent an apartment. In fact, I know he rented a house on the far South Side once. Bill didn't have money because he spent his money freely, and I don't think he had money half the time to pay his rent. The next thing I knew, the landlord was begging him to stay, and the landlord became his good friend. This, I was never able to understand; and adding this to his music talent, Bill was quite a guy. Quite a guy.

It was unfortunate that we lost contact for such a long time. I was going in one direction and he was going in another, and somewhere along the way he did these recordings which were hits. In fact, when I heard it, I didn't know it was him—believe it or not. And I liked it, you know, I heard the recording and I liked it. I said, "Who's that? Very good—who was that?" They said, "Don't you know who that is?" I said, "No." They said, "That's Bill Samuels." The war was on then. I was working in a defense plant and playing all night at the Rhumboogie nightclub. Where Bill was or what he was doing I didn't know until he came back. We got together after he made his recordings, and we did some running around together. We had a little place in the basement of an apartment building—had three rooms. When we first rented the place, it was $10 a month, and then when the war came, they froze the rent. So the landlord couldn't raise the rent all through the war. [*Laughs*.] We had a piano in the front room. This is where we danced. We had a bar in the middle room and a bedroom in the back room and a lot of the acts from the different places; for instance, I got off, say, four o'clock at the Rhumboogie or DeLisa—wherever I was—or the Persian lounge called El Grotto. I was working those three places. Not simultaneous, but among others, I didn't know which one I was at the time, and the different musicians would come down. We would sit around, drink, play, and enjoy. Some of the people from Joe's DeLuxe Club would come down, and Bill would bring some of his friends from the North Side—oh, yes, he was playing some place up there around Belmont. I think that's where the el stopped at, up there. There were a lot of places around Belmont at that time on the North Side. And he would bring a lot of his friends down. So we would have a crowd there about four o'clock in the morning and the three rooms would be jamming, you know? We had to have—so that's the one place I do know, the one thing I do know: he was working the North Side, and sometimes I was working the South Side. But we would meet in the morning at this place and we'd stay there nine, ten, eleven, twelve o'clock the next day—just playing, drinking, dancing, enjoying ourselves, you know? And then after so many years, near the end of the Second World War, Bill moved to another state, Minnesota, and I lost contact with him for the next thirty years. I never saw him again because he passed away. But for a good four or five years during this time just before the war and during the war we had pretty close contact. He was, if you might call it, a gourmet of soul food [*laughs*], and I think he had high blood pressure. He ate a lot of soul food, and he loved pork. He loved these heavy foods, and I don't think he watched his blood pressure too well. I know this happened while I was around him. He loved to eat. He loved to eat. And he ate such heavy food, you know—beans, greens laced with pork of some kind, you know, ham, chops, ribs—all this, I think, this caught up with him quite early because he was overweight, he was a bit overweight. Not too much, but he was overweight. I really felt bad when he died, you know?

Art and Shelly

Shelly: Well, we just kind of hung with him. We just kind of hung on to Bill and we did a lot of singing with him. As Art said, amateur hours, various things like that. The old Regal Theater.

Art: We did one show with him in the Regal Theater. That was great.

Shelly: That's where we got the engagement at the Regal Theater, from winning the amateur shows, you know? We won three of them; what was it we won? And from that they gave us two nights' work at the Regal Theater. Was over there. Over New Year's holiday, wasn't it?

Art: Yeah, because I know Dubb came over there as a star after that. He came back as the headliner. The first prize was fifteen bucks—fifteen silver dollars. The guy would always say, "Here's your fifteen silver dollars." Second prize was $10 and third prize was $5. We went in there and we won second prize. They called us again and said, "Why don't you come on down and do the show?" We kind of insisted we'd have to win the first prize if we were coming down there—you shouldn't print that. [Laughs.] We won the first prize. They called us and said, "Hey, we're going to have a good show—why don't you come on down and do the show?" We said, "Yup!" First prize! We got it. Dubb played right across from the city hall. There was a club—I don't know, you're quite young—but you might know where the Erlanger Theater used to be. Next to the Erlanger was the One Twenty Five Club. He played there for years—and the old Three Deuces here in Chicago—he played there for years.

Sylvester Hickman

There was a big family of Samuelses, about seven or eight of them. All of them could sing. Well, I knew all of them. I can recall Georgia, the one next to Bill, Art and Shelly, and George. Then they had a sister, a sister that lived about Thirty-First and the Dan Ryan. She's retired now. She was a good singer; her name was Gin. And then you had another sister that sang real good. She was young, but she never did go out into it because she married young. Well, Ernie Ashley was Bill Samuels's bother-in-law—he's married to Bill Samuels's sister. I'd been playing with Ernest Ashley and decided to take a trio out; do you remember that old place—Ritz Lounge? Do you remember when it was running? They had the Ritz Lounge at the Ritz Hotel—Oakwood and King Drive. Well, it was real popular—real popular at that time. I can remember when Clark Terry used to come down there and sit in—and some tenor player from Detroit—I can't remember his name. The two of them used to sit in—that's when they allowed sitting in, you know. There was a lot of good times there. That was a good joint—used to jump. Ernest had five pieces in there around '41, '42; something like that—and that's when I ran into Bill Samuels because he came in and started playing too. Then I cut off from down there; I started playing with Sonny Thompson. Sonny Thompson had an eighteen-piece band in the El Grotto downstairs. That's when I went there and stayed a while. Then he was getting ready to come out because Earl Hines came in there with his big band. That's when Bill called me up, and we made a trio. He didn't get Ernest. Ernest played with him later on, but he got Ace Lambert, Adam Lambert, that's when we started playing, out there some place on Broadway and Grace—it was a place right on the corner; that's where we started playing.

Where did name Cats 'n Jammers come from, and who came up with it?

I don't know [*laughs*]—we just had to have a name [*laughs*] so somebody picked out Cats 'n Jammers; we just stuck with it.

Was that just for the recordings, or was that on the bandstand too?

Well, we used that on the bandstand and advertisements.

Even before the recording?

Yeah—Bill Samuels and his Cats 'n Jammers! We played the Regal with—let me see who's the feature—Johnny Otis. That's when he was playing drums with his band and Esther. That's when I first saw her. You had Johnny Otis and featuring Bill Samuels, and they had a dancer or two; that's when the Regal was running regular, and every week they had to change shows, you know—when we finally ended up, we hit New York. And hit the Apollo Theater, and came back and hit Detroit and then do a little round-robin with the Milt Larkins band in our southern tour. Then we came back to Chicago. And by that time Adam had cut out because Adam had come from New Orleans; he had a seven-piece band, and he cut out of his band to go with us. When he come back, he decided to take over his band again And that's when Ernest Ashley came back. We stayed together for a while—one of those things like that.

We did quite a little bit of recording for Mercury. That's when Mercury first started out. Yeah, I think we were the second ones to record for Mercury—closer to '44 I think. Berle Adams—you know, the booker—well, he was instrumental in getting that together. He was booking Louis Jordan at that time. So he got us together. Berle was the president here. We did about fifteen, sixteen pieces. Well we made some records that they didn't put out. I don't know, Mercury might have dumped them, you know? I don't know. And they might have put some back away—you can't tell about things like that. And we did "I Cover the Waterfront." Well, "I Cover the Waterfront" surprised us. But the first time—I didn't know what was happening: he called me up—that's when the South Center was running on Forty-Seventh Street—and said, "You know they're up there playing our record?" I had to go up there and listen. I think it sold maybe hundred, two hundred thousand, [which] at that time was quite a bit. It sold enough for us to get some good bookings. Bill sang it from his heart. "One Hundred Years from Today," he sang that from his heart. He did all these pieces that he sang; he sang from his heart. He really was a good singer—believe me, one of the best. One of the best—could interpret a song. And he was broadcasting on WBBM for a while when Dave was here. What's his name?—Dave Garroway! Yeah, he had us on his program on WBBM—fifteen minutes on Wednesdays, I think it was. We played about three or four pieces, on his program every Wednesday. That's before he went to New York. That was about—I'd say '44, '45—because that's when he heard us, when he heard that record. And then another piece we did that they couldn't play on the air at that time was "Jockey Blues" because you couldn't play those type pieces then. "The Bicycle Tillie"—you couldn't get that on either. [*Laughs.*] Yeah, we had two or three you couldn't play on the air. But we'd go someplace people would want to hear 'em.

How long were you with him altogether?

Oh—I'd say about seven or eight years before I got tired. I decided I didn't want to travel anymore, and I started playing with some local bands around the South Side, North Side too. I talked with him several times when he would come to town. He'd ask me to come up and work in Minneapolis with him. But one of them things—I was kind of set around here. And I was doing all right. All I can say is I had great times with him, believe me. We had some great times together.

Art and Shelly

Art: Well, a lot of it was done right here in Chicago for Mercury records. Berle Adams I think was his agent at the time; you might know of Berle Adams. Mercury wasn't very well known at that time, but then he kind of got it moving a little bit. Because one recording, the one I think most people are familiar with, is "I Cover the Waterfront." You know, the flip of "Waterfront," that was one of the ones that sold the most. We, as a family group, were always a little disappointed that not many people know of his prowess with a piano. See, most of his recordings you don't get much of playing, and that's what we always wanted him to do more: play—play piano for us. But, of course, his voice is the thing that kind of took him over. But he played very well. He was good. Some of the guys used to say, "He's an orchestra"—the way he played.

Berle Adams

I was an office boy for GAC and aspired to become more involved in the industry. They gave me an opportunity to canvass the cocktail lounges in Chicago who were starting to use talent. The breakthrough was the Capital Lounge in Chicago, where they bought the attraction from my boss, the Mills Brothers, and then looking at the number of hours that the cocktail lounge was open and the number of performances that the Mills Brothers would do. And Maurice Rocco was the other attraction there. I realized that they would need a fill-in orchestra, and I wrote to my New York office, and they suggested Louis Jordan, if he would play. So they brought him as long as he would play for scale. And that was the start of my career as a cocktail-lounge booker. I was very fortunate I was able to make friends with the owners of all the clubs, and they looked to me for suggestions as to who they should feature in their cocktail lounges. In those days I was involved with the blues—with Louis Jordan, and I was also Big Joe Turner's agent, and I started Joe Williams. Joe, I started him on his career as a blues singer. So I was very much involved with the blues singers. And in one of my wanderings I found Bill Samuels and the Cats 'n Jammers and I thought he was a very exceptional talent with that great voice that he has; I became his agent, and we were very fortunate in finding additional employment for him consistently.

The last session I remember, the standout was "Open the Door, Richard" on Mercury—it's a comedian's act—Dusty Fletcher. See, I had played this thing with Dusty. That was his act with the Duke Ellington band in '44—he was on the show with us, you know, and I took Sonny Greer's place. Sonny had a problem—he tasted pretty good, you know. So they wired me and sent a ticket to join them here and there. I had a year with Ellington—not running, but when something happened to Sonny Greer. So when Bill did "Open the Door, Richard," I knew how the act went—know what I mean?—and it helped a bit. But the vocals were done by Hickman. "Open the Door, Richard," and we did several swinging things—a little upbeat. But as I say again, I don't remember other than that. They did a lot of singing as a group—but I was just playing rhythm.

Where were the Mercury studios at the time? Do you remember?

At Wacker Drive and Wabash—there was an office building there where booking agents were located, and Mercury had a studio in there. The reason I remember the building, I did a session there with June Richmond with the Sonny Thompson band—before there was Mercury. It was my younger days in the music business. Bill Samuels and I were musical acquaintances, but that's my only association with the group—two sessions. But I knew them individually.

Art and Shelly

Art: He was traveling at that time to different spots.

Touring as a musician?

Art: Touring. Yeah, as a musician. I went on a trip with him to Kansas City, Missouri, once, and from there he was going everyplace: San Francisco, then mostly North Dakota, Minnesota, Wisconsin, Illinois, in this area, and he started traveling and finally he decided to leave Chicago, and he moved to Winona—Winona, Minnesota—and he was quite successful there. That took him from Winona to Duluth. And from Duluth he settled in Minneapolis. Because before he was stable in Minneapolis and I think he was broadcasting from WCCO up there at one time, and I know he had a little fifteen-minute spot from Duluth on TV. I didn't know too much about the guys that he had when he was in Minnesota. I know Red Maddock is on this station. Do you know Maddock? On Saturday night—I was surprised one day—I was listening and they were talking about the guys that were playing, and they said Red Maddock on drums. Well, this was the guy that was playing with Dubb when he died. He never left Minnesota: that's where he died—Minneapolis. That's where he died. That's where he had a cerebral hemorrhage and he died.

Red Maddock

I'm glad that you mentioned the name of Bill Samuels. Brings back a lot of memories to me. Bill and I were together a little over three years. I met him in 1951 at the Jockey Club in Winona, Minnesota. He had left Chicago, and he had his wife, Shirley, and his kids with him. He was playing at a place called the Jockey Club. And I had just gotten off the road. I was ready to quit; I was going to quit playing. I had a real rough time on the last road trip, so I came back to Winona. My family was there, my wife and kids. So I went downtown on a Saturday night [to] the Jockey Club, and Bill Samuels was playing there. And I listened—man, the door to the joint was open, and I could hear him from the street. I went in, had some suds, and I was listening to him; [at] intermission he got off the stand. One of the union members introduced me to Bill and I told him I played drums, and he asked, "Do you happen to have your snare with you?"—which I did. I had my drums in the car, and I set them up and we played together. We hit it off right away—just like we were twins. I anticipated what he was going to do, he did the same. He used to say to me, "My God, man—are you psychic?" You know, I could just feel what he was going to do. We used to scat sing. No rehearsals. Just start out scatting and just fell into it—kind of a miracle. But he sang great. We started out in Winona. He was going to play there two weeks. He said to me, "Red do you know some place where you could book us into around here?" So I said, "Yeah, I know a guy in La Crosse." Earl Grimler, had the Melody Mill, he was a saxophone player. He and his wife ran this joint. So I called him up and he hired Bill and me. And we stayed there quite a while. Packed the joint.

Just the two of you, drum and piano?
Yeah. Yeah, sounded like a band.

Never any other players? Never guitar basses?
No, no. Guys would sit in sometimes. But I said one night, "Give me a C." He said, "Where the hell's that?" [*laughter*]. I said, "Are you kidding?" He said, "No, I don't know where C and D and all that is." That's what he told me. I think he must have been kidding me. But he had learned the piano from his mother from hymns. His dad was a minister. But we played in Winona at Arnie's, too: Arnie's it was called—they had five bartenders. And I'm telling you, a busy person is a happy person. They were really packed. Whoa, that place was packed. And Bill had such a wonderful voice, sang ballads really great. "Flamingo"—man, I wonder where I could get that record. Boy, he did a real wonderful job on that. He sang "Goodbye," Goodman's theme "I'll Never Forget You." Yeah, that

was a beautiful thing too. But we played Minot, we played Fargo and Minneapolis—we played at Augie's up on the avenue there—in Austin, Rochester. All around Minnesota we played. The kicks we had on the road, you know, they were just wonderful. Nothing but laughs and fun—he was a lot of fun to play with. When we were on the road, Bill would do the cooking and I would do the dishes. And he could do more with a bean and a slice of bacon, man, than anybody—he was such a great cook. God, he was a cook. And before we ate, he said, "Now man, I'm going to recite something from the Bible, and when I pause you say 'Jesus wept.'" I'll never forget that. And he would say grace at the table before we would eat—just the two of us. I was kind of embarrassed at first. But not later on—it got to me. What a nice man, I thought—you know? What a great guy. We hadn't been together too long, and one night he was taking a bath and he yelled at me, "Hey, Red! Come on and wash my back!" [*Laughs.*] But I went in and did—I grabbed his washcloth and the soap and I washed his back, you know? I thought at first it was kind of strange. But I thought, "Hell no, man—wash his back if he asks you to wash his back." So I did. [*Laughs.*] Hell of it is, he had me wash his back every time he took a bath—which is once a month, at least. [*Laughs.*] After Appleton we went to Minot, and half way to Minot we had to rest; it was a long trip, so we stopped at a motel. We were the same size. He was black and I was white—no, red—I was red. But we wore the same uniforms even to the socks and everything. Bill, in the room he says, "Hey, man, look what I got." He showed me a jar some kind of a salve—on the label it said Abe Lincoln Hair Straightener. Because he always said to me, "Gee, you're lucky, man, you got straight hair and it looks good." So he was going to straighten his hair. So in this motel he showed me this salve and he said, "Now, this is going to straighten my hair out." He said, "I'm going to put it on, but I can only have it on twenty minutes, and let me know when that twenty minutes is up." So we had a couple of tastes, and we were kind of jolly joking around, having a ball, and we forgot. About forty-five minutes later I said, "Hey, how about rinsing that gunk out of your hair?" He said, "Oh, Jesus, man!" You know, and he couldn't get there fast enough. He went to the sink and rinsed his hair out—the hair came out by the handfuls. [*Laughs.*] He had holes in his head. [*Laughs.*] He said, "Now what am I going to do? Oh, man!" But anyway—it grew back in, but he didn't know what he was going to do. [*Laughs.*]

Everybody loved the guy. He bought a brand new Buick Riviera in Mankato, Minnesota, and he showed me the down payment on the receipt—two-and-a-half dollars he put down on this car. I couldn't believe it. But the guy loved Dubb—the guy that had the Buick franchise. He just loved to listen to Bill play and sing. "Sure, Bill!" He took the two and a half. Bill said, "That's all I got."

[*Laughs.*] When we were in Mankato one night, a guy comes in in overalls, he's standing at the bar drinking a beer, and he said to Bill Samuels, "Bill, if you can sing 'Because' and make me cry, I'll give you a hundred bucks." Bill said, "Get ready to weep, man." And he sang that "Because God Made You Mine," you know that tune, and he sang that, and the guy wrote out a check for $100. And Bill took it to the boss of the joint, and said, "Is that check any good?" and the boss said, "I'll cash all you got of those—he's a contractor"—you know. He looked just like a working man, but things like that happened to Bill everywhere he went—you bet everybody was so good to Bill. I think one woman gave him a grand piano. Yeah! Grand piano. But he didn't take it anywhere. When we played Mankato, he would go in there and he would just play on the piano—she wanted to give him the piano. But he was very well liked. His dad came to visit him in Winona. He was a big man, kind of—plump, you know? So Bill said, "Hey, Dad, you want to watch your diet now." And his dad took out a salt shaker and he shook it on the food. And Bill said, "What's that?" He said, "That's my de-calorizer, [*laughs*] that's my de-calorizer."

One summer afternoon we were sitting in that car he bought. We were about a half a block from the bus depot in Winona. A beautiful day. He's sitting in the driver's seat; I'm sitting over in the killer seat. So anyway, the bus stopped at the bus depot, and a big lanky black guy got off the bus. And he had two wicker satchels, suitcases, you know, those old-time ones? He was tall and lanky, and Bill sees him. And Bill says, "Oh-oh!" Bill called me Brother Andy. "Hey, Brother Andy," he says. "When he spies me, he'll be over here in a second"—because there aren't any colored people in Winona to speak of. Bill is the only one. So this guy sees Bill, and Bill says, "Oh—oh, he saw me." So this guy comes over, sticks his head in the car window, and he says to Bill, "Is we the only ones here?" [Laughs.]

Our last engagement was at Windsor, Canada. And after that we split, and he went to Minneapolis. I played at the Manor, and one night I came to work and the bartender said, "Did you hear about Bill?" I said, "No." "He had a heart attack." I said, "Where is he?" "Mount Sinai Hospital." So I went up there, and when I walked into the room, I knew it wasn't a heart attack. He was tethered to the bed. It was a coma. What he had done, he was playing at the Sheraton Ritz in Minneapolis. It was his second night there, and he was at home getting ready for work. He went to the bathroom and he screamed to his wife, "My God, Shirley, I'm blind!" The vein went back of his eyes. I went over and touched his hand, and I talked to him and he talked to me. He was in a semi-coma. And he said to his wife Shirley, "Give me my laundry, Shirley; I want to go take my laundry." So she scrounged up the sheets and put it in his arms, and he held it and said, "Now, you tell Mike to be a good boy." That was his son, Mike. We'd go and visit him every so often. The night he died, we were in Mount Sinai. He had another aneurysm. I couldn't believe it. It's hard to believe. It was March 23, 1964. A guy couldn't have a better friend than Bill Samuels. And that's the way I'll remember Bill.

Marl **Young**

This is another interview made possible by a *Blues Before Sunrise* listener. I had stumbled across some recordings by Chicago's Little Miss Cornshucks, issued on the Sunbeam label. In addition to Cornshucks's vocals, the records featured some far-out arrangements and a little jazz combo led by Marl Young on piano. That was a name new to me—certainly no one playing down-home blues. I would play the records and then come on the mic to laud the band and the arrangements done by Marl. I remember specifically a listener calling me up on the show, telling me they knew Marl Young and could put me in touch with him if I wanted to do an interview. Marl had moved out to Los Angeles thirty years earlier and been based there ever since. I called him in L.A. and we did an extended phone interview discussing his life and career.

Marl Young signs merger agreement between (black) local 767 and (white) local 47 of American Federation of Musicians, 1953. Photo Courtesy of American Federation of Musicians Local 47.

This interview was recorded September 7, 1987. Marl Young died April 9, 2009.

■ ■ ■

Well, I was born in Virginia, January 29, 1917. My mother brought us all to Chicago about 1924. We came from a broken home; my father and mother were separated. I went to school in Chicago through high school and to junior college. I went to Wilson Junior College. I started playing at a very early age. I started playing by ear and did a few city contests. Then I was enamored of the jazz players and people like Earl Hines, and at that time Claude Hopkins in New York was broadcasting from the Roseland Ballroom. This is in the early '30s. In 1938 I went to Wilson Junior College and there participated in what we called the Spring Music Festival. I wrote music for the jazz band and for the symphony orchestra—all on my own. I taught myself to orchestrate it at a time, for about two years, when I couldn't play because of an injury to my hand. I taught myself to orchestrate. This is the first attempt at symphonic orchestration. It came out well. About 1940 I got married but was playing with some of these gig bands of Chicago. There was Johnny Long, Lloyd Kimbal, and others of that type that were playing local engagements three or four nights a week. Playing like this enabled me to play at night, make some money, and still go to school. In 1940 Sammy Dyer, who was producing the show at the Grand Terrace—sometimes called the Sunset—called me to write the music for a show, and this is the first time that Lionel Hampton came through Chicago with his band. I wrote the music for that and subsequent shows there. Later on, Sammy Dyer went to the DeLisa and asked me to come there and write the shows. In 1942 the Rhumboogie opened, and I was hired just as a rehearsal pianist. At that time, a guy named Buck Thompson, I think from St. Louis, was writing the shows. Joe "Ziggy" Johnson was the producer. I was hired to conduct the shows—to rehearse the shows—and later on I was hired to write the music for the shows. This went on for about two or three years. In 1943—at the end of 1943 we put a band together, which included people like Eddy Johnson, who is a very popular tenor player in Chicago now, a very close friend of mine. Hillard Brown, drummer. Nat Jones, who recently died, and to me was just about the finest alto/clarinetist I ever heard in my life. This also included Charlie Parker and a tenor player by the name of Tom Archia. We put this band together—at this time. I was having political problems with the union, with my becoming the leader. However, because of the antics of Charlie Parker and Tom Archia, the leader quit, and the owner of the club, Charlie Glen, just insisted on my becoming leader because I was the leader of the band anyway and because I was the conductor of the band for the shows and was also writing music for the shows. My first act as the band leader was to fire Charlie Parker and to fire Tom Archia because, although they were very fine players, they were just disruptive as far as the band was concerned. They would turn their backs on the other saxophone players and play something completely different. Charlie wouldn't show up one night and he would show up another. Sometimes he would come there and he wasn't in condition to play. I wanted a band that's going to play and not have disruptive forces. My first act was to fire those two and replace them with two other people. We finally hit it up with John Houser on alto, another fellow named McDonald on tenor, and Eddie Johnson on tenor. Eddie left, and I replaced him with another sax player named Jay Parish, I think. We had people like Gale Brockman, who was then perceived as one of the finest players that I had ever heard. I hired Henderson Smith, who was in Chicago and still one of the greatest trumpet players I have ever heard. I hired a bass player by the name of Quinn Wilson, who is now dead but who was famous for playing with Earl Hines—a very fine player. We had a very fine band at the Rhumboogie.

Before I knew who you were or knew that you were still alive, I had decided, from listening to the records, that you had one of the wickedest little bands that I had ever heard. One of the things that Eddie told me, that you wrote some of the most difficult arrangements that the fellows had ever seen. He told me that they were always complaining that when you had to hit the show—before they were even really warmed up—you had them jumping through hoops.

Except this one thing—I have run into at least ten or twelve of the people who played with me there, including Eddie, and they have said that after they played my music, that everything else that they played after that "was just like A, B, C." That they had no difficulty at all. Eddie told me that after playing my music everything he played after that he had "absolutely no problem." So maybe it did some good.

Was there any kind of really visible reaction when you and he would hand out parts? Would people slap their foreheads or anything like that?

The brass sometimes—the trumpet players. You know that's a very physically difficult instrument because of the muscles in the lips. They are very delicate muscles, and trumpet players have to be very careful or else they can blow themselves out. I would get most of the dirty looks from the brass, but strength enough—after they would play it up they were okay. I insisted—I had to have what I call three first-part players in the band, and I would tell the guys to divide parts. This guy takes some of the first part. You take some of the first part. You take some of the first part. That way it would not overwork any one man. If they did that, there was really no problem.

Maybe you can run down the address of the Rhumboogie Cafe for the folks who aren't familiar with it.

Well, I can't give you the exact address, but it was between Calumet at South Park on Fifty-Fifth Street, and it was on the south side of the street.

Okay. Can you give us a layout of the room? Say, if you just walked in the door—can you describe the Rhumboogie?

If you walked in the door, first you would walk through the lobby. You would walk in the door, you could go up either the left side or the right side.

When you walked in and went down, I think two or three stairs, you were in the main dining room. Upstairs there were seats, and that's where they had what they called the Twenty-Six table. This was a game where you put six dice in a container and threw them out. If you got certain combinations, you won drinks. The bandstand was at the very back of the room, and you could enter the bandstand either from the right or the left; that's where the chorus girls and the principals would enter. If you went to the back of the room—behind and to the right of the bandstand was the kitchen where they prepared the food. To the left was the business office. That's where Charlie Glen had his office. Charlie Parker was playing with us. The bandleader was Carroll Dickerson. Charlie wouldn't show up, say, on a Wednesday night—wouldn't show up on a Thursday. Anyway, Charlie would come in on Friday. Carroll Dickerson would see him coming in the door and would go out, say, the left side. If he went out the left side, Charlie would come in the right side, get on the bandstand, and have his horn out. It really became a game because you never knew when he would be there or what condition he was going to be in. I was always amused by the fact that he would wait for Carroll Dickerson to make his move to the right or to the left. If he went to the left, Charlie came in the right. If he went to the right, Charlie would come in the left. This stuff went on for about three months until Carroll Dickerson got tired of it and quit. That was the way the room was laid out. There were seats on the right, seats on the left. In the middle, of course, was the floor, which was used for the floor show and was also for dancing.

What were the dimensions of the room?

I would imagine that it could seat about 150 people. I could be wrong on that—I don't know how much goes on at estimating that. But I'm sure it could seat about 150 people. Also there was seating upstairs.

Okay. Didn't they refer to that as the balcony?

That's right.

So you could actually sit upstairs and watch the floor show?

You could sit up there and watch the show. The bar was up there too. That's right, I forgot about the bar was there. That's where they gave the drinks to the waiters and waitresses, and that's where they played the twenty-sixes game up there. I very seldom went up there. I think of all the time that I was in the place, I might have gone up there twice in that particular area. But also upstairs, in back, were the dressing rooms for the performers. This is all on the same level as the balcony, although it was completely separated from the balcony and the bar.

Let's go back and talk about the stage shows at the Rhumboogie. If I was a patron and I came down there and sat in for the show, how would the whole thing unfold in an evening's entertainment?

Well, first the band would come to work at eleven o'clock. We would play a set, take a short intermission, and the first show went on at 11:30.

How many pieces in the band at that point?

Eleven. I had four brass, four reeds, and three rhythms. Our first show went on at 11:30—would last about an hour. Then the band would play a set, go back, come off, go back, and get prepared to do the second show. The second show was entirely different from the first show. The principals and show had different singing numbers or dancing numbers, depending upon the talent. In the first show they did three production numbers: an opening; what we call the middle number—which is always the big number in the show, usually an exotic number; and the finale. In the second show there was just the opening and the finale; there was no middle number. The third show—the last show went on at three o'clock in the morning. It was a repeat of the first show. We got off at about four o'clock—except on Saturday night we started at 10:30 and the first show went on at eleven o'clock. Then, after we finished with our shows at about 3:30 or four o'clock Saturday night, we are now into Sunday morning, and we gave a breakfast there, which started about six o'clock in the morning. We would get out of there about nine o'clock. So we would go in there at 10:30 at night and the next time we saw daylight was about 9:00 or 9:30 the next morning.

I see. I guess one of the things I wanted to get to was—we got the band in there and we have the principals. But how would the principals line up? I mean, would you lead off with a singer or a dancer or a comedian? How would you mix that up there?

It would depend upon the producer. He would tell them what order they would—I know when George Lane, who came there with the Milton Larkin band was there—he would always be the first principal to appear. But he was a regular, he was a regular there just like the band was. But the other principals, the order in which they appeared, really depended upon the producer. If a person was designated as the star of the show, of course, they appeared last, and usually the star of the show would participate in the middle number. When the middle number was over, the star would remain on the stage and would go through his or her act.

I understand.

The shows were fashioned like that over and over again.

How often would that show change?

The shows at the Rhumboogie changed every four weeks. The show at the DeLisa changed every three weeks. The shows at the El Grotto changed every four weeks.

Sometimes, especially when I started doing shows at the El Grotto, I would do some twenty-five arrangements in a week and was working every night. But, as I said, those weeks I just didn't sleep.

Let me ask how you would rehearse a production and still stage another one? Was there ever a time off or were you rehearsing during the day and performing the old one at night?

Yeah! I was rehearsing during the day, performing the old one at night, and maybe rehearsing another or two shows at other campaigns at the same time. Also, at the Rhumboogie they really worked me because Charlie was afraid the show wouldn't go right; I also worked—the music you worked six nights a week. I worked seven. Because he wanted to be sure there was somebody there to conduct the show on the seventh night. Now, he paid me well, but he also worked me. I worked seven nights a week.

How long did you have to rehearse a production before you were actually able to stage it?

The shows at the DeLisa were rehearsed two weeks. The shows at the Rhumboogie were rehearsed most of the time two weeks. If there was going to be a very difficult show where they had a lot of things to do, they might rehearse three weeks. But for the most part they would rehearse two weeks.

Did that mean that the principals were already in town and even though—

No. No. When I say rehearsals, I meant mainly with the chorus girls. Also, this is something that I enjoyed; when Charley Markum was there in 1943, he not only had chorus girls but he had chorus boys. This is the first time in the Chicago area, and in fact the only time, but it certainly made for a more spectacular production because of the fact he could play the boys against the girls. But when I said rehearsals, that meant mainly that they were getting the dance routines for the production routines for the chorus girls and the chorus boys. The principals would come in either the day before the show went in and they would go into the rehearsals, or sometimes they would come in on the day the show went in because of other commitments that they would have. But on that day, we had some long rehearsals. Sometimes we wouldn't get out of the Rhumboogie till eight or nine o'clock, and I had to be right back at eleven o'clock. Maybe I'd be at the DeLisa from six o'clock in the morning until time to go to the Rhumboogie, and on the days that the shows went the same time, we would put the show in at the DeLisa. Then they would do it that night; then I would go home maybe write two arrangements, and they would get to the Rhumboogie, and then we would rehearse the final show and put it in that night. They all went in Friday night. During the time at the DeLisa there were people like Sunny and Sunny, the Barry Brothers; we had such great acts there, and this was where the famous George Kirby got his start. He was a dishwasher at the Rhumboogie and would keep running up to us making all these strange noises. We thought he was a little off. He came to the Rhumboogie on Sunday morning for his breakfast there, and I heard him. I said, "Man, I want to write some music for you." So for about a year I wrote music for George, who I think is just one of the greatest talents I ever heard in my life—especially where impressions are concerned. We had people like Jessie Scott, Bill Bailey, who was a very fine dancer. Brother of Pearl Bailey. There was also a very fine performer by the name of Mabel Scott. One of the first dance teams that I ever played for was a team called Russ and McCain. This was a very fine dance team. I got a chance again to write some music for them, but I also got a chance to just play for them every night. We had people like Claudia McNeil in our show. She later became a star in the motion picture *A Raisin in the Sun*. Also, Dinah Washington appeared in the shows there. I did four arrangements for Dinah while she was appearing at the Rhumboogie. That's where I first met a very fine performer named Louise Bryant, who did quite a few movies and also retired in the movie industry as a choreographer for the stars that were being prepared for the motion pictures exhibition.

We talked about dancers—how about comedians that appeared there?

Oh, you know—oh, Pot, Pan and Skillet. That was one of the big acts at that time. Buck and Bubbles and Moke and Poke. These were the teams. As far as the Rhumboogie is concerned, the comedians were teams. Not individuals. I cannot for the life of me think of one individual comedian who appeared there. But I do know that Pot, Pan and Skillet, Moke and Poke, and Buck and Bubbles they appeared there. These are very fine comedy teams. They presented the finest black talent that was available in the country at the time. These talents always came to Chicago, and they would appear either at the Rhumboogie or at the DeLisa or/and when the El Grotto opened, they would appear there.

I would like to say that the concept of the shows that were being put on in Chicago at that time at the Rhumboogie, at the DeLisa, and later on at the El Grotto—and, of course, before that at the Grand Terrace—in performance and in concept were as good as the shows that are seen at Las Vegas through the years. They didn't have the million-dollar costumes. They didn't have the million-dollar scenery. But the concept of producers like Sammy Dyer, Ziggy Johnson, and Larry Steele was the greatest of concepts of any of the shows that I've seen in Las Vegas, and for about two years I was in Las Vegas every other week. Yes, I mean every other week, and I saw just about every show there, especially the book shows at the DOOM, at the Stardust, and at the Desert Inn. People like Joe Johnson.

Also, there was a producer named Charlie Morrison who came into the Rhumboogie at the end of 1943. He brought with him a young lady by the name of Hortense Allen; you might have heard of her. Well, anyway, she became a producer on her own. These people were very talented people, and their concepts were magnificent, as far as I was concerned. I considered it a pleasure to have been able to write music for them. But let me say that I think the greatest of all of them was Sammy Dyer. Sammy Dyer had a dance school at Thirty-Fifth and State. Every year he would put on a show. I think they called it the Dyerettes?—or something like that. He would present these very talented young black kids who just had magnificent talent. For about two or three years I was sort of the house musician for that because of my ability not only to play jazz but to play classics. He dealt a lot into classical backgrounds. I got a chance to play a lot of his shows. Of all the producers that I've worked with, to me he had the greatest concepts. Other producers admit that.

Larry Steele, of course, put on very spectacular shows, too, and—as you know for years—every year during the summer he was on the boardwalk in Atlantic City. I think I was fortunate as a musician during the time to have those guys as my colleagues. We experienced the type of show business that really prepared you to play almost anything. I know when I came out here and I worked for Lucille Ball, we did what we called musicals. I would rehearse it just like we did at the Rhumboogie. I would make the sketches then I would write the music. The only thing here—it was better because we would put the music on tape at a pre-score and our music department would go over it. In Chicago we had to do it live! All sorts of things would happen on that first show. [*Laughter.*] Sometimes the producer might be finishing the finale at eight o'clock at night, or nine o'clock at night and we're supposed to hit the first show at 11:30. It was pretty wild, but it was the greatest experience in the world for a musician. The young musicians that come up today just do not get that kind of experience, and it's a crime. It's a shame, really, because if they have to come out here and play in the studios, they just are not as prepared as I was.

Since this program that I do is basically a blues show, my main point of reference is T-Bone Walker. I was wondering if you could help recreate how T-Bone fit into these production numbers. Do you have any recall of what he would do

exactly when he was there? What kind of a person he was to deal with and anything of that nature?

The first number that T-Bone ever did at the Rhumboogie was in 1942—it was "Evening." That was the middle number of our production number. That's the big number in the show. This was one of his main numbers that he did. Joe Johnson built this production number around T-Bone. During the numbers he would come out with his guitar and get to the microphone and he would sing "Evening." We had a guy there called Matlock who did the lighting, and he was absolutely a genius. He should have been out here in the motion picture industry. I remember the beautiful lighting that Matlock would give on this number. That was the first number that he ever did at the Rhumboogie, and of course after the production number of "Evening" he would then go into his act. They talk about Elvis Presley. I don't know if Elvis put the guitar behind him or did the splits while he was playing.

T-Bone would put the guitar behind his back, play it backwards—and do the splits! He was just a fantastic artist. If he had been white, he would have made two billion dollars. Because the things that white guys were doing, they copied off of T-Bone. You never heard Elvis Presley do anything on the guitar, but T-Bone—he was a good guitar player for the genre that he was in—the blues idiom. He was an expert guitar player for that type of music. Sometimes when there weren't too many people in the place, after he would get through with his act, he would just sit up and jam for ten or fifteen minutes. He would play, and he was a good player. He was a great visual performer because of the physical gyrations that he went through while he was playing. He should have been in the movies and he should have been doing the things that they were having Presley doing because he was a better performer than Elvis Presley.

From what you've said, the amount of your work schedule, you don't sound to me as a guy out carousing a lot. You probably didn't catch up with T-Bone on that end of things, did you?

No! [*Laughter.*] I couldn't keep up. Well, first, I didn't try to keep with him; I was married. I got married in 1940. Also, I was in school most of the time besides this. I was either in school or else I was studying orchestrating music with someone. I just didn't have the time to do all these things. He and I, we went out maybe three or four times during the whole time we worked together. I know one night we were on at the DuSable Hotel for quite some time before we went to work then. Other times after we got off of work; usually, I went home, but sometimes you sort of have to unwind so you go someplace to have breakfast, and he was there. But I couldn't keep up with him on the schedule. First thing, I just had too much to do. Also, usually, after we would get off at work the other guys could go home or they could go out. I had to go home and write music. [*Laughter.*] Or else I had to go home and grab a little sleep and go to the DeLisa to rehearse the show. I just didn't have time to do all these things. Also, I didn't drink. I didn't smoke. I just wasn't a carouser. Not that there's anything wrong with being a carouser; I don't want you to think I'm a prude. I just didn't have the time to do it. Probably if I had the time, maybe I would have.

It seems like so many of them are gone and you're still here. I think the no-smoking, no-drinking policy must have been a good idea.

Well, it certainly helped me, because at the time I could get no sleep. At least one week out of the month I would stay up at least two days, and I mean with absolutely no sleep. Sometimes four, five, six days with absolutely no sleep. I was either rehearsing, writing, or in my car going somewhere to rehearse or play or conduct. I was always careful of having a heart attack. When I got a pain, I would say, "Well, I've overdone it." I lucked out nothing ever happened to me. I was able to go on like that, year after year. After staying up three or four days, I could go to sleep and sleep eight hours, wake up, and go right on. I've been very fortunate. But I did know that if I decided to drink and smoke and carouse with some of the others that I wouldn't have made it. I'd have been gone a long time ago.

They said that Charlie Glen owned the Rhumboogie. It was supposed to be owned with Joe Louis. But Charlie Glen ran it. Charlie Glen started the Rhumboogie label. Because we rehearsed the records right in the Rhumboogie, and we were all working in the Rhumboogie when we first made the records. T-Bone Walker and George Ling, the singer, and I worked for a full year; all the way through 1944 into 1945 at the Rhumboogie. It was during this time that we made the record of T-Bone, the one that was to keep popular, "I'm Still in Love with You." Horace Henderson had made a big-band arrangement with fifteen pieces. We recorded with only eight pieces, so I made the orchestration for the eight-piece band. We also had on the other side a thing that I wrote and T-Bone put the words to, called "Sail On Boogie." We featured this in the show. At the same time we featured this in the show, I'd written him an arrangement on "Rhapsody in Blue," which featured not only instrumentalists, but I had four people singing the slow themes. We kept these two numbers in the show for two or three months because they were so popular. We made some more records with T-Bone in '45 and '46. These were six-piece arrangements. I had Eddie Johnson, Nat Jones on saxophone, and Quinn Wilson, of course, on bass. I forget who played trumpet; I think it was Charlie Greene, and then I think Henderson Smith. These records were distributed in Europe. About three years ago I got some letters from people in Europe saying that they were still playing the records and wanted to know more about it. Of course, by this time T-Bone Walker was dead, and there was no chance of taking in on these.

Do you remember any of the titles we're talking about in these particular sessions? I've got some titles that I could run down. Run 'em down.

Okay, we did "Sail On Boogie" and "I'm Still in Love with You." There was also "T-Bone Boogie," an arrangement of "Evening," "You Don't Love Me," and "Mean Old World Blues." Yup, the "Mean Old World" he and I wrote that together. Of all the blues, that was my favorite. I think that's one of the finest arrangements I've ever done. The arrangement on "Evening," again, was written for sixteen pieces at first. I had to reduce it—I don't know who did that arrangement. But I did the orchestration for the record. We did all these things with T-Bone. Also, T-Bone did "Stormy Monday." I can't remember the year for that, and I did the arrangement for that. That remained a standard all through the years. We did that out here.

That was on Black & White, wasn't it?

Yes.

Was Ralph Bass included in that somehow? Was he the A and R man at that point?

I don't know who the A and R man was.

That was Paul Reiner's label, wasn't it?

I just don't know. All I know is we did it out here, and I know that I did the arrangement.

Let me see if you have some recollections of another session of T-Bone. For Imperial?

Yes. He did a lot of things for Imperial.

Now, I have a listing of only one time for you on Imperial. A session called "I Walked Away."

Yeah, that was a good one.

"No Reason."

Yes.

"Look Me in the Eye."

Yes.

And "Too Lazy."

Yes—again.

Were there more than just those four sides that you recall at Imperial?

I thought we did eight sides, but I'm not sure. I know I did two or three sessions with them out here. I thought we did about eight sides for Imperial.

The one from Imperial that I have the information on is from 1950. Would you assume the other one was right around that vicinity?

Yes, '50 or '51, in that area. I remember one, "I Walked Away," because of the numbers on the session, and that was my favorite. The fellow that owned that label was Lew Chudd, and that was the same label that Fats Domino was on. Anyway, I was hired by Imperial—you know, these guys didn't put these things on paper—they would do them. Then Lew Chudd would give me the records and I would have to take them also to get the copyrights. They were all blues numbers. I would have to take off what they were singing as the melody and lyrics and make copies so they could send in and get the copyrights. I don't think anything was written in those sessions. Now, the T-Bone sessions—the things are written because I wrote them.

Maybe you can tell me about Charles Gray. Who was Charles Gray, and do you remember the titles that he did?

Well, he was the trumpet player that we did the six-piece things that we did with Nat Jones and Eddy Johnson. He was the son of the president of the union, Harry Gray. He's a trumpet player.

Do you remember the titles he did?

No, but I tell you what I'll do: somewhere here buried under something, I do have those records, and if you will give me an address, I will send you the titles.

I have one here "I'm a Bum Again" and "Crazy Woman Blues." Was there more than one?

There were at least four. In 1946 my brothers Harry, Chester, and some other people formed the Sunbeam recording company. We did some things, novelties and instrumentals, which probably the public didn't buy too well because they were too far ahead of the public's taste. Anyway, we recorded Little Miss Cornshucks. At the time I was working at the DeLisa with Fletcher Henderson, who, although he played the piano, hired a piano player to play the shows. I was also, of course, writing the music for the shows. Mike DeLisa wanted Cornshucks to sing only blues, but I had made an arrangement on "So Long," which was a regular part of the shows. Every time she would do the number, he would come steaming up the aisle, saying he only wanted her to sing the blues. But every night I would call the number, and when he would come steaming up the aisle, I would turn my back and continue directing the band. So this went on—when we decided to record her. I decided. It was my decision that we were going to do "So Long," and we put another blues on the other side, but ironically it was "So Long," the traditionally popular number, that became very popular in Chicago at the time. Which indicates you just can never tell what record or what tune is going to be a hit as far as records are concerned. Anybody that can predict that, I guess; the recording companies would put him in an office and give him a blank check and tell him to predict a hit. Nobody's been able to do it yet, and that was an indication. There she was, a blues singer, but the most popular record she did in Chicago was the original popular number.

How many titles did you do altogether with Cornshucks?

Let's see, we did "For Old Times' Sake," which was a number written by my brother and I. "When Mommy Sings a Lullaby," which was written by my brother and I. Two blues; one on the other side of "So Long." I just don't remember the names of them.

"I'm Gonna Leave Here Walking?"

That's it, that's it. "I'm Gonna Leave Here Walking."

The flip "For Old Times' Sake" — "Have You Ever Loved Somebody"?

The blues that was on the other side of "For Old Times' Sake"—that was the blues.

On the other side of "Lullaby" was "I Don't Love You Anymore."

Yeah! That of all the blues that we did that was my favorite because of the type of arrangement that I did on it. It was a real wild arrangement. I think that is the total of tunes that we did with her—we might have done a couple more, but I'm not sure. But those were the ones that we did put out for publication.

I have a copy of one that you were probably talking about the band things on Sunbeam. An instrumental called "We're Off."

Yeah.

A vocal on the other side by a fellow, Bill Greene, can you fill me in on him?

He had won a contest. At that time they were holding some sort of contest on radio for young singers. I heard him on the radio. He had won one of the contests, and we decided to record him. He was very young. I would imagine Bill was no more than twenty-one when we did that record. The record didn't get anywhere, but I thought it was a good record. I thought he was a good singer, but, you know, most of the records that are made don't sell. Nobody knows why they do or why they don't.

Was Sunbeam distributed anywhere other than Chicago?

Yes. I went to places like Indianapolis, St. Louis, Detroit, and others and arranged for distribution. And then later on there was a company there—I think it was M & B distributors. I'm not sure. But anyway, we arranged for them to distribute, and that way they distributed nationwide for us in the certain markets.

So the titles for Cornshucks, then—I probably don't have any other ones to chase if I have these—

Those were the main ones.

You don't happen to know of any other off the top of your head, if there were any others that I might . . .

Not that we did. As I recall now—when we did the last two—"I Don't Love You Anymore," whatever was on the other side—"For Mommy Sings a Lullaby": that was the day we also recorded Bill Greene. We did those in the same session. That's why we didn't do more.

You also have another very famous vocalist on record. Maybe you can go into that a little bit. You know who I'm trying to get to here.

Was that John Hartman?

Right.

Yeah, we did four things with John, with strings. I guess this was about 1947. I first met John in 1945. A friend of mine, Walter Dyett, he was a teacher at Phillips High, very good musician. Then he formed a casual band. Walter brought him by my house. John had just gotten out of the army in 1945. I did his first arrangements; I did "You Go to My Head" and I did "Without a Song." I think these two later on in '48 out here he recorded with Dizzy Gillespie. I do know he recorded "You Go to My Head." The other one, I'm not sure. I just thought that John had one of the greatest voices for popular music I've ever heard, and it's just a shame that neither one of the records was able to hit into the general market. But we did four things with John. One was "What Have You Done to Me?"/"Always Together," which was written by a schoolmate of mine. Her last name was Watkins. I forget her first name. Another number, "The Songs I Sing," was written by Luther Hill, who was a columnist for the *Pittsburgh Courier*, and myself. The other was a tune that I heard played at the Rhumboogie. I never did know who the author was, but we thought we would do the tune anyway because it was such a beautiful tune. We just did four things with John.

Were these the first things that Hartman had recorded?

Yes. Of that I'm sure. Because he did these things in Chicago. Now, he did the things with Dizzy Gillespie out here.

As long as we're talking about records, let me follow up. I see another one here—I don't know if this one is on Sunbeam. The Marl Young trio?

Oh yeah. We did some things with Gene Ammons. Is his name on there?

Yes.

Yeah. Yeah, I forgot about those. I forget how many things we did there. What we did, we were backing a singer by the name of—hmmm—Petite Swanson—a female impersonator who had worked at Joe's Music Café at Sixty-Third and South Park. I don't know how long you've been in Chicago, but in the early '40s Joe Hughes had a café at Sixty-Third and South Park, which featured female impersonators. I worked there with a band with Paul Keene, D. Q. Robinson, and Quinn Wilson for about a year and a half, just before I went into the Rhumboogie in '43. I heard this singer, and I thought that we would like to do some things with her; it was the Marl Young trio behind her. Then we did some things with a guy named Carter—the Bob Carter trio.

How did you get from Chicago to the West Coast?

Well, 1947, my first wife and I broke up. I had wanted to come California for a long time because I don't like the weather in Chicago. The winter of 1944 I got pneumonia. I darn near died, and I said, "Somewhere and somehow, I'm going to leave this town." So when we broke up, our agreement was that I would keep the apartment, where we had the business office with so many records, until I came to California, then she would move back in. Around this time Wild Bill Davis, the organist, was playing with Louis Jordan. He had decided, he told me, "I'm going to become a Hammond organ artist." I saw him again; he said, "Look, I'm going on playing organ, and Louis needs somebody who can play and write." Bill was playing and doing the writing for the band. He said, "I think you're the one for the job." So I talked to Bill but I never talked to Louis. I thought that I could get to Los Angles anywhere before December 1. I got out here November 24. I walked into the studio where Louis Jordan was recording a Decca on Melrose, and I told him who I was. Then he gave me the news: "Well, I expected you out here before this, three or four days ago," and said, "when you didn't come—" Of course, I was driving all the way there; he couldn't get in touch with me. He said, "I hired somebody." He hired a fellow named Bill Doggett, who later made a recording called "Honky Tonk." Really. So I came to town with no job. But strangely, when I walked into the studio, a girl waved to me and said, "Marl—Marl." I said, "Who is that?" I went over. It was a girl by the name of Martha Davis, who was a very popular pianist and singer. She said, "Look, what are you doing out here?" I said, "Don't look like I'm doing anything. I thought I was coming out here to work for Louis Jordan. Evidently, Bill didn't tell me just when to get here, and I don't have anything to do." She said, "Well, I'm going to do some recording with Louis, and we don't have anybody to do the arrangements. Would you do them?" I said, "Of course I'll do them." I did those. He did "Daddy-O." I forget the title of the other number. This was pure happenstance. I walked in—I can't even remember where I met Martha, but she certainly knew me. I walked in; I hadn't been in town ten minutes and I got a recording session. But I also lost a job that I thought I was coming to. I got in touch with a former entertainer named Ginni McGown. I got a room there. She had a studio here, and I did some teaching. Then I got in touch with Louise Bryant, who was doing some work out there. I did some work with her. I got in touch with Benny Carter, with whom I had done numerous arrangements in Chicago. I was sending them to him all over the country. He had me do something with Freddy Slack. You have to be in a town for three months before you can go to work regularly on a job. I got married out here. My wife and I worked together—vocalist Judy Carol. She had sung with Duke Ellington and Lucky Millinder in the years past. We stayed together for a turbulent eighteen months. I got groups together and worked; I was always busy. I had a six-piece band at a place called The Down Beat; my wife and I had a six-piece band. The economic conditions became such that you just had to cut down. So I cut down to a three-piece band. Then I cut down to—yeah, three pieces. It was my wife, myself, and a bass player at South Hamilton. We worked until we broke up. Then I hired another girl named Estelle Edmonson, who was also prominent in the amalgamation movement. We worked until 1958, '59, and then in 1963 I started doing a single. I worked as a single for ten years in the Beverly Hills area. I played good jobs in the Beverly Hills area, in the Santa Monica area and the Palms Spring area. I also decided to go to UCLA out here and get a degree from the university. But in 1958 I started working with Lucille Ball. I started working for the Workshop Theater. Then, in 1962, she and Goodman Bass went back on the air with what they called *The Lucy Show*. I started out just as a pianist in the warm-up band. They would have a band that would play for the entertainment of the studio audience while they were filming the show. In '64 I started playing piano for the background music for the recording sessions. In '66 I started writing the music for the musicals where you would have people like Tennessee Ernie, Dean Martin—people of that kind on the show. About '68 Wilbur Hatch, my boss, just turned this aspect of the operation over to me all, the pre-scores; I not only did the rehearsing, the orchestration, but I also did the conducting. In '69 Wilbur died suddenly. I suddenly had to take over his duties and became the composer on the show. I had never done music like that, but I learned fast. I remained the composer on the show until it went off the air in 1974.

You were not affiliated with the band when it was in its real heyday. What was it, '53 to '56?

No. I started in '58. This is when they had just changed the format of *I Love Lucy* to what they called the *Desilu Playhouse*. I don't know if you remember that. At the same time they established a *Desilu Workshop*. They had people like Ken Berry, who was later on *Mayberry RFD*. He's on Saturday night now. Also they had people like Carol Cook preparing these people to perform. At about 1959 we did a review on the lot with these kids. That was the 1959 *Desilu Workshop* "Christmas Show." I did a lot of—I didn't do the orchestration—I did a lot of the arrangements for that show. Rehearsed the show and played the piano on the second. About this time she and Desi were breaking up, and in 1960 they actually broke up. They were getting a divorce. She decided that she was going to do a play on Broadway called *Wild Cat*. I rehearsed and prepared her for the audition for that and played the auditions for the male lead out here. But I did not know them during the time they were doing *I Love Lucy*. I came on right on the tail end of that. I certainly wish I had been there at the time.

Somebody told me you have a law degree.

Yes. I have a law degree from John Marshall, but I was always so involved with music, I never was able to study successfully for a bar. In fact, I really wasn't that much interested in it because I was always busy. I'm still eligible to take the bar out here. I don't know if I'll ever do it or not. You know, you get busy in one thing. But let me say this; the knowledge came in very handy out here because at the time we're talking about, in those days the music and unions were segregated. There were black unions and white unions all over the country. We started a movement out here to integrate the unions, and my knowledge of the legal things stood us in good standing. In fact, I wrote the merger agreements that brought the then all-black Local 767 and the then all-white Local 47 together in 1953. It was my merger agreements that both unions voted on that brought the two unions together. Later on, I became the first black member of the board of directors of 1957. During all the years that I was there I was chairperson of the legislative committee, which is responsible for writing the bylaws, and most of the bylaws that we're operating now under the merged Local 47 were written while I was the chairperson of the legislative committee. I was on the board for four years. I ran for secretary and lost. I got busy—these were during the years then when I was really working for Lucy and at the same time I was doing nightclubs. In 1972 I ran for the board of directors again—and won (also during which I was chair of the legislation committee, though). I went back in '73 for two years, then I ran for secretary. We still had not had a full-time elected black executive officer. I ran in '74 and became the executive secretary, full-time elected officer. I was there for eight years. In 1982 I ran for president; I lost by 220 votes. But I lost. When I came out of there, I just decided to take some time off and rest.

Are you at all active now? What are you doing these days?

These days I'm doing as little as possible. All those years that I was abusing myself and the type of regimen that I carried on in Chicago, I continued out here—staying up for days with no sleep. When I came out in 1983, in January, I just decided to rest. It's only now that I feel like I might start trying doing some things. But I just decided to take my weary body and rest it for a while.

Scotty **Piper**
(The Mayor of Forty-Seventh Street)

In 1941 blues pianist Roosevelt Sykes wrote "47th Street Jive," an ode to that Chicago street which was the center of black nightlife from the late 1930s to the early 1950s. It was the main street for music, stage shows, and dancing. Forty-Seventh Street was the home of the Regal and Metropolitan Theaters, and the Savoy Ballroom, and dozens of other night spots that hosted music. On one particular program, after playing "47th Street Jive," I received a call from a listener asking if I was familiar with Scotty Piper. I had never heard of Scotty. Scotty was known as the Mayor of Forty-Seventh Street. He worked as a tailor to many of the black celebrities in Chicago show business, which gave him a celebrity status all his own, and he was a regular on the club scene. The caller put me in touch with Scotty, and we did the following interview.

This interview was recorded July 1984. Scotty Piper died May 22, 1987.

Scotty Piper. Photo courtesy Scotty Piper Collection, Chicago History Museum.

■ ■ ■

My real name is Louis V. Piper. V is for Vernon. I was born in New Orleans, Louisiana, May 18, 1904. I came from New Orleans to Chicago in 1916. My mother and father were separated, and when my mother died, my father sent for me to come to Chicago. I went to Douglas School just a short time because my mother taught me to fight to take care of myself, and when I came here to go to school, the kids was making fun of my lingo. I would whip their butts, and the teacher would send a note that I was fighting, and my father wanted to whip me because I was protecting myself. I said, "Well, they're making fun of my words and fun of my lingo." I would say "chunk" for throw, "snapbeans" for stringbeans, "Irish potatoes" for white potatoes, "banquette" for sidewalk, "gallery" for porch. And in addition to the words they laughed at my brogue because people down there have that French brogue. They're mixed-up down there—that's why they call those pretty girls Creoles, because they're half mixed—Spanish and negro, Italian and negro, Indian and negro. And they're all mixed-up. So I stayed with him a short time, and then I ran away from him during the Chicago race riot of 1919. I was an instigator during the race riot. I was there when it started. We used to ditch school and go to Thirty-First Street and swim, Thirty-First and the lake. And the white boys used to swim around Twenty-Ninth Street. They had a foundry down there where the water would come out and was warm. So we went down there one day and one of our friends was floating on a log. Some of the white boys threw a rock and knocked him off the log, and he drowned before any of us could get to him to save him. In the meantime, a white truck driver hit a little colored girl at Thirty-First and Cottage Grove, and the policemen didn't want to arrest him. So the race riot started from those two things in just a few days. I was shining shoes out at Fifty-Fifth Street, which was an all-white community, and I had to come down the alleys to slip back to my neighborhood. By traveling through the alleys with my cap on, they couldn't tell whether I was black or white. That's the way I got back to 3216 Indiana Avenue, by going through the alleys. Back in that time blacks didn't get any farther south than Thirty-Ninth Street—from Twenty-Ninth to Thirty-Ninth and from Wentworth over to Cottage Grove—they call that the "Black Belt." And then all the young colored boys who had jobs in the Loop lost their jobs. They brought bums over from Madison Street to wash and bus dishes, and they fired the colored boys. The only place that kept colored help was the Palmer House because the old man had it in his will to always keep colored help. But the blacks lost most of the good jobs in the Loop and on the North Side. I was just fourteen years old when the riots started. I left town, and they thought I got killed in the race riots—but I ran away and I joined up with the circus, Ringling and Barnum and Bailey Circus. I traveled all over with the circus. Watering elephants, that was my job with the circus. When I was eighteen years old, I had been in every state in the union, running on the road, traveling with the circus. When I got to Minneapolis, I decided to quit the circus. I stayed there in Minneapolis, and I started dancing around in nightclubs, doing the Charleston and bring the white girls over into the black neighborhood. I'd sit around the hotel and with my cap on, they couldn't tell whether I was black or white. Then the girls would pay me money and the guys would pay me money to bring the girls over to them. There was an old man that taken a liking to me. He said, "Son, you're making a lotta money now. There's a place they call Idlewild in Michigan. Lots are very cheap up there. If you go ahead and buy you some lots, when you get to be a man you'll have you some money." I didn't pay any attention to him because I was running wild. I was wearing good clothes—I was always dressed well. So I didn't pay any attention to him. And that came to be the head summer resort for the black people, Idlewild, Michigan. And when Roosevelt put the CCC camps into existence, me and an Italian boy were hoboing on the road together. We'd gotten to Rockford, Illinois, and they had the camps out there. At that time they had the little tents out on the street for the recruiters. So we decided to sign up, and they took us out to Camp Grant in a jeep; when we got out there, they asked our nationalities. The Italian boy was darker than me. He said, "I'm Italian." I wasn't paying any attention, and I said, "I'm a negro." He said, "We're not enlisting negroes." So my friend didn't sign up either. It was eleven miles from Rockford to Camp Grant. We had to walk all the way back to Rockford—they wouldn't even bring us back. That's when I came back to Chicago. I started out in the wholesale district. It was around Franklin and Van Buren, and Market Street and Van Buren. And then, after the Merchandise Mart was put up, practically all the wholesale people moved over to the Merchandise Mart. There's a few over there now, but not much. Well, I started over there at Van Buren and Market. I started out making dresses, and I finally got into the clothing business. A company that had stores in every principal city, they called the Wohlmuth Tailors, they came here and opened up a store at Forty-Seventh Street and King Drive. I got to be manager at that store. I did a lot of business for them. Then Joseph H. Cohen Vanity [Clothing] at Seventy-Fifth Street and New York came here and opened up a store right next to them and called it Scotty—that's how I got the nickname Scotty. I started doing good business for them. The tailoring business was real good back in those days. The show boys had beautiful costumes when they came out on the stage—they dressed real well. They'd do two or three shows then go back and change costumes and come back out. When show boys wanted something loud and styled up, they had to get it made to order. So after I started working for Joseph H. Cohen I gave them an idea to use a lot of scrap goods and they made two-tone coats and two-tone jackets. Then they got into the high-style business making clothes in the high styles and high colors. Well, by being a dancer and dancing all around and getting these show boys to know me, they'd come and get their clothes made.

That's why they call me Scotty Piper, The Dancing Tailor. Some call me the Mayor of Forty-Seventh Street. In 1910, when Jack Johnson fought Jim Jeffries and [took] the heavyweight boxing title away from him, he was the black heavyweight champ. And at that time when they had something special happen, the newspapers had "extras," and we boys would go out and sell the papers and holler "Extra—extra!" I was selling these papers and yelling "Extra—extra, the new black heavyweight champ of the world." And a bunch of white boys grabbed me and took my papers away from me and whipped me. So I didn't have an idea that I would ever see Jack Johnson. But one day I saw Jack Johnson, and when Joe Louis came from Detroit and he fought over at Bacon Casino, Jack Johnson was sitting down front, and he said, "That's gonna be a great champ one day." Well, a week after that I saw him in Walgreen's drug store, and I told him what had happened to me when he took the championship. I told him I was measuring Duke Slater up for an overcoat—Duke Slater was an all-star America football player and later became a prominent judge. So Jack said, "Where are you located son?" I said, "Right across the street at 414 East Forty-Seventh Street." He said, "Well, I'm gonna come there and let you make me a suit." That was the biggest thrill I ever had in making someone a suit. The last time I saw Jack Johnson was in the '30s in Walgreen's drug store—that's the old drug store that was on the South Side. I made clothes for the Club DeLisa—all the acts that came in there—and Red Sanders for over twenty-five years. I made clothes for the Step Brothers, the Ink Spots, the Mills Brothers,

Scotty Piper outside his Forty-Seventh Street shop. Photo courtesy Scotty Piper Collection, Chicago History Museum.

Horace Henderson, Fletcher Henderson, and "Fatha" Earl Hines, who just died here not so long ago. He was the first black band that had a national hookup on NBC, and I made him uniforms to open up that night. He was playing at the Grand Terrace at Oakwood Boulevard and King Drive. I got all the suits made up, and the boys in the band came into the store to pick up their suits. But I said, "You can't pick up the suits—I ain't got the money yet." So Earl Hines came in and said, "Why didn't you give the guys the suits?" I said, "I can't give them the suits unless I get the money." He said, "Well, I'm Earl Hines . . ." I said, "I'm Scotty Piper—I'm responsible for these suits. I got to either have the money or the suits—that's what my boss wants. If I don't get the money and you got the suits—I'm in bad." [*Laughs.*] I made up stuff for Louis Armstrong—he and I were raised up together in New Orleans, so he gave me business when he came into town. We used to run around the streets barefooted. We didn't put on no shoes until Sunday. He wasn't a bad boy, but he was what you call a mischievous boy—always getting in a little trouble, and they put him in a boys' home, what they called Jones Home in New Orleans [also known as the Colored Waifs Home]. And that's where he learned to play the trumpet. Then, when the longshoreman or Odd Fellows would die, they would let that band out to play the deadmarch to the cemetery. And then they would jazz all the way back to Jones Home and kids would get behind the band and dance. They had dances out there they called "Ballin' the Jack" and "Shakin' the Shimmy." They used to follow the band back doing those dances. I made stuff for one of the Queens of the Blues singers—Mamie Smith. She had me make her daughter an outfit—just an evening gown. And Ma Rainey, I did work for her. And Ethel Waters and I were friends. When she was a dancer she was real thin and I had a beautiful picture of her, but a lot of my pictures got stolen. I just hated that because they were talking about how fat she was, but they didn't know how streamline she was when she was a dancer. No, I didn't make any clothes for her; I wasn't in the clothing business then. She was a hot number in her days. I made clothes for Frankie "Half-Pint" Jaxon. I made him just a regular suit. "Half-Pint" Jaxon—he worked over at the Metropolitan Theater when the Metropolitan had stage shows there at Forty-Seventh Street and King Drive. He worked at the Metropolitan and he worked over at the Club DeLisa, too. Another little kid that used to work there was Rhythm Willie—used to play harmonica; he could play that thing so good, he didn't need no band. I made a graduation suit for Joe Williams—and I made a graduation suit for our mayor, Harold Washington—also, Sammy Cooke, I made his graduation suit; Lou Rawls and Nat King Cole—I made his graduation suit. He had a black pair of pants made and a white coat, and all of his friends said, "Man, why'd you ever get a graduation suit like that? You look like a fly in a bowl of buttermilk!" [*Laughs.*] I made up clothes for Duke Ellington. I made up stuff for Cab [Calloway]—also, Mack and Mack, Buck and Bubbles, I made clothes for them. So there were very few people that I missed. I should have a lot of money today, but I suppose I'm blessed—I have my own home and plenty of food, plenty of clothes, and I have plenty of friends in the church where I belong; and I have peace of mind, so I suppose I'm rich! I'm soon going on eighty-one years old, and I can still dance—a lot of theatrical folks who came up around my time can't. They even stopped Sammy Davis from dancing. They told him to stop dancing. And I've got a few other friends younger than me that had to stop dancing—and I'm still gettin' down! I do the boogaloo, the boogie-woogie, do a little bit of Charleston, and I can get down. I'm doing the twist like all these other ones do [*demonstrates a few brief dance steps*]. Back in the 1920s when the Charleston came out, they used to hold contests in the different theaters and ballrooms, and I danced all around the different places. Chilton and Thomas—Claire Chilton and Maceo Thomas—they were the greatest Charleston team there was. They danced over for the Queen of England. I was on a contest with them one night down at the Chicago Theater—and I got out there and my legs wouldn't move and I said, "Holy Christmas...." My legs wouldn't move, and I don't know what happened. [*Laughs.*] That Chilton and Thomas, boy, you talk about a team that could dance.... They finally separated, and he got to be a drunk, but that girl and boy could dance. Claire Chilton went to school with my wife. They went to McKay School out on Sixty-Sixth Street and St. Lawrence. But they were the dancingest Charleston couple I ever saw.

It was a very outstanding street in the 1920s and 1930s and into the 1940s. That was the most outstanding street because they had the two theaters there.

Scotty Piper PR collage. Photo courtesy Scotty Piper Collection, Chicago History Museum.

154 BRONZEVILLE

They had the Regal Theater, and they had the Metropolitan. They had live shows at both places. When the Regal opened up in 1928, they brought Fess Williams in from New York to MC the shows. All the outstanding acts would always hit the Regal Theater. Duke Ellington played there, Claude Hopkins, Jimmie Lunceford, Fatha Earl Hines played there, Erskine Tate and his Sweet Taters [also known as his Vendome Syncopaters] played there, Louis Armstrong played there, the Whitman Sisters played there, Leonard Reed, Ralph Cooper, Willie Bryant and the Step Brothers, the Lightning Flashes—they were a dance team—Butterbeans and Susie, Mack and Mack played there, Billie Mitchell, Chippie Hill, the Chocolateers. But then it began to go down. When that closed, that stopped the traffic on Forty-Seventh Street; the Savoy Ballroom closed up, and that stopped a lot of traffic. A lot of the buildings were vacant—those that were boarded up. People began to move out of the neighborhood. It just melted away little by little.

It really started from State Street and went over to the 700 block of Forty-Seventh Street. They had the Savoy Ballroom. That was the place all the social clubs used to rent for their affairs. Then Eddie Quick was in his prime, and they used to hold the fights—boxing matches there. That was on Tuesday nights. Joe Williams started out at the Savoy Ballroom singing the Star-Spangled Banner on Tuesday nights. And then on Halloween they held a Halloween Dance with all the female impersonators. White folks would come from all over the North Side to try and get a parking space to see the masquerades. At Forty-Seventh Street and Prairie they had an outstanding tavern there, and then as it went down, then at the 400 block, there upstairs they had a place called Stairway to the Stars. Joe Williams sang up there—Lil Green, too. Then there was the 708 Club in the 700 block, which later became a pawn shop, and I worked there when it was a pawn shop. Just a few months ago they bought the pawnshop out and put a furniture store in there, but that used to be an outstanding nightclub there at 708. Muddy Waters played there, and Johnny Long, Eddie King gigged there sometimes. And I think you should know something about Gerri's Palm Tavern. That's at 444 East Forty-Seventh Street—still going strong. All the celebrities still stop in there when they come to town. That was Jim Knight's place—he was a policy king; he opened up the first exclusive tavern on the street, and he was the first black mayor of Bronzeville. The *Chicago Defender* used to hold an election each year to elect a particular individual to be mayor of Bronzeville—which sold a lot of papers. The ballots were in the paper you would buy, the *Defender*, fill out your ballot and send it in to the paper. Some folks actually spent a lot of money to run for mayor of Bronzeville and some didn't—just like me when I ran. I didn't spend any money. One year there were

SCOTTY PIPER

three or four running against me and I came in third, but I didn't spend any money. I never did get elected, but I was just as popular—even more popular than some who made it. Then they had another outstanding tavern at Forty-Seventh Street and Calumet, they called it the Brass Rail. That was Old Man Smith's place, and then Nelson Sykes took it over. All the outstanding celebrities used to go in there. But they just had a piano player; it wasn't a nightclub, it was just a tavern. But that's gone now. And I think that Nelson Sykes [who] had that place is in the cleaning business in the Loop, cleaning stores. The 211 Club, they had there on Forty-Seventh Street. I don't remember who played there then. There were a lot of other nightclubs surrounding Forty-Seventh Street. They had a club down there at the Forty-Seventh block they called the Club Congo, down in the basement. That's where Al Benson's daughter died down there in Club Congo.

I should have a lot of money now, but I don't have anything but a wife I've been married to for fifty-six years—and we're still sweethearts. We go to bed in peace and we wake up in peace. A lot of mornings she gets up and says, "What do you want for breakfast, Daddy?" I say, "Get up, Girl—your breakfast is on the table." She's been a good wife and a good mother, so I do all I can for her because she deserves everything I can do. So I say if I ever get a family, I'm gonna make my children happy at home. And that's what I did. You can give a kid everything in the world—automobile, bicycle, motorcycles—if you don't give that kid love and companionship, you haven't given them anything. You got to be a friend to your child as well as a parent. And you have to make their friends welcome in your home and treat them nice when they come to your home because they'll always want to be home and you'll always know where your kids are. And when they wanted a party, they always wanted to know if I was going to be there. I'd say, "Why—do you want me there?" and they'd say, "The kids like you—you're a lot of fun." So I'd turn the lights down dim for them. I'd tell them, "If you smoke at your house, you can smoke here—but if you don't smoke at your house, don't smoke at mine" . . . and I would call and find out. When they were invited out to a party, I'd call up to see if there was a party there. If there was a party there, I'd say, "Daddy will be at home waiting for you to call. If you haven't got anyone to bring you home, I'll be here waiting for you and I'll come and get you." When my kids were going to school, when they went out to parties—if they stayed out, when they came home I had a midnight snack for them. If they had their friends with them, I had a midnight snack for them, too, and made them all welcome. And I know when my daughter's period was as well as my wife did. That's how close I was to my girls—I had all girls—and I always gave them love and companionship.

I always was close to them, and I'm still close to them. I just had a grandchild born last week. I had all grandsons and I just had my first great-great-granddaughter born last week. So my children were always happy with me—and they're happy with me now!

I worked with all the different organizations—community and NAACP, the Urban League, Joint Negro Appeal, Committee 100, American Friendship Club. I helped out Providence Hospital, and Elliott Donnelley's Boys Club and different churches. I'd donate my services modeling for them and helping them with their teas. I received a lot of plaques and citations. But I think that I earned it because I worked helping out kids and talking in different schools, trying to tell them right from wrong and putting them on the right track. I talked to the students at the school over at Forty-Ninth Street and Indiana. I told them, "The most important thing when you're in school is to listen to your teacher. Respect your teacher and comprehend, and she'll give you all that she has. But the most important thing is your education. There's no more common labor today. Everything is computer or robotics—so you have to get that education. You can finish grade school, high school, and college—that's the right road. But you can be on the right road going the wrong way. The wrong way is getting with gangs, stealing, drinking, and getting on dope. You only have one body to last you a lifetime, and if you don't take care of that body, that body's not going to take care of you. And when you go out looking for a job, you've got to go neat and clean; otherwise, they won't hire you. And they judge your intelligence according to your clothes. There are a lot of people in show business that are really good, but when they apply for a job, they don't look so neat, and [people] don't hire them. But then another group applies—they're not as good as the first group, but because they dress right, not only do they get hired—they get their asking price." So I tell all young people keep themselves neat and clean. And when you start on a job, you have to learn to take orders, because if you don't learn how to take orders, you may never be able to give them. And you have to learn how to respect the other fellow, because someday you may be the other fellow. You got to start at the bottom and work your way up. I always try to give young people good advice—because I didn't have no one to give it to me. . . .

As far as I'm concerned, I think Jesse Jackson is a great black man. A change has got to come. If he doesn't win, he's done great things for the black race. He's given black people courage and strength, and he's caused a lot of young black people to vote—people who've never voted before. Many of them thought if they registered, they had voted, but Jesse Jackson and our mayor Harold Washington have enlightened the young negroes that voting and owning land is power. But you have to use it in the right way. By getting their education, Jackson and

Washington have shown them the right way—just like Dr. King. And then the young will get away from that violence—you can't win anything with violence. Everyone is created equal—and everyone who's trying to do something good is criticized. They even criticized Christ when he was performing miracles. If he were here today and nailed to the cross, they'd be stealing him off the cross. At the time I came here, the only good job the negroes had back in those days was the stockyard, Campbell Soup, Argo Starch, the post office and the railroad. Those were the only good jobs the negroes had—before the race riot. If a guy worked in the post office, that was a good job. Also, many of the large hotels had black help in those days, and many of the rich white folks would have black chauffeurs driving his Cadillac or his Rolls Royce. And back in those days they weren't too many white men that had Cadillacs—very few. People had a hard time during the Depression. Right now, there are so many ways they can get help that weren't available during the days of the Depression. They've got Social Security and Medicare—they didn't have either of those back in the Depression. People would sit out on the streets in those days. They sat out so often in those days, they had to get curtains to match the sidewalk [*laughs*]. Things have changed for the better. We've got more opportunity than we ever had but we worked hard for it. We were held back for so many years. It seems as though the northern white man was more prejudice than the southern white man. Up here they're fighting—a white man lives over here and a black man lives over there. There was nothing like that when I lived in New Orleans. A black family lives here, an Italian family next door to them, then another black family and an Irish family right next door to each other—we didn't have any trouble like that. That's why I don't understand the situation today. Things are better for us, but I think we're entitled to it. In our race we have outstanding baseball players, football players, outstanding basketball players, outstanding boxers. We're on television and on commercials. And this has been a miracle for black people. We've got a black mayor and a black superintendent of police—and we really upset it when we got a black Miss America—and the runner-up, too! When I first came here, a black policeman was lucky if he got to be sergeant. Now we've four or five station commanders and detectives on the force—things we never had before. But we had to struggle to get those things, nobody threw it in our laps. . . .

Like I said, many years ago I made Mayor Harold Washington a graduation suit, and just recently we were at a party out at Reverend Cotton's beautiful church, way out south, and the mayor came in while I was sitting there. The mayor said, "And there's Scotty Piper—the Mayor of Forty-Seventh Street!"

Part Four **Short-Order Chicago**

Little Brother **Montgomery**

By the time I got on the blues scene in Chicago, blues piano had taken an awful beating. Otis Spann, the preeminent blues pianist on the Chicago scene, had died a few years earlier at age forty. The jukebox had rapidly replaced the piano as the preferred source of musical entertainment. There were virtually no pianos left in black neighborhood bars and taverns. And the changing style of music in the second half of the 1950s only added to the problem. Bands playing Little Walter–style harmonica rarely included a piano, which tended to handcuff their free-wheeling style, and then came the string-bending style of blues guitar, popular in the late 1950s, which omitted piano as often as not. All these combined to present a real dilemma for many of the Chicago blues pianists—jobs were so few that many people were actually starving. In fact, in the late 1950s and throughout the 1960s several of the better-known Chicago blues pianists ultimately moved to Europe. For almost a decade these blues pianists made regular tours to the United Kingdom and Europe. Overseas, these musicians

Little Brother Montgomery and Edith Wilson. Photo courtesy The O'Neal Collection.

found steady employment, were free from segregation, and were regarded as celebrities. It was easier to bring over a single pianist than to bring an entire band, and a clause in British Musicians Union rules allowed for "Intermission Performers," which provided ready work for the solo blues pianists. So when jobs dried up in Chicago, Memphis Slim and Willie Mabon moved to Paris, Eddie Boyd to Finland, and Curtis Jones to Germany. All made Europe their permanent home, finished their careers and their lives there. But there were still a handful of Chicago Blues pianists who chose to stay in town. Sunnyland Slim, a wild and wooly pianist who sang with leather lungs, was as talented in hustling gigs as he was playing piano. He would find gigs in the black neighborhoods when nobody else could. He would take his portable electric keyboard and hire a band. He worked steadily on the North and South Sides to the very end of his life. A pair of other pianists, Blind John Davis and Little Brother Montgomery, made a living playing solo piano for the new white audience listening to the blues. They would play mostly in North Side blues and folk clubs. I saw all three of these guys on a regular basis. I would see Sunnyland Slim in my work as a drummer on the blues scene and worked with him on several occasions. Sunnyland was sort of the social nucleus for a handful of postwar blues veterans, including Floyd Jones, Snooky Pryor, John Brim, and several others. It was always great to be around Sunny and all of his blues friends. Blind John Davis would listen to my radio show and was a regular caller on the program, always checking in with stories of the musicians he knew and worked with. Little Brother, on the other hand, never appeared on the blues scene. Most of his work was formal blues piano recitals performed for white audiences, usually at folk clubs and rarely a blues club. I'd seen Brother several times in concert, bought and played as many of his records as I could get my hands on. As time went by, I realized that Little Brother was regarded as the best blues piano technician in Chicago and was among the elite players in the wide field of prewar blues pianists. Sunnyland and Brother had a mutual admiration society. Brother, who rarely handed out compliments to anyone, once told me that Sunnyland was "such a great piano player that Sunny himself didn't know how good he was." And Sunnyland proclaimed Brother to be "the ass-wiper"—the highest compliment any musician could aspire to hear from Sunnyland. Another pianist, Erwin Helfer, as a teenager went to the South Side to learn piano from one of the legendary house-rent pianists, Crippled Clarence Lofton. Erwin, who was white and a generation younger, was a friend and protégé to the three veteran players and often managed to find them work on the North Side. In reading the liner notes on Little Brother's albums, it became clear to me that he had a colorful and extensive personal history. I was interested in doing an interview with Brother for my radio program and asked Erwin if he could arrange it. Erwin pitched the idea to him, and Brother agreed to be interviewed. We made arrangements to meet in the radio studio of WBEZ, Chicago's public radio station, then located at the southwest corner of LaSalle and Wacker. I was to meet Brother outside the building and take him up to the studios. It was quite a scenic location, right next to the Chicago River and spanned by the heavy ironwork of a 1930s art deco drawbridge. As I stood on the corner, I spied Brother crossing the bridge. He was short, maybe 5'4", and stood out immediately as probably the only guy in the state of Illinois wearing a derby. We made our way upstairs and got situated in the studio. Brother spoke in an unusually high, raspy voice but expressed himself in the same manner in which he played piano—concise and exacting.

This interview was recorded October 16, 1981. Eurreal Montgomery died September 6, 1985.

■ ■ ■

I was born in Louisiana. I was born Tangipahoa Parish. Louisiana is the only parish state of the United States—the rest is all counties. There ain't no difference between a parish and a county. I was born in Tangipahoa Parish, Kentwood, Louisiana. That's eighty-three miles north of New Orleans, Louisiana. My father's name was Harper Montgomery, and my mother's name was Dicey Montgomery. My real name is Eurreal Wilfred Montgomery. They used to call us after our father's first name—they used to call me Little Brother Harper when I was in kindergarten and public school—they called my older brother Son Harper—that was his nickname. My father was a log pond farmer at the sawmill. He played coronet, and my mother played concertina—squeeze boxes, I call them. His uncle had a band in New Orleans—his name was Gunzy Montgomery. He had Gunzy Montgomery and His Big Four Band. He had a band back there in New Orleans with Piron and all them—those kind of people—Buddy Bolden, Bunk Johnson, and all of them. Willie was my older brother and then Leon Montgomery. Olivia was my older sister—Paul Gayten, you might have heard of him—that's my nephew. That's my sister's son, Paul Gayten. He's a terrific piano player himself. My father had two pianos. He had a barrelhouse, they call it—a juke over in Reed's Quarters—that's the quarters where people live—and he had a piano over there—a Junior Heart piano—he had over in that place. And then he had a baby grand in the house, the Decker Brothers—that was the name of that. Well, I was playing ever since I was four years old. Guys used to set me up on their knee and pull me up to the piano and pay me to play, you know, a quarter, fifty cents. Now, if they didn't pay me to play—I wouldn't play. They'd ask my mother could I play: "Can Brother play a piece for me?" they'd say. She'd say, "It's all right with me." But I wouldn't play unless they paid me. Now, if they'd give me fifty cents or a quarter, a dollar, whatever—they used to give me those silver dollars they called bow dollars back then. If they gave me a bow dollar back then, I'd play whatever they asked me. I could play anything—the music they had at that time. So they'd pull me up to the piano on their knee and I'd play a bit, you know? When I got to be about seven or eight years old, I could play, I'd compose. When I was eleven years old, I ran away from home—and I've been on my own ever since. I was playing then—I'd play barrelhouses, sawmills jobs, honky-tonks, house-rent parties—I played everything. I hoboed, rode freight trains, and everything. One guy tried to make me jump off a freight train on the VS&P—between Vicksburg, Mississippi, and Monroe, Louisiana. I was going from Vicksburg to Tallulah, Louisiana. I had come over to Delta Point just riding hobo—me and another little piano player, Eddie Majors. This guy tried to make us jump off—he was a brakeman. Well, we weren't supposed to be on there—but he wasn't supposed to make us jump off, either, with the thing running that fast. It was making about seventy or eighty miles an hour—we was dead before we hit the ground—telegram posts were flying and the ground was running from the train. So by the help of the Lord and everybody else he fooled around and let me stay on there until the train stopped. It stopped in Bond, Louisiana, to go into the hole for another train to pass. So when it stopped we got off and walked those eight or nine miles on into Tallulah. I ain't hoboed since that time.

    I used to see a lot of guys when I was a kid—Jellyroll was a guy I used to see when I was a kid—Jellyroll Morton. Papa Lord-God—he was a piano player. Another one named Ford—I never knew his first name—his last name was Ford. He was a great piano player. Had another one named Riptop—Loomis Gibson. He couldn't play but about three or four pieces, but he could play them—they were good. I made "Crescent City Blues" out of one of his numbers, Loomis Gibson. I learned that from him when I was about ten years old. And Son Young—George Young—he was out of Arkansas. He influenced me—he and Joe Martin out of McGhee, Arkansas, Bob Martin from Kentwood—my home. He was a great piano player. Cooney Vaughn—he was another one. "The Tremblin' Blues"—I made that—that was one of his numbers, his blue numbers. He was from Hattiesburg, and he was a terrific piano player when I was a kid. He was about twenty-five or thirty years old when I knew him—I was about seven or eight years old. I had a lot of guys that influenced me. I came along with great guys that played piano, like Red Cayou—he was from New Orleans. All of us—Fats Pijon, Walter Pijon. His name was Walter but they called him Fats Pijon. They had another guy there that played piano—a great piano player, he was from Kansas City and played down there then. His name was Eudell Wilson. And Friday—Long Tall Friday. I never did know his first name—that's where the "Forty-Four Blues" came from—me and him and Ernest (Robert) Johnson. He was from Cannon, Mississippi. They used to call him Big Brother and me Little Brother. They called him Delco Robert.

The first time I came North, I came with a band. It wasn't my band—it was the Joyland Revelers, out of New Orleans—Clarence Desdune and the Joyland Revelers. At the time I was in that band, there were fourteen pieces. We had some great musicians in that band—great trumpet player Alvin Alcorn's half-brother was playing trumpet in that band—his name was George McCullen. That's Alvin's and Oliver's half-brother—the older one, but he was their half-brother. So Oliver was in the band, and when George left and went back to New Orleans, we sent and got Alvin—when he was about fifteen years old. And we had Harold DeJohn—he had a marching band in New Orleans. And we had Raymond Johnson on trombone. We had a good band. Clarence Desdune was a violinist. His father was a band master in Omaha, Nebraska. He would go to the radio station [and] they would give him an armful of music, like stock arrangements—Frank Skinner was arranging back then—Archie Blair, and all those kind of guys. We'd rehearse a number—like "White Heat," "Business in F," "Business in Q," and all those kind of things. We had that number—Dave Payton wrote it, him and King Oliver wrote it—that "Mule Face." It was a big-band number, you know, so I learned to play it with the band. I played the arrangement like it goes, and then I made it a piano solo. "Mule Face"—I made a rag out of it, just piano. When I got ready to leave the band, Clarence Desdune got mad with me because I was going to leave the band. "You mean to tell me you're going to Chicago? What am I going to do for a piano player? You rehearsed all this music we got and we can't get nobody else to read." "You ain't got nobody who can read now," I said. I wouldn't know a note if it was as big as my hat. He said, "Aw—you don't mean to tell me you can't read? You've been playing with me this long?" I'd been playing with him about a year or better. I said, "Man, I can't read nothing." I could just hear like the Devil. [*Laughs.*] And then he asked George McCullom, "You mean he don't read nothing?" Harry Fagner was playing banjo, and he said, "No—he don't read nothing." "I'd have bet my life he was one of the greatest readers!" But I didn't read nothing. So I was playing up until the time I was twenty-three or twenty-four years old before

I ever took a music lesson. I just play from within me—they call it "by ear," but there ain't no such a thing as "ear." It's musical incline. If you can't hear nothing—if you can read it, you ain't gonna play it all that great, either. [*Laughs.*] And then I could beat half of the guys in the band who were reading. But if they played that number down one time, the next time around I could play the whole thing! I left that band in Omaha, Nebraska, and came to Chicago.

I stayed in Chicago. I played at a place called King Tuts at Forty-Seventh and Michigan. I played house-rent parties. I played at 5009 Vincennes Avenue on the South Side for Miss Lumpkin on Sunday nights for $1 and spaghetti supper. Then I played for Harry McNeal at Forty-Seventh and Champaign—I got $3. I played for Buddy McGhee at 4048 South Indiana on a Saturday night, I'd get $3—I'd do all right. I'd make $10 or $15 a week. This was around 1928–1929 and 1930. They had some good guys around then. Fats Waller lived on Sixty-Second and Michigan at the time—he was playing organ at the Regal [Theater]. They had a good piano player here named Tiny Parham. Erskine Tate—Ted Weatherford—he was a great piano player. He was playing up there at Thirty-First and State. Clarence Jones—he was a piano player, and he had the band at the Grand Theater over in front of the Vendome. And Jellyroll was here—he was playing at the Owl Theater on Forty-Seventh and State. Pinetop Smith, the guy who made "Pinetop's Boogie Woogie"—we were playing all that kind of thing before he ever named it boogie-woogie—you know. We used to call that Dudlow Joe back around 1920—during World War I, before anybody ever recorded it—before he ever recorded it—but we were all playing it. Jimmie Noone's band and King Oliver, Charlie Spand—there was a lot of us around then. Will Ezell—Blind Blake—me and him run together every Monday! He was a great guitar player. He could play rags, blues, anything on that guitar—he could play anything. So him, me, and Charlie Spand got together every Monday. Black Bob—his name was Bob Call—that's his real name, but they call him Black Bob. Jimmy Blythe. Cow Cow Davenport—he was livin' at the old ——— Building. His wife was Lillian Davenport, and he had a girl working with him; her name was Ivy Smith. And we had Arnold Wiley—he was a great piano player, and his sister [Irene] was a vocalist. And Reuben Walker. And Sippi Wallace's parents—they had thirteen girls and boys. Their home was in Houston, Texas. The older brother was named George W. Thomas—he wrote that "Up the Country Blues" and "Shorty George Blues" and all them kinda things. His daughter's name was Hocial Thomas—you might have seen her name on records. Hersal Thomas was the baby. He and I ran together because we were around the same age. He was a great piano player—he was a terrific piano player. Hersal wrote "Suitcase Blues."

There's a lot of songs that get stolen—they didn't write the number, but they're gonna record it before the person who wrote it does. The "Forty-Four Blues"—that's the "Vicksburg Blues": me and Friday and Delco Robert—there were three of us—we made that number up when I was around eleven or twelve years old. We were playing it in all the barrelhouses down there—and we had another guy that could beat us playing it—his name was Ernest Johnson. We called him Flunky [*laughs*]. We called him Flunky because he flunked flunking on the Y&V railroad—trying to get to be a brakeman. They called him 44 Kid. See, Ernest learned it—everybody was trying to play it. There's so much to that particular number—if you don't *teach* it *to* somebody—they ain't never gonna learn how to play it. The bass that I put in that thing—other people can't make that bass because I learned how to play it when my hands were small—I shut my hands and opened them to make that bass. But your hands get too large to make that bass like that—so most guys that try to make that bass make it overhand—and it's hard for them to do. But since I was playing it ever since I was a kid I could still do it as my hands got larger. But if I had to learn it all over again—then I couldn't learn it. I tried to show it to Lee Green—we called Lee Green "Porkchop"—that was his nickname. He was pressing clothes with one of those big old irons. If Lee Green was living today, he couldn't play it—and what little bit he learned, he taught it to Roosevelt [Sykes]. Roosevelt can't play it either—he just mess it up. And they beat us up to St. Louis and recorded it. I believe they recorded it for the OKeh Label. Roosevelt and all those people—they know I composed it.

The first numbers I ever recorded, Fats Waller wrote them. J. Mayo Williams was the talent scout for the people up there then. So we recorded for him up at 666 North Lake Shore Drive—me and Tampa Red and Georgia Tom. Irene Scruggs—I recorded with her.

They called her Chocolate Brown. And Minnie Hicks—her husband, I didn't know his first name, but he played guitar. I recorded on my own in 1929—that thing you heard called the "Vicksburg Blues"—and "No Special Rider"—they didn't release that until 1930.

That was the Paramount Label out of Grafton, Wisconsin. Well, Aletha Dickerson, she was the talent scout for Paramount then. Art Laibley and Williams had been with that company, but he'd left there. Her husband was a good piano player—his name was Robert Alexander—we called him Bob—Bob Alexander. On recordings they called me Little Brother. I'm E. Montgomery on some records. I made "Louisiana Blues," "Frisco Hi-Ball"—all them kind of things. I made them for the Brunswick and Vocalion labels, and they had a third label—Melotone. I recorded for RCA Victor in 1932 and 1933—but I

LITTLE BROTHER MONTGOMERY

never did come north to record for them. I was living around Jackson, Mississippi, then—that's when I had that band the Southland Troubadours. RCA would come down there and bring me down to New Orleans at the St. Charles Hotel—and that's where I would record for them. The man of the day was Eli Oberstein, and I made all those records you hear in one session. I made about twenty different numbers in one session. He would ask me what I wanted to do and then just turn the machine on. He would just let me record—and when I got through with one record he'd say, "Just go to the next one." And I just kept going—twenty numbers in one session! People like me and Walter Vinson, Monkey Joe, Tommy Griffin, Annie Turner—I accompanied her. The things I did with them were around 1934 and '35 for RCA Victor #2—the Bluebird label.

The Depression came on, and I went on back south in '31. Anybody would have left here if they coulda got away at that time, you know, because Depression came on and neckbones was five pounds for twenty cents—that was four cents a pound and your room rent was $3 a week—and you couldn't hardly scuffle up that $3 to pay for your room. Yeah—times was rough. I went down to New Orleans and stayed a little while and then went back to Jackson, Mississippi—and that's where I formed the band myself—the Southland Troubadours. I had a good band. I had one of the greatest trumpet players there ever was—his name was Doc Palmer. He'd been playing on the shows—on the Georgia Smart Set. And his brother was a bass player—his name was Edmund Palmer. I had Louis Jordan—he came from Arkansas. He played with us about a week and then he went on north. Not too long after that, we heard a record that he made—he was a showman. All those kind of people were showmen with their music. Louis Jordan would crawl all around the stage when he played his saxophone—on his knees while he played and rolled his eyes—but he was a showman! It went over well at the time. I left the Southland Troubadours and went out in Texas and stayed. I went to Beaumont, Texas, and played in a whorehouse. My old lady was the lady of the house—she ran the house. I call her my old lady, but that was like a wife now—her name was Nettie Lindsey. That was in the red-light district—on Crockett Street. I made a lot of money—I made $50, $80, $100 tips a night. The women—they'd be crying about somebody they loved, and I'd play songs for them—they called them Torchin' Songs—you know? They'd get you to play different things for them and they'd pay $10, $15—whatever.

Then I left Beaumont, Texas, and came back to Cannon, Mississippi. My father had moved up there. I went back to Hattiesburg—that was Cooney Vaughn's home. I played there at a nightclub. I started Otis Spann out to playing—he and Johnny Jones—when they were little kids. I was playing over in East Jackson at the pool room and Otis Spann's mother was named Miss Josephine—his father was Friday Ford, and little Odie looked just like him. He was a little half-hand piano player himself. His father died, and then old man Spann married Miss Josephine, and Otis took his name—Otis Spann—but his real name was Odie Ford. So when he got to be about eight or nine years old, he would slip off and come over to the pool room where I was playing—and just listen. Then Miss Josephine would catch him and whip him all the way home. He just kept coming out. I said to him, "Your mama's gonna beat you to death if you don't stay away from up here." He said, "I sure want to learn to play—I can play a little." So I went to showin' him when he got a chance to come over there. And Johnny Jones was the same way. I remember when Odie was born—I remember the midwife that birthed him into the world—Miss Candacey. She had a son we called Kansas City—he tried to play the piano too [*laughs*]. Sunnyland is one of the best old time players that's living today. He can play the blues—and he can play a boogie-style piano, too. And Sunnyland is a piano player that don't know how much he could play hisself—because all those B naturals and A naturals and D naturals—Sunnyland plays in all those kind of keys just like you'd play in the original keys—make him no difference. That's why all those guitar players like him. Most of those guitar players, you buy him a guitar and he can't tune his guitar where it's supposed to be tuned, so he just play his guitar open—and Sunnyland can play right there with them!

I came back to Chicago in about 1939—I just got tired of being down South and came to Chicago. I didn't like to stay in any one place too long—I'd get tired. So I came back to Chicago in 1939, and I haven't left Chicago since then. I been living here ever since.

"Robert Jr." **Lockwood**

Sunnyland Slim set this interview up. I was around Sunny a lot. I worked with Smokey Smothers each Sunday at Blues on Halsted doing the matinee. Sunnyland Slim and his band did the nightcap, but Sunny showed up almost every afternoon, even before the matinee got started, and kept us company. I remember one Sunday he told me that Robert Jr. Lockwood was coming to Chicago in the next week, saying, "Whenever he's in town, Robert stays with me." I mentioned I'd like to interview Robert for my radio program, and Sunny said he'd put us in touch. Later in the week I got a call from Sunny. He said, "Hold on a minute . . ." and he put Robert on the phone. I told Robert I'd like to do an interview with him. He replied that he didn't do interviews for free. I asked him how much he would charge me for a sit-down interview. He said, "My wife Annie takes care of the business. Here, I'll let you talk with her." Annie came on the phone and we agreed to a dollar a minute—which was fine by me. We made arrangements to meet at the radio station which was located in downtown Chicago's Loop at 2 p.m. on a Friday afternoon. Robert Jr. Lockwood was in great demand by everybody because of his associations with several iconic blues figures. His

Robert Jr. Lockwood. Photo courtesy the Robert G. Koester Collection.

mother spent time with the legendary Robert Johnson, from whom Robert Jr. learned to play guitar. It's why he was referred to as "Robert Jr." He also worked with Sonny Boy Williamson II (Rice Miller), who took Robert on the road throughout the 1940s, and together they pioneered the broadcast of live blues on radio, performing on the *King Biscuit Time* radio program on KFFA in Helena, Arkansas. He continued to perform and recorded with Sonny Boy during the 1950s. He also played and recorded behind harmonica genius Little Walter. Everybody wanted a piece of Robert, or a moment of his time, or a short conversation—and everybody wanted to ask the same questions about Robert Johnson, Sonny Boy, and Walter. While Robert Jr. was by nature—according to his friends—a warm, friendly, intelligent person with a sharp sense of humor, over the years he had adopted a rather salty, standoffish persona in public simply to ward off the onslaught of these same questions. He wasn't particularly patient or tolerant and was often short with the clamor in general. I hoped to talk with him about lesser-known aspects of his career. I knew, for instance, that he'd spent time and come to Chicago with Dr. Clayton, an obscure blues figure who had a major influence on B. B. King, so I was looking forward to our interview and hoping to cover new ground. If Sunnyland gets credit for arranging the interview, he narrowly averts blame for scuttling the event. Our agreed start time was 2 p.m., but Sunny didn't get them to the station until 4 p.m.—which put them in the Loop during the evening rush hour when traffic was in close to total gridlock. In addition, what little on-street parking is available in the Loop during the day disappears at 4 p.m. Robert was forced to park in one of the downtown parking lots, which even thirty years ago was frightfully expensive—$12 for the first hour and only escalated after that. When they finally showed up Robert was mad as a wet hen—not a great way to start an interview. But he quickly calmed down and we got to business. We recorded in the talk show studio sitting at the round table with a half-dozen microphones. Sunnyland sat at the table with us and occasionally joined in the conversation. The interview lasted approximately an hour and at the end I kicked in an extra twenty-five bucks to help with parking.

This interview was recorded June 1982. Robert Jr. Lockwood died November 21, 2006.

■ ■ ■

My first instrument was an organ—one that you pumped the air into with pedals. I started trying to play that at eight years old. Then I saw Robert Johnson when I was about twelve and a half. And I heard him play the guitar and support himself—I didn't think that was possible—and when I heard that, I liked it. So I started pestering him about his guitar—I wasn't asking him to learn me—I'd seen him doing it and I just wanted to try and do it. So every time he'd set the guitar down and get his mind occupied doing something else, I'd pick up the guitar. So, finally, he decided to teach me. I've been playing guitar ever since.

Had you seen other people play guitar—before Robert Johnson?

I saw a lot of people play guitar, yeah—but I wasn't interested. I always wanted to play something that I didn't have to have no help.

Was it just that he was in the vicinity—or was it the way he played it?

It was the way he played it—otherwise, I'd have tried to play guitar before. See, my people wasn't in too bad a shape—they could afford to have bought me a guitar.

How long was Robert actually around?

About ten years.

So you associated with him for ten years—you had that much time to learn from him?

I learned to play inside of three years.

Did you ever work with him?

Yeah—I played some with him. I did a couple of short tours with him—one up through Arkansas—one up through some parts of Mississippi—different times.

What was your reaction when you learned that he had died? Had he left your house by that time?

Well, he would always come and go—just like all musicians do. When we heard that Robert had been poisoned to death—me and my mother always expected that, anyway. Yeah—I don't know why, but we always did expect that. He didn't seem to value people too much, especially females—just another lady; he'd see one today, and tomorrow he'd walk right on away from her, right here—and go to another one. That's why we always expected somebody to do something to him, you know?

How long was it after he died that you made your first records?

Two years. Well, I already knew about record companies by being affiliated with Robert—and I could play. I'd listen to other people's records—and I already knew that I was better than a lot of people I'd heard—so I didn't see where there was anything in my way. I was down South—I didn't have a style: I had Robert Johnson's style! My style started changing after I started making records. Before I made records, I didn't think about style; but Robert played all kinds of ways, so his style was very broad.

Was it a lot different than we hear on the records?

Well, he played jazz and ragtime...

I left from Helena, Arkansas, and went up to St. Louis—which I had people in both of these places—St. Louis, Helena—and Memphis. When I got to St. Louis, I started working in Ninth & Chestnut Garage—and I ran into Dr. Clayton. Clayton and me worked around the city there for about a year, I guess. And he mentioned doing some recordings—but there were no labels in St. Louis recording black talent. So Clayton and I came to Chicago in 1940. When I came to Chicago—the first night I was here I slept in the park, and it wasn't because I didn't have any money: I had a pocket full of money. I came here with a thousand dollars in my pocket—and a round-trip ticket! Me and Clayton slept in the park just because it was nice out there. And it turned over cold out there in June or July—and I caught a cold. You know, when I recorded my first records I was hoarse—and I sung above that. I been trying to figure out how I done that. Anyway, we slept in the park—and it got cool and we went and registered into the Rhodes Hotel—I think that was on Thirty-Fifth Street—yeah, Thirty-Fifth and Rhodes. We came here to record for Decca, and we ran into that Lester Melrose bunch—which was Memphis Slim and Memphis Minnie—Little Son Joe and Big Maceo, and Tampa Red. We went up to Tampa's—that's where we met Melrose at—on State Street over there. When Melrose heard Dr. Clayton sing, he went crazy. And these people were fighting over talent—like they always do. Mayo Williams was black, Lester Melrose was a Jew—and they were fighting each other like dogs [*laughs*]. See, we came to see Mayo Williams—and he was in New York. So Lester Melrose wanted to make sure he recorded Dr. Clayton before Mayo Williams got back. In the meantime, he and Clayton got together. He recorded Clayton right away. When he got ready to record Dr. Clayton, he designated Big Bill to be the guitar player. Dr. Clayton refused to record. He said we'd had been playing together for over a year—why should he let Bill play, when I had put in all the time helping him arrange his stuff? And Lester Melrose used everything he could think of to stop me from playing on that session. Then he came up with, "Well, he has to have a union card."—and I had one! [*Laughs.*] That was real funny! Doc looked down at me and said, "Ain't you got a card?" I said, "I got something—." I pulled it out of my pocket, and Lester Melrose turned red as a beet. Anyway, it came to the point where he was still trying to insist that Bill play. So Clayton told him, "He's gonna play for you—and you're gonna do the singin'." He said, "I'm not gonna do the singing.

If this is gonna be my recording session, it's going to be conducted like I want it to be." Plus, Clayton had a very good education, too—you know? So anyway, I ended up playing on Clayton's first five recordings—me and Ransom and Blind John and Judge Riley—that's right! Then, after Melrose heard me play, he asked me about doing a recording session for him. At that time they were only getting $25 per record—$50 for a session—which was four tunes—two records—two 78s—and 13 percent of one-cent royalty. Did you hear what I said? I told Melrose I wasn't interested in the royalty—13 percent of one cent? I'm not even interested. I told him he'd have to give me $500 to record. He said, "Nooo—No way!" And I said, "Well, I didn't come to see you no way." So we fell out—we never did get along—but he ended up giving me $500 for my recording session, and he gave me $400 for helping Clayton—and Dr. Clayton got about $5,000 out of him. I don't think anybody had got that kind of money out of him. Oh man—he cried like a baby! [*Laughs.*]

You know, in St. Louis Clayton didn't drink like that. I really think that he just got overjoyed from being able to record records. See, some people just can't handle that fast success—you know? So in St. Louis he didn't get drunk. I had to go home. I had to go back to St. Louis to get a Social Security card—I didn't have a Social Security card when I came here—and I couldn't collect my money. So I had to go back to St. Louis and get a Social Security card and come back to Chicago and pick up my money. And when I got back here, Dr. Clayton didn't have no shoes and just one pair of pants—and one shirt. The people had done took all his money from him and he got drunk. He came down to the bar that was next door to the hotel over there at Thirty-Fifth and Rhodes. He went into the bar and had the bartender lock the door—and they didn't let nobody out and they didn't let nobody else in. I guess there was about eighteen people in there, and he bought food and drinks for everybody—and they still took his money. When I came back here to get my money, he didn't have a quarter.

Charlie Jordan is what sent me to Chicago—that's right! Charlie Jordan had a blues club there in St. Louis—and Charlie Jordan made demos on me and Dr. Clayton, and he sent them up here to Chicago—and he never got any response from them. You know, that's really pitiful—that man should be rewarded for Clayton—and me. And he never was rewarded—I don't know why he was wasting his time like that. He was supposed to be working for Mayo Williams—and we came to Chicago to see Mayo Williams from Charlie Jordan. He was an invalid, and he was on crutches. He played the guitar and the piano. Yeah—I knew him so well.

Did you lose contact with Clayton — with you and Melrose having fallen out, and Clayton under contract to him?

Well, he was just somebody I knew—I didn't depend on him. In fact, I've never been the type to depend on nobody. I've been kind of a lone wolf all my life anyway. I've been around Sunnyland Slim more than I've been around anybody. When I first came here, I played with Curtis Jones—but Curtis Jones had a thing going on that I didn't like: he couldn't go nowhere without smoking pot [*laughs*]—and all that shit, you know? And I just cut him loose. And I finally ran into Sunnyland, and me and Sunnyland stayed together for a long time—and finally I went to work with Walter. I went to work with Eddie Boyd first and then with Walter. Me and Sunnyland had a trio around here for a long time. Sunnyland and me [*laughs*], we had a trio, and we played for a dude over on Indiana Avenue who was a very hard pay—I tell a lot of people about that, and it cracks them up. Sunnyland and me hired to work for him—and most of the people coming in, we knew them because we done played all over the city and we just about knew everybody. So everybody who came in—whatever they drank we put it on our tab and collected their money—do you remember that Sunnyland? [*Laughs.*] When time come for us to get paid [*laughs*], we owed the man money! [Laughs.] Oh—that man really didn't know what to think; we were the only trio that man ever paid, and when time came for us to get paid, I think I owed the man about $80—Sunnyland owed him eighty and Alfred owed him eighty! [*Laughs.*] The man said, "I don't know what's happening here...!" [*Laughs.*] So we just paid him down to our salary.

Well, I met Sonny Boy [II] because Robert Johnson knew Sonny Boy. Sonny Boy came to my mother's house with Robert. Now, Robert was another one that never ran around with nobody—and I don't know how in the heck they got together and just came by there. Somehow or other Sonny Boy ended up in Helena—and came home with Robert. And Sonny Boy got a chance to see me when I was—I guess I was about fourteen. And then two years later Sonny Boy came back after me; I was sixteen. I'd been in Mississippi with Robert—and I'd done been in Arkansas with Robert. Sonny Boy came by and begged my mother to let me go to Mississippi, and she finally said I could go. From then on, I been playing with—helping him to make his records—and everything. We got arrested in Sawdust, Mississippi—we got arrested for disturbing the peace. A fellow—I don't know, I guess maybe he intended to kill me—but I caught his hand and his belt—and the gun. I got my hand in my old pocket and got my knife out. He was a big man, too—he was as big as Sunnyland. He reached for his gun on me, and I caught his hand and his gun and his belt. He couldn't get his gun out of the belt because I had his hand and I had my thumb under the belt. [Laughs.] I finally got my old knife out, and I think I stuck him a little, and he broke loose from me and the gun fell on the floor. And Sonny Boy was coming in the door when the man broke to go out the door. Sonny Boy jumped on the man's back—that man ran almost half a block with Sonny Boy—Sonny Boy was on his back [*laughs*] eating him up! So they throwed us in jail—that was on about a Thursday. That Saturday came—Sonny Boy said, "Hey, Robert Jr.—get your guitar. Let's make us some money." There wasn't but one person in the jail—the person in the jail was a trustee, and everybody called him Jewel. I got my guitar, and me and Sonny Boy got up in the window upstairs and started playing. And the jail got surrounded by people! In that time there were very few radios, and they didn't allow no jukeboxes in Sawdust [Sandhurst]. And that jailhouse got surrounded, and those people threw—they must have thrown over $200 over that fence. Well, the trustee brought us about $230, and I know he put some of that money in his pocket: I know he didn't bring it all to us—I know he didn't. So we got about $230 that Saturday. And the next week we did the same thing, and we collected up about $350, and I know Jewel had about $30—$40 or $80 of that money—I know he did! And through the weekdays the police officers started taking us out every night, having parties. And every time they took us to a party, we would make $50 or $60 apiece—we got out of there with almost $1,000 apiece! These officers—I think one was named Ed Manee and Sid Harris—highway patrolmens. So we stayed in there about eighteen or twenty days—something like that—and we were living first class. We had company coming to the jail, and they were letting them in at night, letting them out the next day—that's the silliest thing I ever seen [*laughs*]. And we had corn liquor—in the jail, that the cops gave us—a whole gallon! When that run out, they gave us another. They finally just felt ashamed of themselves—holding us. We weren't doing no work: we were just making money playing, coming back to the jailhouse, and eating out of the hotel. So they came in that day and said, "Robert Jr." I said, "Yes, sir." They said, "If we let you all out, are you going to stick around, or are you going to leave?" I said, "As soon as you let me out, I'm leaving." Sonny Boy said, "Oh-oh-oh-oh—I-I-I think I'll hang around." I said, "Well, you're going to hang around by yourself!" He just wanted to get out. [*Laughs.*] Now, they really didn't want us to go—they wanted us to stay! Because musicians were very few, and Mississippi was—well, it still is—a funny state. See—all the things that take the money out of the state, they try their best not to allow that. So they didn't have jukeboxes, they didn't have slot machines, they didn't have none of that in Sawdust and Como—they didn't have none of that! And me and Sonny Boy playing that harp and guitar, that was very rare.

So they let us out, and we went to the hotel and ate. And then we walked out on the highway and started hitchhiking. I think we were gone about two days. We got down to Hunnianna [Hernando]. Well Hunnianna is just before the line in Tennessee. So we went home with some people that lived in Tennessee.

That night—I don't know why, but I always seem to be the one that's up—and I'm curious, you know? Sonny Boy just went on in there and laid down and went to sleep.

I saw the police car pull up in the yard, and I said, "Oh, what in the hell is this?" So they stood out there and talked to me and explained what they had come for. They said, "We're having a fish fry, and we want to take you all back down there to play for us—and we'll bring you back!" I said, "Okay." He said, "Where's Sonny Boy?" I said, "He's asleep." He said, "I'm gonna scare the shit out of him." So he goes in there where Sonny Boy was sleeping and shines the light on him. "All right—get up, let's go!" Sonny Boy says, "Oh, Lord—what I done done now!?!" [Laughs.] After Sonny Boy found out who they were, he wasn't frightened anymore. And they carried us all the way back to Sawdust, Mississippi, and we played for that party; $28 was a lot of money back then, and they gave us $28 apiece—and brought us back. We left Hunnianna and came on in to Memphis. Yeah—that was true.

I knew Little Walter ever since he was about twelve or thirteen years old. Walter was down there in Mississippi and Arkansas. Walter used to get on the spare tire when I'd go out in the country to play, and he never could work. He'd get on the spare tire, and when we'd get almost to where we turn off where the house was, he'd get off and brush the dust off of him and stay out of sight until the house got full of people. Then he'd come in and ask me to let him play the harp. That's why I had so much control over Walter. A lot of people never understood that, but Walter respected me like a father because I would knock him down. Many a time my old lady would cook me a T-bone steak, and I'd give it to Walter—in Marianna and Helena, Arkansas. AND I DON'T LIKE NO HARP! I only helped Walter because he needed help—and I knew I could help him. I don't like no harp—I ain't never liked a harp! You know, I played with the other Sonny Boy, too—John Lee Williamson. I just played with them because they needed help, and I was the best help available, you know? And I got paid well. I just don't like harps—I'm sorry—they're so limited. There's a lot of things I want to play, and if they're on the harp, I can't play them—so why be bothered with that?

I tell a lot of people about Ike Day. Ike Day was a drummer—you hear a lot of people talk about drummers. Ike Day was a drummer, but he had a habit. And Ike used to come where our trio was playing and sit at the drums and play by himself on our intermission. And when time came for us to go back to work, the people would ask us to let Ike keep on playing the drums by himself. You see Odie Payne trying to roll the bass drum pedal? Ike Day was doing that. Ike Day had two or three sets of drums in the Loop. He had a set at the Brass Rail—I know. He had these drums down there because he was a junkie and his set was always in pawn. So the people who wanted him to play at these clubs bought him a set of drums and stored them in the basement and wouldn't let him take anything out of there. Buddy Rich was playing at the Brass Rail one time, and Ike Day came in there. He tried to speak to Buddy, and Buddy wouldn't speak to him. And Ike Day asked him to let him play one, and he told Ike he couldn't blow his nose. So from one thing to another—he finally jumped up and put the sticks in Ike's hands and jumped down off the bandstand. Ike jumped up on the bandstand, and the bartender started hollering, "No—no!" Buddy didn't know that the man who owned the Brass Rail had a set of drums in the basement that were for Ike—when they could catch him straight. I think Buddy called him a name and said Ike was pestering him. And the bartender told him, "Well, there ain't no need of you trying to play anymore tonight if you're gonna let him play. And Buddy didn't go back. When Ike played there wasn't no need of anybody trying to play! [*Laughs.*]

Sippie **Wallace**

From the very early days of my exploration of blues I was fascinated with the classic blues singers—the women who pioneered blues recording during the 1920s. In the late 1960s and early 1970s what little material was available by classic blues singers on microgroove recordings was available largely due to the accompanying jazz players— Louis Armstrong, Fletcher Henderson, King Oliver, and the like. One of my favorites was Sippie Wallace, who was still living at the time and had resumed performing after many years away from music. Sippie was part of the Thomas clan, a musical family raised and based in Houston. Her oldest brother George Thomas was a pianist, a composer, and made his living as a sheet music publisher based in Chicago. Then came Sippie (her real name was Beulah Thomas) and her niece Hocial, George's daughter, who were a year apart and raised together as sisters. Finally came Sippie's younger brother, Hersal, who was a teenaged prodigy of blues piano and was raised by Sippie and Hocial. George composed several classic blues piano pieces including "The Rocks," "The Fives," "The LaSalle," and several other enduring tunes—all popular with blues pianists of the 1920s. Together George and Hersal are given credit for developing the style that was later

Sippie Wallace. Photo courtesy the Robert G. Koester Collection.

known as boogie-woogie—only then it was known as "Fast Western." The family followed George to Chicago and later moved to Detroit. Sippie and Hocial recorded for the OKeh label as classic blues singers, often singing tunes composed by their brother George and accompanied by their brother/uncle Hersal. Hersal was the rage of Chicago's rent-party circuit, despite his youth, and had many admirers, including a couple of local teenagers who aspired to play in Hersal's style—Albert Ammons and Meade Lux Lewis. After a handful of successful years recording, tragedy struck the family when Hersal, still a teenager, died of food poisoning in 1926. Both Sippie and Hocial were so disheartened by his death that they left blues singing and joined the church. Their older brother, George, died in Chicago in 1937 after breaking his back. Sippie has always maintained that he did this stepping off a streetcar. This interview was recorded at two separate sessions. The first was in 1981 at the Lake Shore Drive Holiday Inn in Chicago, where Sippie was performing at the music venue Rick's Café, located within the hotel. I was accompanied by Bob Koester on this session, and we lugged his Roberts reel-to-reel recorder with us. The second session was held at the Blackstone Hotel in the South Loop in Chicago. I was solo on this session and recorded with a cassette deck borrowed from the radio station.

This interview was recorded April 11, 1981, and October 27, 1984. Sippie Wallace died November 1, 1986.

■ ▨ ▧

Them days gone forever, child—*them days is gone forever!* Well—I learned to play piano self-made—just like Hersal. Hersal played the piano from watching Buddy [George] play, and I learned how to play the piano from watching Hersal play! [*Laughs.*] And then Hocial watched us play, and Hocial played. So the three of us played piano—we just took it up.

I was nothing but a gospel singer, and so whenever Mama went to church and go to the Lord's meeting, there used to be a man next door to us in Houston, Texas—where I was born—and he had a Victrola, and he had all these records there. I would hear these records—and I loved those records. I heard Ma Rainey and I heard Mamie Smith sing the blues—and I liked them blues! I kept on—I'd go over every evening and listen to those records until I learned how to sing those songs. Then I learned how to play them! And after I learned how to play them—there used to be a tent show not far from my house, and all the girls used to come over to my house to rehearse—I had a piano—after they found out they could come to my house to rehearse. Well, the piano player couldn't come up to my house to rehearse them and they found out I played the piano; I used to play for them when they'd come up there and sing. They'd say, "Sippie, why don't you come up and join us?" I'd say, "Child—I can't dance." So they kept after me until I went up to the show—and when I went up to the show to see them dance on the tent show, I liked it! But I still couldn't go until Mama went to church: I'd slip out the windows and go to the show, and I had to come back and get in the window before Mama came back from church, and Mama would never know I went to the show. So they finally got me to sing on the stage.

When I started singing I had to sing ballads—that's what my brother wrote was ballads. He wrote "Come Share Your Life with Me, Sweet Baby Doll." He moved to Chicago and stayed here for years. He started writing blues after he got to Chicago. "Muscle Shoals Blues" made a big hit here in Chicago—and "New Orleans Hop Scop Blues," and the "Houston Blues," and several other blues—you know, "Draftin' Blues," "Uncle Sammy Blues"—my brother wrote that. "The Rocks" was his main piece then—at that time "The Rocks" was the main piece—and then he wrote that "Bullfrog Rag." He wrote "The Fives"—you know, our mother was sick and my sister wrote him to come on home—we called him Buddy—she wrote, "Come on home, Buddy—I think Mama's going to die. She's very, very sick." But Buddy didn't have enough money to come home. So he wrote this number, "The Fives," and it was a hit and he was selling copies—sheet music. He was wishing he could get the money to come home to see my mother. But my mother died on the 28th of January—and my brother didn't get home until the 10th or the 12th of February—so he didn't see Mama at all. And that's where "The Fives" were born—see, it sounds like a train: "Da-da da-da da-da da-da"—you know, trying to make the bass sound like a train. Buddy wanted to come home so bad to see Mama—so he got the fastest thing he could get. "Here comes Number Five—she makes a mile a minute." I was a little girl—just four or five years old—but I remember so well. "Number Five" wasn't supposed to be sung—it was a rag to dance by.

I was about thirteen and my mother had died, and I thought my brother was going to take care of me. My brother said, "Get you a husband." Well, Mama never let us receive company—you know? I didn't know how to get no man— how was I going to get a husband? Go tell a man to marry me—that's no way to get a husband—is it? *Is it?* [*Laughs.*] You have to do something worse than that! I made a song about "For so many years I didn't know what love was all about—I'd never been loved but by my Ma and Pa." I wrote, "But after Mama died a man stepped into my life—he hugged me and he kissed me and my eyes flew open like an electric light!" [*Laughs.*] "I love that man—I love that man—I did all I could to keep that man. He told me he loved me too. But as soon as he got me he loved everybody but me—But still I kept on loving that man." I said, "But that man walked off and left me for a woman who looked just like you!" [*woman listening to the interview*]. So I was downstairs cooling off, and the woman had a little girl—and she said, "My Mama stole your man." [*Laughs.*]

Mama had died, and I had met my first husband, Frank Seals. He had been in the army, and he married me before he went into the army. When he went into the army, he forgot he had married me—and he wanted everybody but me. And after he came back from the army, he met some woman—see, they had a variety of women over during the war—and he couldn't see me, because I was nothing but a little child bride. So when he came back to Houston, he had met a woman—A REAL WOMAN—and she gave him a silk shirt. He wanted me to give him some Stetson shoes. YOU KNOW, IF I GOT ANY MONEY I'M NOT GOING TO BUY HIM SOME STETSON SHOES!! I'D BUY THEM FOR MYSELF!! So he quit me because I wouldn't buy him any Stetson shoes—I let him go!

It hurt me so bad—I cried, I couldn't eat: I tried to eat, and my supper would lodge in my throat—I couldn't swallow—I couldn't eat! [*Laughs.*] I said, "I love Frank." I went and got my divorce—I paid $13 for my divorce—it like to broke my heart. I went before the judge and he told me my divorce was granted—I didn't want it. I prayed to God I didn't get it! [*Laughs.*] I loved Frank so hard! [*Laughs.*] But that boy gave me the blues! [*Laughs.*] I said, "I know what I'll do—I'll take some carbolic acid; if I take some carbolic acid and I kill myself, then Frank will know I really did love him." Now wasn't I a fool? Wasn't I a fool? [*Laughs.*] Wasn't I a fool!?! I told my sister Lucy what I was going to do. I said, "Lucy—I'm going to take some carbolic acid." I didn't know where I was going to get the carbolic acid because I didn't have any money to buy none. I said, "I'm going to show Frank that I did love him—but I'm going to kill myself, and he's going to know I really did love him!" She told me—she said, "Sippie—don't do that. That's a crazy thing to do that. You will find a man that you love better than you ever loved Frank. There's as good a fish in the sea that have never been caught. Forget about Frank—go 'head on and get you somebody else." And sure enough—I met Matt Wallace in about two months' time. I met Matt, and I married Matt—and Matt carried me to Chicago. And my brother gave me and Matt a job typing and writing music. He taught me how to use a typewriter. My brother would have put me on record—he would have let me sing his "Muscle Shoals Blues"—but he let Bessie Smith sing it. But Mr. R. S. Peer came to my brother George when his "Muscle Shoals Blues" made such a big hit. He came to Chicago and he said, "George, the world's gone crazy about blues. Have you got any more blues on hand?" George said, "No—but I got a little sister here, and she may have something that would suit your taste."

Now, my brother George Thomas was a songwriter, and he wrote all kinds of songs. Everybody was looking for me—and I didn't know they were writing for me. They said, "We can't hear from Sippie. We wrote all kinds of letters to George, and George doesn't seem to know where Sippie is." But George was lying—George knew where I was, but he didn't tell me—until one day I happened to get the mail, and there was a letter in there from the OKeh people. It said, "I guess we'll have to comb everywhere until we find her—and give her another contract. We can't find Sippie." And that's when I wrote them a letter. And that's when they told me they had been trying to find me so long and everything. And my brother told me that's because I wasn't putting any of his numbers on record. So I guess Buddy told them why he hadn't told them about me. But then they demanded that I—every time I record—make at least two of Buddy's numbers—maybe more, but at least two of Buddy's numbers. And I've been hearing from them every since! My songs made a hit—they didn't know me, but my songs made a hit! They didn't know anything about me, but my songs made a hit—that's what gave me the job!

I had twenty-eight hits—one right behind the other! It was through my brother—my brother plugged me. Mr. Peer told me that my record had outsold the "Crazy Blues"—Mamie Smith made the "Crazy Blues." My record, "Shorty George," had outsold the "Crazy Blues"!

I didn't know what that meant; I said, "It has!?!" I didn't even know what they were talking about! [*Laughs.*] R. S. Peer must have had an argument with the OKeh people, because I was sold to the Victor people—without my even knowing it, I was sold. And he changed my name from Wallace to Thomas—well, Thomas was my name right along. I got a contract from the Victor people and the first record I made was glass—and I was the first person that made a glass record.

Hersal wasn't nothing but a little boy, and I kept him with me all the time. But between us two—me and Hocial—we'd carry him with us all the time. Hersal would work with me and work with Hocial—he worked with Butterbeans and Susie—and Sara Martin. He'd play piano for anybody that came along. Hersal played on about twenty-eight records for me. Clarence Williams wouldn't let him play too much—until I got Hersal a contract from the OKeh people. Clarence Williams wasn't much of a piano player—he'd just complement. Hersal stayed with my brother Buddy. One time he went out, Buddy told him, "Don't let nighttime catch him outside"—be in when the streetlights went on. So Hersal was out there playing ball with the boys and didn't come back on time. Buddy got so mad, "Yeah—I'm gonna get me that six-shooter! Yeah—I'm gonna give him that six-shooter!" I said, "You aren't going to do anything—you aren't going to touch Hersal!" So I called up my cousin Fanny—she was living then. I said, "Is Hersal over there—has Hersal been there?" She said, "No, Sippie—he's not here but if he comes over . . ." "If he comes over there tell him to stay there. I'm coming after him!" So I called anywhere I thought I could find Hersal to tell him to go by cousin Fanny's house because I wasn't going to let my brother touch him! I kept Buddy off of Hersal—and I kept him with me all the time! He stayed with me—Mama wasn't living—he had to stay with me or Buddy, one. So he stayed with me all the time. He stayed with me in Detroit, too. He died with me in Detroit, too. He was sixteen when he died. He ate some pork and beans and died of ptomaine poisoning—that's what killed him. And I never ate pork and beans from that time up until about two years ago. I had been scared to eat them because Hersal died. He should have taken them out of the can—but he was playing at a cabaret and he worked until two o'clock [A.M.] and he was so hungry, and being a kid he couldn't buy food like we could—he couldn't buy himself a sandwich. So he bought himself a can of pork and beans—and ate out of the can. It killed him—ptomaine poisoning. I carried him to the doctor two or three times, but the doctor said he had ptomaine poisoning.

Hocial is my brother's child. He really wasn't working around music—he was working at Ford's in Detroit. You know back then they paid off the sixteenth of every month—but now they pay off on the first. So Buddy came home to bring his little pay home. He gave the money to his wife, Octavia, like he should, so she could pay the grocery bill—Hocial was about three weeks old—but his wife never did come back. And that like to worry him to death. And Mama began to come to his house every sixteenth, and my brother would give my mother the little change to take home to the family. He tried to wait until Octavia come back home with the money—he was going to give my mother some money—but Octavia never did come back. So he said, "Mama, you can go on home until Octavia come. I'll come down there the first thing in the morning." So he said, "Take the baby with you." Hocial was a three-week-old baby. She brought Hocial home, and Octavia never did come back. When she saw Octavia, Hocial was ten years old. My mother raised Hocial—I thought Hocial was our sister all the time because Hocial nursed Mama's breast like I did. Mama kept telling us that Hocial was George's child—she was raised up as my sister, but she was my niece. She died in 1942. After I made "Shorty George"—well, nothing was going to stop Hocial from recording. After my brother put me on record, he would have had to kill her if he hadn't put her on record! [*Laughs.*]

Hocial had one of those low-down men for a husband—Dewey was his name. He never bothered me, but he tried to have every woman he met. He told Hocial he went to bed with her sister Queen. Hocial got the gun to kill Dewey—but instead of the gun killing Dewey, she killed her sister. Now, she didn't intend to kill her. I had been there three months, and I had just left—going back to Detroit. If I had been there, that wouldn't have happened—I had too much God in me, too many prayers—it wouldn't have happened.

I got home, and I didn't even unpack my bag and Dewey sent me a telegram saying, "Hocial have killed Queen. Hocial is in jail and Queen is in the morgue." They were doing all right when I left them there. I didn't have any money—I didn't know how I was going to go back. But I went to the Eastern Stars and I told my Grand Mason—I let her see the telegram. She said, "Well, Sippie, you've got to go back to bury your sister." And I didn't think you could get a reservation on Sunday—but you can. So she made the reservations, and I left Sunday evening at six o'clock to go back to California. When I got back there, they had Hocial in jail—and Queen was in the morgue. I went to the jail, on the ninth floor in California, and the man had some big old chains that hit the floor just about scared me to death. I said, "Hocial, couldn't you get around killing Queen? I know Mama turned over in her grave when you shot Queen." She said, "Sippie—I thought she was going to dodge; I didn't mean to kill Queen." And she told Queen—even though Queen was dead—she was talking to Queen: "Queen, I didn't intend to kill you." Well, if you don't intend to kill—don't shoot. Don't stab! Because you don't know which way that knife is going—you don't know which way that bullet is going. So don't play with no guns and don't play with no knives!

Bernice—Bernice Edwards—she stayed with me and Hocial; she wanted to play like me and Hocial. So Hocial, Bernice, and I made a song called "Barrelhouse Man." Hocial would sing one song; we'd write another song, and Bernice would sing that; and then we'd write another song, and I'd sing that. That's how we would do.

Joe Pullum—yeah, I know Pullum! I know him like I did my own brothers. He was there in Houston—going to school with me and Hersal and Hocial. His poppa was a preacher—Reverend Pullum. Pullum took Hersal's song. We named it the "Hersal Street Gouch"—and Pullum renamed it "Black Gal"! [*laughs*]—that was Hersal's own song, and he had changed the name of it. I said, "Well, let him go—he wants to sing on some records." So we let him go ahead and have it because we had a variety of songs, you know? I never did tell my brother George—because he would have tried to do something about it. Yeah—he named it "Black Gal," [*sings*] "Black Gal—Black Woman—Woman what makes your head so hard?"

I sold Sara Martin the props from my first stage act—a life-size Victrola—with me singing in the Victrola and I'd open the doors and step out. I sold it to Sara because I wasn't going to sing the blues anymore. I sold it to Sara because she used to come to my house. She got holy sanctified before she died.

Among the classic blues singers, who were your contemporaries, who were your friends? Who did you know?

Butterbeans and Susie, Sara Martin, Ma Rainey, Bessie Smith, Clara Smith . . .

Was Clara here [in Chicago]?

She stayed with Ma. Ma would invite us to her house. She had a girl working for her, and she'd tell the girl, "Bring a drink for Sippie and her company." She was very nice—Ma was nice to get along with.

Let me tell you something. We all are short of the glory—and the Lord won't let you stray too far until he turns you around. Now, you can be so-o-o-o jazzy—but when the Lord says, "Come in," you're going to come in. The Lord wanted Jonah to go preach to the wicked men in Nineveh. Jonah didn't want to go. If you go to church right now, you'll find that most preachers don't want to preach—they don't want to preach. But, honey—if it's for you to preach, you're going to preach! You know one thing that tells me I'm going to be a preacher—and I begin to believe it [*laughs*]—she told me about a month ago, "You're preaching right now! You just ain't got your papers. But you're preaching right now!" I sing a song called "Adam and Eve Had the Blues." And the way that I did it, I said, "You find it in Genesis—second part of Genesis and some parts of the third chapter of Genesis—read it sometime!" If it's for you to preach, child—you're gonna sure preach it!

Johnny **Lewis**

Bob Koester, the renowned jazz and blues collector, was a film enthusiast as well and held regular Friday night screenings in his store. It was at one of these sessions he screened a documentary, *Chicago Blues* (1970), by Harley Cokeliss. Bob had served as guide and advisor on the film, assisting Harley by recommending and helping him to make contact with musicians of interest. In the film was a thirty second clip of Johnny Lewis, the obscurest of the obscure, an unrecorded country blues stylist in Chicago. It happened that Johnny was a house painter by trade, and he did some neighborhood painting for Harley's parents. When Harley discovered that Johnny played blues, he decided to include him in the film. As the clip played, Bob explained how they decided to include him in the film—and that he was still around, living on Chicago's West Side. I found Johnny in the Chicago phonebook and made arrangements for him to come down to the radio station, where we recorded the following interview and about half an hour's worth of in-studio performances.

This interview recorded March 1981. Johnny Lewis died October 6, 1992.

Johnny Lewis. Photo courtesy The O'Neal Collection.

■ ■ ▪

I was born October 8, 1908, in Eufaula, Alabama, that's eighty-nine miles south of Montgomery. I never did believe in nobody taking care of me. Even as a boy, I always wanted to take care of myself. That's the reason I left home so early. My playmate was named Johnny Upshaw. I went to church one Easter Sunday, and he had on a pair of black and white shoes, which were the prettiest shoes I'd ever seen in my life. And he had what you would call a white pinstripe suit. He had a white straw hat. He asked me on the church grounds—they called me Wayne for a nickname—he said, "Wayne, what did your daddy get you for Easter?" That broke my heart! He was just one boy, and my dad had thirteen of us. My dad couldn't buy two or three suits for us like his dad could buy two or three suits a year for him. I could only get one suit a year. So I told him a lie—I told him my dad bought me a brown suit, because I always liked brown, and he bought me a hat and shoes to match it. I told him it looked like it was going to rain, and I didn't want my new stuff to get wet. But I didn't have any. I left right then from the church, and I went home and fell across the bed. I cried and cried and cried. When my mother and dad got home, she came in there where I was. She said, "Wayne, honey what's the matter? What are you crying for?" I called John Upshaw "Tad" for a nickname. I said, "Tad had a brand new suit—out and out—and he asked me what did papa buy me for Easter. I told him papa bought me a brown suit—out and out—and I didn't have it and it just hurt me to my heart. Mama, will you ask papa will he let me leave and go—because I want to be dressed up like everybody else. Let me go where I can get me some clothes like I want and help y'all." She said, "Son, you're too young. You know you're not old enough—but I'll ask your dad." I was afraid to ask papa, so mama went and asked him, and he came in and said, "Boy, what was that you told your mother?" I said, "Papa, I want to leave and see if I can get a job." Well, being out on the farm he couldn't see where I could find a job. It didn't look like there were any jobs. He said, "Boy, you know there aren't any jobs. Where can you go and find a job—and you're too young, anyway, to be talking about leaving." But I kept on, and I said, "Daddy, just let me go." So the third time I asked him, I said, "Papa—I feel just like God is with me: he says where there's a will there's a way. I feel that he is in front of me. I feel that he's behind me and he's on each side of me. If you let me go, I believe I'll get a job before this time next week." He said, "Well, all right—go ahead." He didn't think I knew where to go—and I didn't. I was on my way to my uncle's house. He lived about a mile from my dad. I met a man named Jew Mitchell on a red horse. He was a white man and he was on a red horse. When I met him, I said, "Hi, ya'!" He said, "All right—hi, boy! Where are you going?" I said, "I'm going—but I don't know where I'm going." He said, "What are you looking for?" I said,

"I'm looking for a job." He said, "Do you really want to work?" I said, "Yes, sir, I really want to work." "Can you climb?" I said, "Yeah, I can climb." "Can you flail pecans?" "I can do that too!"—which I had never flailed any pecans. I had eaten plenty of them but I never went up in the tree and flailed them. In fact, I didn't know hardly what he was talking about. "Well, then get up behind me on this horse." So he took me to his farm and said, "I pay 75¢ a day for flailing and 50¢ for picking them up." So I went on and worked for him. Let me tell you what they call flailing pecans. You go down to the creek and find a reed. Find and cut yourself a reed that's about eight or ten feet high. You take that and just hit the limb on the pecan tree and the pecans will fall. If they're ripe the hulls—the shells—will open up. The minute you hit that limb, all the pecans fall—that's what you call flailing.

We used to cut hay. At that time most everybody slept on hay mattresses, not cotton mattress. Pull a whole lot of hay. Cut the hay, leave it out in the field where the sun can cure it. Then you carry it home and put it in your mattress—and it slept good! So then I left there and I picked cotton. They started me off with 30¢ a hundred. I stayed there and he raised me to 40¢ a hundred. He had a man by the name of Loca. The boss bet me Loca would beat me picking cotton. What happened was that every time Loca would pick four hundred, I picked five hundred. So then he gave a job for 75¢ a day and three meals—good meals, too! Then I worked at a shaving mill. They cut hardwood and take it to the mill, shave it, and take all those shavings anywhere you got oil or anything to wrap and pack it in those shaving; that way, if anything got busted the shavings would catch that oil.

Then I got it in my head to go to Columbus, Georgia. I stayed with my sister and her husband. I had about a quarter in my pocket and couldn't find a job, so I was on my way back home and I came across a man by the name of Charlie Grant. I asked him what he was doing, and he said he was making ironing buckets and selling them. They didn't have electricity for electric irons; instead, they used these buckets full of charcoal. I had never seen anybody make ironing buckets, plus he had his guitar sitting on the side. I asked if he would play me a tune. He said he didn't mind. Then he played me a tune, and when he played that tune, I didn't have but one quarter, and I gave him that quarter. He was going over to Alabama to play for a dance, and he asked me to come with him. I said I would go with him. I went back to my sister's house and told them about this guy playing guitar, and everybody seemed to know him in Columbus. He was about the only musician that was around there. My sister said he was all right, so I went with him over there in Alabama—just across the Chattanooga River. Right around from the river there was a police station, and the people he was playing for lived right behind the station. We went over there, and he began to play—and I never will forget if I live a hundred years: the first piece he was playing was about "... it's so cold up north until the birds can't hardly sing." He played another piece about "... the water pipe done busted, the water's running cold, I just want some good girl to come give me jellyroll." I didn't think they had any colored women as nurses. That was the first black nurse I ever saw, and she was all dressed in white. She was as pretty as a speck of turkey. She said her husband had just quit her and come north with another girl. I thought if she would take any one home it would be me—because Charlie didn't ever dress up, and I didn't think she would even look in his direction. But she jumped up and fell in love with Charlie right then—and it surprised me. That was on a Saturday night. So I said, "Lord, if you let me live to see Monday morning, I will go and buy me a guitar." That Monday morning about 5 o'clock I was standing outside Patterson Pawn Shop on Broadway in Columbus, Georgia. The first guitar that I ever owned was a value—it cost me $15. Then I started playing. My first piece I started out behind Charlie was "So Cold Up North." The next piece I played was "I Howled until I Made My Tonsils Sore": "If I can get what I want, you won't hear poor Lewis howl no more." It seems to me that Charlie got a little jealous after people started to say I could play as good as him, because I did have a little better voice than he did. So he quit carrying me around with him. If he played for a dance, he wouldn't tell me anything about it until he got back. So then everyone went to calling me. And he and I were called about the best guitar players that were in and around Columbus there. I never knew him to make any records. He's been dead about three years now. Every time I went home, I would go to see him. I played a lot of Blind Lemon pieces, and then I heard Blind Blake. On all those tunes I just heard the records—I never did meet them in person. Now, I saw T-Bone Walker in the '40s. He came and stayed a week. He had a guitar with that tin plate in the middle—anyway, it was something like steel. You'll notice that the tuning I play most of my pieces in—that's the tuning he was in. That's where I learned to play with my fingers. Before that I mostly just played with the slide. I met up with a lot of good musicians. I met Buddy Clayton—he was a mighty good musician. He made a record years ago, but I never could get a copy of his record. But I knew him good from a boy on up until we got grown. They had a fellow by the name of Bo Fagan, and he was playing a blues about "Mama don't allow it—Papa won't have it here. I don't care what your Mama don't allow, I didn't come to see your Mama no how. Mama won't allow it—Papa won't have it here."

I will tell you if I'm on my dying bed—because that hurt me to my heart and in my heart. As I said earlier, I didn't want anybody doing anything for me. I wanted to bear my own expense. While I was out there looking for a job, a white lady called me, "Hey, boy—are you looking for work?" I said, "Yes, ma'am—I sure am." She said, "I got a kitchen. Can you paint?" I said, "Yes, Ma'am—I can paint"—which I knew I was wrong—I couldn't do it, but I just figured God was going to be with me. Just like I figured when I told my dad that God would be with me, and before I could get to my uncle's house I met that white man and he put me to work. So I just had faith in God that he would do what he said—where there's a will, there's a way. She said, "How much would you charge for painting my kitchen?" I didn't know about any price, so I said, "Whatever you give me." She said, "I'll give you $5." So we went to the ten-cent store, which was Kress & Silver's in Columbus, Georgia. I bought some brushes, and I didn't know anything about painting. So she bought the brushes. And I didn't know anything about thinner—back then it was turpentine—and yellow enamel paint. I put the whole gallon of turpentine in the enamel paint [*laughs*]. There wasn't no such thing as a roller as that time. So I started painting, and when I got through, I had about as much paint on me as I did on the wall [*laughs*], and being so thin, the paint just run down like water. She had two nice boys—they were twins about my age. They liked me, and I liked them. She said, "Well, Mr. Bickerstaff won't be home before six o'clock, so I'm going to feed you all now." That was about five o'clock—I never will forget it. She had me sitting between those two boys—one on one side of me and the other on the other side. Just as we got about half way through eating, Mr. Bickerstaff walked in. He came home early, and he hadn't called her. He walked in and he looked at her, he looked at me, and he looked at the boys. So I started getting nervous because I could see that mean, low-down look on his face. She said, "Honey, what's wrong? You're home early and you didn't call. Why didn't you call me?" He said, "Do I have to call you?" "No." "What's this nigger doing with his feet under my table?" She said, "Honey, there wasn't anybody here but the boys and they love him. . . ." Then he looked at the job—which I couldn't blame about the job [*laughs*] because the job was terrible. He said, "Who did this painting?" She said, "John did." "Did you pay him?" "Yes—I paid him. I gave him $5." He said, "Boy—get up from here." I had already got up from the table because I could see that he was real angry. He said, "Where's that money?" I reached in my pocket and showed it to him. He snatched it out of my hand and said, "I ought to make you pay $5 for messing up this kitchen. Now get out on the back porch and eat." So I went out on the back step—and I never will forget—I sat out on the back step, and he came out and stood up and looked over me. He stood so long until that fear just left me. So I jumped up and took the plate and just broke it up. I couldn't eat any more after that—I was just holding it. I took the plate and threw it to the ground and just kicked the plate. And I jumped up and looked him in the eye. I said, "I'll be back!" I took off running—I never will forget it. I ran down the alley, and when I got there a piece it looked like to me something just struck me. I said to myself, "If you go home and get your gun and come back and kill this man, your people, your mother and father and brothers and sisters probably won't see you anymore. So I stopped, and while I was standing there the boys come running up behind me. They were calling me, and I was getting ready to fight them because I thought they had turned on their dad's side. The boys said, "John—Here's something mama sent you." Lord help me speak these words—she sent me $10 with those twins brothers. Plus she sent a long waiter full of chicken and turkey and food to take home. I took it and went on home. The next day the boys come and played with me. The boys is up in Cleveland somewhere, and I'd just like to know where they're at so I can give them something and let them knew I still appreciate what they did.

The reason I came to Chicago—I don't often speak about this—was Mr. Homer Jr. Diamond. At that time his dad was the mayor, and I started working for him. He had a bowling alley. He called me "Lightning." I set pins so fast that I could set pins in two alleys faster than a lot of the fellows could set one. I worked for him, and one day he said to me, "Lightning—will you promise me that you will work for me as long as I live?" I said, "Yeah, if you'll promise me that you will never fire me." He said, "I sure will." That was the agreement we made. Well, after a while he left and came to Chicago, but before he left he told me that if I gave him $600, I could have the bowling alley. So he gave me the title to the bowling alley, and I ran it for three or four years. I had ping-pong, I had shuffleboard outside. I added a new room with a pool table. I was doing pretty good. I was the only black person I knew that had a bowling alley in Columbus, Georgia. Another man and his wife had moved in, and I thought we were really good friends. His name was John and his wife was named Miss Mary, and I would say right now that she was as good a white lady as there was in the world. She was crazy about my wife, and the two of them were together every day. And our kids got along lovely together. I had about two or three hundred chickens that I had ordered from Sears & Roebuck. I don't know if they sell chickens now or not, but they were selling biddies at that time. I got up one morning, and all my chickens were dead! This was after they got big enough to be fryers—and they were piled in my yard! I didn't have any dream that he was the one who did it. He came in and he looked around and the next morning my chickens were dead. So the next morning all of his were dead—I killed every one of his! I got some food and started feeding it to them until they came in my yard and I killed every one of them. And you can just about guess what happened after that—we had a shooting scrape. I told my wife, "Baby, I'm going." She said, "I hate to see you go." I said, "Well, God is with me." When I left my house and my wife went with me all the way to the Greyhound bus station, I was playing "Baby Please Don't Go"—back to New Orleans. "You know I love you so." Then I talked a little bit about "turn your lamp down low before I go—you know I love you so." I left home the 16th of February 1949. I got to Nashville, Tennessee. When I got there, someone asked me if I could play my guitar. I told them, "Yes." They said, "C'mon and play." I told them, "I'm not allowed to play it in the bus station. I can go outside and play you a tune." He said, "If you can play it good, I'll give you a dollar." I told him, "I'm going to play it [*laughs*]; I don't know how good it's going to be. It'll be good for me." So I started playing for just this one person, and before I got through, the crowd blocked the sidewalk and someone called the police. In just a few minutes there were five or six policemen with clubs and guns in their hands like someone had committed a hanging crime. They told the people, "Scatter!" Everybody left but me. And one policeman said, "Hey, boy—what's wrong with your feet that you can't run?" I was surprised to hear the police that far up north say the word "boy," because I was always told police up north didn't say "boy." I said, "Officer, there's nothing wrong with my feet. I'm a citizen of the United States. I'm not doing anything wrong. I don't see why I should run. I've eaten many a rabbit, but I don't have a dammed bit of his blood in me. If you want to take me down—take me down!" He said, "Well, you're taking money." I said, "Yeah, and I'd take it from you if you give it to me. You don't see any signs that I'm charging people to play." He said, "Do you live here?" and I said, "No—I don't, and I wouldn't live here." He said, "Where are you from?" I said, "I'm from Columbus, Georgia, born in Eufaula, Alabama, eighty-nine miles south of Montgomery." Then he said, "If all of your people were like you, it would be better." Then they signaled all the people to come on back, and each one of those police gave me a dollar. So I sang a song for them "I'm Scared to Stay Here—I'm Scared to Leave This Town"—because the police is on every corner in town. I made so much money, I missed my bus. My brother was supposed to meet me here at the bus station, but I called and told him I was making so much money down there, I wouldn't arrive until the next day. [Laughs.]

I had heard all my life you can't teach an old dog new tricks. Now, I wouldn't say I was an old dog—but I was an old man. There were so many people that came to hear me play, and when I got through they all gave me tips. There was a young couple there who didn't have any money to give, and he felt bad, so he gave me his harmonica and told me to remember he and his wife. I didn't want to take it because I had never played a harmonica and didn't imagine I ever would. I offer it to my nephews and they didn't want it, so I took it and locked it up in my dresser. One morning about three o'clock that same little boy that came to me in Columbus, Georgia—he was the same—he wasn't any older or bigger or taller—he came up blowing that harmonica. He was blowing a tune, and I didn't know the name of that tune. But I jumped right up out of bed and started blowing it. My wife said, "Don't blow it this time of the morning—look how early it is. You'll wake the neighbors." And I said, "Well, if I disturb them, they disturb me sometimes. If I disturb them, I'll just have to disturb them. If I wait until day, I'll lose the song." That's how I write my tunes. That same boy brought them to me in my dreams. All those tunes you hear on my record, that's how I wrote them, and if I wait, the tune won't come back again. I've got my harp here now if you'd like to hear me blow it [*blows a little*]. I used to hobo to Birmingham, Atlanta, Macon on the train. And one time while I was on there, the conductor came back and told us, "Hobo, y'all get off here, you can't ride this train!" So he put us off way up there by Loca Hill, and when we got off, there was this woman that was up there in a little old house that sat up on top of that hill. She was baking some good butter biscuits. We boys, there were two or three of us, and we could smell those biscuits. We went up there and asked her for one. She wouldn't sell us any but she gave them to us because people down there—they just give you. That had been several years earlier, and I dreamed about it and so I wrote about it: "Hobo, You Can't Ride This Train."

Here in Chicago, I knew Magic Sam. I knew Howling Wolf. I was playing at Turner's, Fortieth and Indiana—right under the el station, and Howling Wolf was playing at Thirty-Fifth Street and Michigan. When he got through playing, he used to come up there and hear me play. Sometimes he would come up and play a number or two. When the people saw him play, they would just go wild. I was playing with a guy named Roy Skill—him and me and his brother. I would do a little dancing there, too. I'm still a pretty good dancer. Then when we got through, we'd go down to see Howling Wolf. And I met Tampa Red. I played at the C&A Hotel on Prairie, down in the basement. He allowed me to play with him there. The people used to say they couldn't tell his playing from mine. I could play just about like he could.

When I left home about fourteen years old, I had a little money and I had a few friends. When I got where I was going, my money ran out and my friends walked off and left me. I returned back to my home, and I saw my dad out there building a fence, and I said, "Hi, Dad!" and he said, "Hi." I said, "Do you know me?" He said, "No." "Have you ever seen me before?" He said, "It seems like I have. . . ." I said, "I'm your child." He said, "No, son—you're not my child. You couldn't be my child." I said, "Do you remember having a boy that left home by the name of Johnny Lewis—nicknamed Wayne?" He said, "Yeah—but that's been a good many years ago." I said, "Well, there's as many stitches in my pants leg now as there is in yours." That meant I was as tall as he was. I said, "Is mother in the house? Tell her to come to the door." The moment my mother came to the door and saw me she knew me, but she was afraid to call my name. So I wrote this tune—

My mother wouldn't own me,
My father wouldn't even call my name,
I hadn't done nothing wrong,
Wasn't that a crying shame.
I went to my mother's house
And asked for one piece of bread,
She closed the door,
And this is what my dear mother said:
Now son—you take the world as you find it,
Don't no one want to be your friend,
When you're broke down and out,
No one in Chicago will take you in.
You know your father he wouldn't own you,
And your mother's scared to call your name,
But you know I still love,
Oh child isn't this a crying shame.

Homer **Harris**

With all the interview contacts generated over the years by phone calls from listeners, this is yet another phone contact—but with a slight twist. In most cases the calls were from friends, relatives, or acquaintances of the blues people who helped put us in touch, but in this case I played a record by bluesman Homer Harris, and Homer himself gave me a call! We had a short conversation, exchanged phone numbers, and set a date to get together, again, at the radio station in downtown Chicago. Homer was an extremely obscure blues figure with only one recording session to his credit—and that wasn't available until twenty years after it was recorded—but he sang with Muddy Waters, playing guitar behind him, and so the session was one of the more amazing footnotes in Chicago blues history.

This interview was recorded June 24, 1994. Homer Harris died October 16, 2000.

Homer Harris. Photo courtesy The O'Neal Collection.

■ ■ ■

I was born in Drew, Mississippi, May 6, 1916. I had a mother, two brothers, and a sister. None of them were musical. My daddy was a farmer for a living. He worked for the railroad before he passed, and he worked for Streets and

Sanitation in Memphis, Tennessee, before he passed. I was a baby when we left there and went to Tutwiler, Mississippi.

Did you go to juke joints or see local musicians there?

No—I was too young. I was only about eleven or twelve when we moved there—too young to go to any of those places. I was in Tutwiler until I went to Memphis when I was about seventeen—old enough to get in the clubs! [*Laughs.*] I got a chance to see a lot of the musicians, guys like Rufus Thomas, Memphis Slim. I saw Memphis Slim at what they call the Raff Club in Memphis, and it's been so long that I almost forgot about it. I used to see Slim at a place called the Matinee Club. I used to see him there. That's where Elvis Presley started playing.

Were you singing at that point?

No. I wasn't singing. I didn't start singing until after I came to Chicago.

What were you doing for a living in Memphis?

I was working at a place they call the Tire Mart. I was fixing tires. I worked for the Newsome Tire Company there. I was a tire regroover. I did that by hand. After the tire wore down slick, I could cut the grooves back in it. You do that with a hot iron. I could cut any design by hand. Bring me a slick tire and if it's got enough rubber on it I could cut a design on it—any kind you want—Firestone, Goodyear, Goodrich. Anything you wanted I could put it right back on there by hand. I still have those tools a regroover with a 200-watt heating element in it.

Can you still do that with today's steel-belted tires?

No you can't do it with steel-belted tires.

But you could do that with the tires from the early days?

Yeah. Everybody wanted to do that—all the used car dealers. I had it made. Then I left there and came to Chicago and went into business for myself, doing the same thing with tires that I was doing down in Memphis. I came to Chicago in 1943 after my dad died; I came here on a train they call the City of New Orleans. I had an auntie living here at the time at 2962 South Wabash. I lived with her—Louella Sharkey—that was my mother's sister. I came up here because I wanted a job making more money. I came up here and started regrooving tires for the used car dealers, and I made money. In Memphis I was doing that in a tire shop, but I wasn't making any money—$11 a week, that's all. I was in the tire business a long time up here. I had my own shop at 2962 South Cottage Grove, Expert Tire Service—that was the name of it. I had already opened my business in Chicago when President Roosevelt died in 1945. I had the shop up until 1960. Then I had a truck with everything in there. I could take tires off, set them in my stand and work them over—just like that. I had a closed-in van. Tall as I am, I could stand up and walk from here to the door. I could do a tire in ten minutes. I would charge a dollar and a half a tire—some places I'd get more than that. I was making good money then. I was taking care of truck tires and passenger tires. That's one of the reasons I wasn't interested in going into music, because I was making money anyway. I was self-employed, and when it got cold here, I worked my way west where it was warm. I worked my way all the way to Los Angeles, California, and back. I was on Figueroa Avenue and all over Los Angeles. Then I worked my way back when I got ready to come back. I was up in St. Paul, Minnesota, for a time. I went out to Rockford and sold the truck there, but I still kept my tools—the Honeycutt machine and all my hand tools.

But you've had other jobs as well, haven't you?

I had a hardware store at 3957 West Roosevelt Road, H & W Hardware, at Roosevelt and Pulaski. I had it in 1957 and had it about seven years there. Then I turned it into a lamp store, Lamps Unlimited. Then I sold out and went to Pulaski and Lake, where I opened up a grocery store. That was in 1973. I sold that, and then I had a dry cleaners. My dry cleaners was on Cicero and Madison, right down from the public library.

Did you perform and sing in the clubs around town?

Oh yeah! They used to call me up at the different clubs. Memphis Slim used to call me up to sing—and then I could play a little piano too, you know? Elmore James used to call me up to play at Sylvio's Lounge on Lake Street—Lake and Oakley. At the Zanzibar, Muddy Waters used to call me up to play, Thirteenth and Ashland. They all liked to hear me sing, that's all.

At any point did you ever have your own gigs or your own band?

No, I didn't. I just sat in with other people. I never had the ambition to have my own band. I just wanted to do something for myself. Besides, at the time I already had my own business.

Who were some of the big names you saw here and were friends with?

Roosevelt Sykes. Tampa Red, Big Maceo, Jimmy Rogers, Little Walter, Baby Face Leroy—but all those guys are gone . . . Dr. Clayton, he's gone. Do you remember Dr. Clayton? I used to go see him at Thirty-Fifth and Giles. I've forgotten the name of the club now—but that's where I used to see him. The Plantation, that's where Sonny Boy got killed, at the Plantation. That's Thirty-First and Giles. He was living right down the street from there. I was with him the night before he got killed. He was good. Tampa was with Roosevelt Sykes at Tom's Tavern on Roosevelt Road. That was the last time I saw Roosevelt Sykes play. He was a one-man band by himself. Memphis Slim was at the Triangle at that time. And Memphis Minnie was at the Triangle Club at Fourteenth and Blue Island. And Johnny Jones—Big Maceo was supposed to have been his father because he could play Big Maceo's stuff. Big Maceo had a stroke and he could only use his left hand, and Johnny helped him out with his right hand on the same piano. They went like that for some time, and Johnny was a good piano player. He could play with anybody. L. C. McKinley, I knew him. Lonnie Johnson, all those guys—now they're way back. I used to keep up with all of them. I was with them.

Tell me about Memphis Jimmy. How did you meet him?

Well, Memphis Jimmy's from Memphis. I met him at 2962 South Wentworth [in Chicago] with a lady they call Florida. He was working at the Flame Club on Indiana Avenue. I didn't know him in Memphis. I used to go where he was playing and started singing with them. I used him for my piano player because he played like I wanted him to play, that's all. He was good. He had a piano at his house. I used to go there, and we'd rehearse at his house on South Wentworth—3962 South Wentworth. He'd play piano for me, and I'd sing. I got with Muddy Waters and Sunnyland Slim—all those guys, and they loved to hear me sing. I could sing at that time. I made a record in 1946 with Lester Melrose. I rehearsed it at James Clark's house. Lester Melrose interviewed me, and we went down to the studio for Columbia and we recorded. The studio was somewhere downtown, but I don't remember an address.

Who brought you to Melrose's attention?

James Clark and Sunnyland.

Who was on the record date with you?

Muddy Waters and James Clark.

Did you do any more than just those three sides?

That's all I did. Muddy had some on there and James Clark had some.

To the best of your knowledge, those weren't released when you cut them, were they?

Oh, no. They weren't released. I was listening for them. I have them copywritten too—with Columbia. Those were my arrangements. "Atomic Bomb," "Cut Your Head," "Tomorrow Will Be Too Late"—I wrote those myself and rhymed everything.

Where did those ideas come from?

"Atomic Bomb"—I got that idea—that's the bomb that ended World War II between this country and Japan. I remember that so well, and this was the story of it. I wrote the words up and thought that tune would really make a hit.

I was surprised it wasn't a hit, because I loved that tune. "Cut Your Head"—I wrote that up with "Atomic Bomb." That idea came from a girl I used to mess around with [*laughs*]; her name was Berniece. That's who I had in mind—that was down in Memphis. I told her about it and she wanted to hear it, but she never did get a chance to hear it. That last one was something I just made up, but Lester Melrose was crazy about it.

Did you have all three of these in hand before you scheduled the session?
Oh, yeah. I rehearsed those records at James Clark's house on Wentworth. Then we rehearsed down at the studios, and Melrose said, "That sounds good. Let's cut it." I got paid $35 per side. Cash after the session—and I was glad to get it! [Laughs.]

How many sides were recorded altogether that day?
I cut my three, Muddy cut three, and I think James Clark cut two vocals, but only the James Clark sides were issued. My sides and Muddy's sat on the shelf for twenty years . . .

After you did the session for Melrose, did you do any other sessions?
No—I didn't.

Had you prepared any other songs that didn't get recorded?
No—just those three. I got paid for the session, but I got a little disgusted because I thought those would make a hit. If they had made a hit, I'd still be going today!

What made you put the music thing down? Did you continue to go out on the scene?
I couldn't do what those guys were doing. They were drinking, and I couldn't do it. I wanted to be in that blues life, but I didn't want to do what they were doing to be in it. You have to drink to get the feeling—and I never was a drinking guy. I didn't smoke no reefers or anything like that. A lot of guys used to call me chicken because I wouldn't do it. So today I'm a live chicken and they're dead. That's why I'm seventy-eight years old today and they been gone a long time . . .

What did you find Lester Melrose to be like? Did you see a lot of him? I've read that he had a black girlfriend.
Yeah. He had a black woman—but there was nothing wrong with that. It was unusual for those times, but he was all right.

Was he out at the clubs a lot?
Yeah. He was a tough man, though—he was tough. I liked him, but he was kind of rough. He was a hard guy to deal with.

Blind John Davis

Blind John Davis was a Chicago blues pianist and a good friend. I used to hear from John at least twice a month while I was doing the radio program. If he hadn't played earlier in the evening, he was usually at home with a girlfriend—in fact, he went through several girlfriends during the time I knew him. John was raised in Chicago and first started recording during the 1930s. John was on scores of recordings as an accompanist, most produced by Lester Melrose. He played a standard template, sort of a signature set of riffs—if you heard two bars, you knew it was him. He played that same template on 80 percent of the records. After the war he made a half-dozen recorded sides under his own name, but as the Melrose roster of artists hit the end of the trail, much of John's blues work dried up. Ironically, one of the places John worked for many years during the 1950s and '60s was Otto's Restaurant located in suburban—and segregated—Forest Park, the town where I grew up. He played piano and sang, accompanied by Judge Riley, a renowned blues drummer who had switched to bass in his later years. This gig ended, as the owner is alleged to have burned the club down rather than serve black customers. Blind John started appearing on the North Side

Blind John Davis and Lonnie Johnson. Photo courtesy the Robert G. Koester Collection.

of Chicago during the 1960s, and I began to see him perform during the early 1970s—first at Elsewhere on Clark and Belmont, then Blues on Halsted, Lily's on Lincoln, and The Piano Man. In his final years John became the self-appointed guardian/caretaker of his old pal Tampa Red. Tampa had fallen on hard times after the death of his wife and was a resident at the Sacred Heart nursing home on Chicago's West Side. John visited regularly and encouraged us all to visit as well. He took care of Tampa's funeral when he died and then died himself a few years later. Our interview was arranged during one of our many phone conversations and was held in the studios at WBEZ in the Banker's Building located at Clark and Adams.

This interview was recorded in August 1981. Blind John Davis died October 12, 1985.

■ ■ ■

I was born December 7, 1913, in Hattiesburg, Mississippi. My parents moved to Chicago around 1916. I had three sisters—no brothers. I could see up until the age of nine years old. I stuck a twenty-penny rusty nail through my foot. In those days lockjaw was a sure thing for a rusty nail, but the doctor said instead of giving me lockjaw—with my grandmother's little home remedies—it settled in the weakest part of me, and that was my eyes. I would say the blues was my birth. Before I learned how to play the piano—when I was just a boy—my father used to have me sing Bessie Smith's numbers and Ma Rainey's numbers. When I was just a child, people liked to hear me sing. And I took music through jealousy. My father used to have two or three speakeasy spots during those days, and I'd see him paying his piano player. And I asked him, "Say, Pa—if I learn to play, would you pay me?" He said, "Oh, yeah, you know I will."—just one of those things.

Well, I gave him plenty a sleepless night with me practicing [*laughs*]. And my mother told him, "Leave him alone—you told him you'd pay him." [*Laughs.*] There were great players in those days—there was a fellow named James Patterson, Mayo Williams, Willie Wesley—guys like that. Oh, God—if they'd have been recording in these days, they'd have been great! I played house-rent parties and made a dollar and a half a night—and all I could eat and drink. But that was good money then because you could get a room and board for two and a half—two meals a day. I've played for $10 for six days and nights. When taverns and things first come back, I played for taverns for $10 or $12 a week.

Well, I'll tell you what happened. I called RCA Victor and told them I was blind and I'd like to make a record. They told me, "Well, we don't have anything to do with that, but I'll give you a fellow's number to call." And he gave me Lester Melrose's number. I called him and made an appointment with him—and that's when he took me to Washboard Sam. And we couldn't get along [*laughs*]: Washboard Sam would rehearse a set today this way—and then come back the next day and he had changed it all around.

I know I wasn't wrong because I was writing it all out in braille. So I guess here's what Lester Melrose said to himself: "I'll take him around to Tampa Red—because Tampa writes some pretty rough stuff—if he can't cut that, I'll be through with him." So he took me around to Tampa's—it was just like Brer Rabbit and the briar patch—he took me just where I wanted to be. At that time the Prince of Wales had married Wallace Simpson, and Tampa had made a number "She's More than a Palace to Me." It was a minor number. So when I get around there, Tampa says, "I don't know—I've had six or seven piano players around here, and they just couldn't cut it—so I don't know if you can cut it or not." His wife was sick in bed at that time. I said, "Play down a chorus and let me hear it." He played down a chorus, and when he got through, I played it down. And his wife hollered out of the bedroom, "Tampa, he's the one!" And from that day in 1937 we were close, up until his passing. Our rehearsal spot was at Tampa's home. He lived at 3432 State Street, and he had the house all the way from the back to the front; he had about three rooms that he used to put up musicians that came into town—all the Bluebird and Vocalion musicians would rehearse there and stay there if they were from out of town. What I used to do—the musicians would rehearse their stuff, and when they got it down like they wanted it, then they'd call me in. And when they called me in, I'd have them run it down for me—and when they ran it down for me, then I'd go ahead and play it. I lived on the West Side and he lived down south, but I was there every day. We were just buddies, and I was there when we were playing—and when we weren't. He could close his eyes and run across the street and run right into the place he worked at—The H & T. He worked by himself for a long time until I went in to work some weekends with him. And Tampa could play some piano—just like Lonnie Johnson. When Mrs. Tampa died he died with her in a way—because she was his mother, his wife, his sister—she was his whole family. He worshipped her—and she worshipped him. I was really surprised how few musicians visited him during his bad years, because he was a great guy—he fed many a one of them—and slept many a one of them. Tampa put up so many of them and helped so many of them.

I knew all those fellows—there wasn't anybody that I couldn't play with. Sonny Boy I—that was a great guy! I met him—he was in Chicago to do recordings, and Mrs. Tampa introduced me to him and his wife. Someone told

Sonny Boy that I was a piano player, and he asked me if I would run down a few numbers with him, and I said, "Sure—I'd be glad to." So we ran down those few numbers, and when Lester Melrose came, Sonny Boy told him, "Man—I'd like to have this man on the piano with me." So from then on it was he and I!

My first session was done for Vocalion—around 1937, I'd say. I was recording with either Sonny Boy Williamson or Dr. Clayton. Sometimes I'd have five or six to record with. Anyway—I was just monkeying around with the piano, and this fellow who was from New York heard me sing and heard me do a few things—and John Hammond was there, and they asked Lester Melrose, "Les—why don't you let him record?" I didn't have any idea I'd get to make a record for myself—because I was playing for all the other artists.

My father had all these speakeasies, but he had a day job—he was a molder by trade—and he and Big Bill worked at the foundry together. They worked together for five or six years at the Griffin Wheel Foundry. And they and my uncle and cousins used to pool—ride in the car together. So Bill and I met when I was quite young because he would be at my father's place—Lester Melrose and Big Bill. See, they both were working on the W.P.A., and Lester Melrose got Bill interested in recording. And after Bill started making records, he asked me about it—and I made some records with him. And from then on I was Big Bill's musician. You know, Big Bill used to be a little minister [*laughs*]. Anyway, Big Bill was the first one who carried me to Europe—I was the first blues piano player to play Europe. I've been to Europe—this coming September will be thirty-three times! Sometimes I was there four and five times a year! My favorite color is green, and they talk my language!

Dr. Clayton was born in Africa, and he was a fellow that never talked too much about himself. Oh, my God!—that man had a beautiful voice for all kind of classic numbers—a lovely voice. He had a beautiful voice and could ad-lib, and he was a good entertainer, but he let drinking get the best of him. He was in kind of a pitiful state. And he caught double pneumonia.

I knew Sunnyland before I knew Dr. Clayton. I played piano for Sunnyland when he first came to Chicago—because he wasn't in the union. St. Louis Jimmy—no, I never worked with St. Louis Jimmy, but we were quite good friends. And Jazz Gillum—oh, God, yes! I worked with Jazz Gillum on his first recordings. No—I never met Leroy Carr. When I first heard his recording of "How Long, How Long Blues," I think I was about fifteen—and I liked it! You see, "How Long, How Long Blues" was originally a slow song they called "Jailhouse Blues," and it didn't have the type of bass that Leroy Carr put with it. It was fabulous, and it really gave me a great lift! I imagine Clarence Williams or Jellyroll Morton—I imagine all those guys did it—but Leroy put a brand new suit on it, and I wouldn't be surprised if it didn't sell up in the millions because every place you went you heard it.

There was one fellow I couldn't play with—I had to refuse—that was Arthur Cruddup—Big Boy Cruddup! He made a lot of nice numbers, but I just couldn't work with him because he had no conception of chord formation—or anything like that.

The first time I met Billy Boy Arnold—he knew I lived on the West Side—he was a boy, I guess about thirteen or fourteen. His father's buddy had a vegetable truck. There was a fellow who lived around the corner on Maple—I lived on Leavitt Street. Billy asked Mr. Upchurch, "Do you know Blind John?" And Mr. Upchurch said, "Oh, yeah—I know that boy ever since he was two or three years old"—and he did. My family had a coal business, and he told him where my people's coal business was located. He went over there and asked my uncle about me, and my uncle pointed my house out to him. So he came over and introduced himself to me. We talked, and he told me he was interested in the harp and asked if he could come around. I told him, "Sure!" And after he started coming around me, his dad would be looking for him to sell vegetables—and he would be sitting up in my house [*laughs*]. We struck friendship since he was just a child.

Me and a boy named Leander Walker—he was going to Crane College—he was a trumpet player. So we got together and we started talking. I said, "Hey Lee—why don't we get us up a band?" He said, "That don't sound bad—OK!" We started sing with different fellows, and we got a guy on saxophone named Ray Flemming. Oh, he was great—he was another Johnny Hodges. We had Leander on trumpet, David Lane on guitar, Bill Stevens on drums, and August Beck on bass. We had a great group! I was booked by Fredrick Bros Incorporated—and I was on the road with my band for about eight years straight! We traveled from the late 1930s until that Japanese war was over—that was 1946. We played all kinds of pretty music. We mostly played for white audiences all the time—they wanted songs like "Red Wing"—stuff like that, you know? We played standard blues—things like "Basin Street," "Wabash Blues," "Memphis Blues"—that kind of stuff. And back then guys would laugh if two guys started taking a solo at the same time—"What do you think you're playing, Dixieland?" But mostly all those boys are passed now—they'd be surprised how Dixieland has come back. We never were lucky enough to record together; I've regretted that many a time.

Then I did recordings of myself with MGM. That was for Walter Melrose. You know, there were three brothers over there—Lester had another brother that was a pretty fair piano player, barrelhouse piano player—Frank Melrose, their baby brother. He was killed out in Calumet City. But I never had the opportunity to meet him because he got wasted before I joined up with the organization. Walter Melrose contacted me around 1949. I cut about three records—six sides.

Well, I'll tell you something—it's a pity what some of these guys out here do to music. It sounds like they're hitting the drums with the piano leg—and each one of them's got a big amplifier! Oh, God!—but they're selling . . .

Arbee **Stidham**

Arbee Stidham was not your stereotypical blues singer. He had a "pop" hit record that registered with the blues crowd. It was the only hit of his career, and it came at the tail end of the Lester Melrose era—the two or three years after World War II. By the 1980s, when I conducted this interview, he was no longer performing. His hit "My Heart Belongs to You" was the single recording under his name available to record collectors of the era. There was very little background information available on him or his career. But he was still alive—and listed in the Chicago phonebook—so I simply called and invited him to come down to the studio and tell me his story. It seems unlikely that any one person could save Bessie Smith, lasso runaway houses, and pal around with Elvis, but it was his story to tell—and here it is. . . .

Arbee Stidham. Photo courtesy The O'Neal Collection.

This interview was recorded September 4, 1981. Arbee Stidham died April 26, 1988.

■ ■ ■

I was born in DeValls Bluff, Arkansas, February 9, 1917. My family on my father's side was all musicians. There were three brothers, Lutie, Ernest, and Isaiah.

They had a band down there, and they played all down through there. Isaiah was a violinist—he was a great violinist, but it was too early for guys like that to be recognized at that time. Ernest was playing a coronet. Lutie, my father, was playing slide trombone. Two of the boys left—Ernest and Lutie—and they settled in Memphis, which was ninety miles from DeValls Bluff. When they went to Memphis, they graduated to alto saxes. That's where I began to go and watch them play whenever I could sneak away. That's when I decided to play the saxophone. Well, the first thing I really played was clarinet that was given to me by a merchant in DeValls Bluff. That's what I learned to play, and after I learned to play clarinet, then I went to the saxophone. I always loved blues. It's a thing that just came up in me. They didn't call blues *blues* when I was a boy—they called them *reels*. My Mother used to tell me, "You're singing those reels. You don't do nothing but sing those reels—and you're going to hell. There ain't no way for you to go to heaven singing those reels." But I was kind of like that song, "I'm going to sing those reels anyhow." So I kept on singing them. I had a hard time with her. She put me out of the house—she took my records. I'd ordered these records. The only records I would be interested in were Louis Armstrong and things on that kick. The rest of them were blues like Bessie Smith, Mamie Smith, Sara Martin, Blind Blake, Tampa Red, and Georgia Tom—all those guys. Those are the only thing I was interested in. And then she'd take my records away from me. My grandfather would steal them back and give them right back to me. So the only way I could get away with playing them was late at night. You wind that Victrola up, you know, and then you push that button and the volume would be low. But then she'd hear me and get up and confiscate my records—and then my grandfather would have to steal them back for me [*laughs*]. She threatened to kill him when he took me to Little Rock and bought me the first saxophone. I had the saxophone two or three months before she knew it. The only way she knew it then was they built a place down there for basketball and they hired us to play. The only way she knew that I was playing a saxophone was she had to go to the doctor. The doctor's office was right above this place, and when they got close, she heard this music and she asked my father, "Who is that in there? Stop this car right now." She got out of the car and came in, and there I was, playing saxophone. Man, was she mad! She went back out. She made my father sleep in another room that night. So when I got home, she always would leave my dinner in this pot that she'd hang up so I could eat when I came in. So when I got in that night, I didn't have no pot hanging up there [*laughs*], so I had to go to bed hungry. Papa got up early the next morning. He woke me up early and said, "You get up and get out of here"—because she had switches this long. I was a big boy then, and she was going to beat me to death [laughs], and when she got up, I was gone! And when I made my first appearance with my band at the Ninth Street Theater, she came in. She never sat down. When I came down off the stage, she grabbed me and hugged me and kissed me. She said, "I'm proud of you in a way, but you're still going to hell singing those reels."

Dr. Jordan and His Mighty Minstrels originated from Arkansas. At that particular time my father was playing saxophone in a band for Dr. Jordan. Bessie Smith came through DeValls Bluff. She was opening at the Ninth Street Theater in Little Rock, and she was looking for my father. There was a guy there that knew me and knew that I had this band. He was a white fellow, and he thought an awful lot of me. I was playing for them just like my father and my uncle had before me. Bessie wanted my father, Lutie, to go with her and open with her in Little Rock. But this white guy told her, "Lutie's not around but he's got a son that can play saxophone just like him." I was living across the tracks, as usual, and they sent across the tracks for me to come downtown. Bessie talked to me and told me if I could get to Little Rock to make rehearsal, I could play with her for a few nights. So she hired me and let me play. At that particular time there was Bessie, Mamie, and Sara Martin. Just like they package different artists for shows now, they did that back then. Back then, the top artists would choose who else they would like to have work with them. Bessie was regarded not only as a great singer but also as a way-back fashion plate. She wore some clothes, man! And that helped put her over. I mean, she could sing the blues—no doubt about it. But a lot of the high fashions you see today, Bessie Smith was wearing it then!

At that time she had an old guy with her—Clarence Williams—on piano. Also, Miles Martin on violin. Clarence used to make me come back home when it was time to go to school—because all I wanted to do was play music. I didn't want to come back. I didn't want to go to school. I just wanted to play music. But at that time you had to do what you were told to do. There was a chorus line, and Bessie protected me from the girls in that chorus line. She couldn't have protected her own son better than she did me from seeing what went on in that troupe. I never did witness all that went on. I didn't know anything about it because she saw to it that I didn't know. That's what she had promised my grandfather—and she kept her promise.

During the 1927 flood, that's when Bessie Smith made "High-Water Blues." I was about sixteen I guess. I was working for a game warden down there. I knew how to handle a boat, and I knew how to get around on the river—the White River was down there. It was just like the Mississippi River—long, deep, and wide. The Arkansas Game and Fish Commission had two boats, and they were fast as lightning. I operated one of these boats. It was equipped just like an automobile. They had big six Studebaker motors in them. Ignition—forward—reverse—sit up in the seats with a steering wheel. It was a beautiful boat. What happened was the levee broke and houses were just swept off their foundations and would float down the White River—sometimes going five or ten miles an hour. That's just how swift the river was carrying a whole house. You'd see people up on top of the houses yelling for help, yelling, "Save me!" It was a pitiful thing. The law, we called him the Town Clown, he came over. He said to me, "You're the only somebody who can handle a boat in that type of water." He said, "I've got to take him—I have no choice." So they took me to the boat. I'd chase these houses as they traveled downstream. I'd swing the boat close to a house and start slowing the boat down. When you get close, you get a rope on it. And you'd hold that boat next to the house until you got those people off the top of the house and into the boat. Then you'd snatch the line loose and that house would take off down the river.

I was ready to leave Arkansas and come right here to Chicago, and that's what I did. That's when I began to meet the guys here in Chicago that I heard on records and never had met—guys like Big Bill Broonzy, Tampa Red, Washboard Sam, Josh Altheimer, and all those guys like that. Also I met Sonny Boy Williamson—Johnny Lee, not Rice Miller—also Big Joe Williams—not Joe Williams who was with Count Basie, Big Joe Williams that played nine-string guitar. Those are the guys that I met. I would follow them around and listen to them, but I couldn't get in on anything. After I was here a while I met Fletcher Henderson and Horace Henderson, and as the song said, "That when I got a break." Fletcher was still leading a big band at that time and beating out the tune "Christopher Columbus." I would go down and sit in when they'd rehearse down at the Ritz. He decided I could play and begged me to get a group of my own, you know, a bunch of young guys, and get these guys together and organize another band here in Chicago—and that's what I did. The first gig I had with that was at the 5400 Club, at 5400 Broadway. I fooled with that a while and then I dropped it. The way it happened was one night on the West Side. A fellow I had known for a number of years from traveling around was playing there. He played tenor saxophone, a guy by the name of T. S. Mimms. He called me up to do a few numbers with him, and Lester Melrose happened to be in the audience. Melrose asked me if I wanted to make a record. I told him yes. I didn't pay it any attention because I had that so much—guys were always offering to record me, and I'd never hear any more from them. I had a habit—I was a hell of a reckless driver, and I'd get out here on these streets and I'd raise more cane than a little. I was always getting traffic tickets—nothing but speeding—but they'd grab me and take me to jail. So Melrose came to the house one evening, and he was an Irishman, and so, naturally, my wife thought he was a cop. So when I finally came home, she said to me, "What did you do today?" I said, "Nothing." She said, "Oh, yes, you did, because a great big policeman's been looking for you twice." I said, "Honest to God, I haven't done a thing wrong today." "So you didn't get a ticket?" "Nope!" "You didn't run from the police and outrun them?" "No!"—and just about that time the doorbell rang. It was him and she went up and answered the door and came back and said, "That cop's out there looking for you." [*Laughs.*] I went to the door and "Ahhh, Mr. Melrose!" [*Laughs.*] "Come in!" He came in, and I told her who he was. Melrose said, "I'm ready to do a session on you. Have you got any songs?" "Sure, I've got five or six!" I didn't have one! He said, "Do you think you'd be ready to do a session if we rehearsed the rest of the week?" Now, that was on about Wednesday, so I had to sit down and write those songs. I sat down one night and wrote four songs. So after the rehearsal was over he approached me and said, "I want to buy one of those songs." The number was titled "I Found Out for Myself." At that time I had Tampa Red, Bob Call, Ransom Knowling, and Judge Riley, that was the RCA Victor house band. I said, "No, I wouldn't sell you that song, but I'll tell you what I will do. I'll sell you the other tune, 'My Heart Belongs to You.'" He said, "No—I wouldn't give you a quarter for that." Bob Call grabbed me and took me into another room and said, "Don't sell him that one, Arbee, that's going to be a hit. Don't sell that song." I said, "That tune's nothing. I just wrote that at the last second. I had three done and needed one more, and I wrote that in just a couple of minutes." "Don't sell him that record!" So, OK, they released the record "My Heart Belongs to You." When it was released, they sent it to Zenas Sears in Atlanta, Georgia, WGST. He played it one night, and they flooded the station with calls. Zenas calls Gene Noble in Nashville and told Gene what happened. Gene played it, and they had 181 requests to play it that night on Gene Noble's radio show. This is the way "My Heart Belongs to You" got started. The funny part about all this—I knew nothing about trade magazines. I'd never made a record, so what did I know about it? And music is slow, so I'd taken a job at Wendigo Construction, at 600 West Twenty-Second Street, as a torch man. I was gigging at night and working days as a torch man. So Lester Melrose called me one night and said, "When can I see you?" "I've got to work tomorrow." So he says, "Can I come over tomorrow after work and see you?" "Sure." "Well, in the meantime, take a look at *Billboard* [a music trade magazine]." What I thought he was talking about was the big billboard they had up at the elevated train station—that's what I thought it was. And on this billboard was a woman kneeling down drinking scotch! [*Laughs.*]

So I went and took a look and went back home and called him: "Man, there's nothing there but a big picture of a woman kneeling down drinking scotch." You should have heard him laugh! He said, "Stidham—do you have a quarter? Go back up there to the station to the newspaper stand and tell the man who works at the newsstand to sell you a copy of *Billboard*. I'm going to hold the phone!" I was at 4741 South Prairie, so I just walked to the corner to the station and bought the magazine. When I got back, the phone was still off the hook, and he was waiting. He said, "You are listed in *Billboard*. Turn to page so and so." I turned to that page. "Look at the top of the page where it says R and B. You see where it lists your name? That's because you made a good record. You are #1 in *Billboard*! I have a contract from Gale Agency [an entertainment booking agency]. I'll be by your work tomorrow." And that's where I signed the contract with the Gale Agency to go on the road. After "My Heart Belongs to You" became such a big hit, Lucky Millinder took me over and we did "Your Heart Belongs to Me." "Stidham's Jump" and other sides were made under the supervision of Lucky Millinder in New York City. Now, the other recordings made for RCA Victor were done right here in Chicago. Lucky Millinder was working for RCA Victor then, and Lucky selected me from all the artists RCA had. I was the only one he wanted to record. So that's how I got hooked up with him. One of the guys who played with me was Hal "Cornbread" Singer—also Mundell Lowe, Tab Smith, Sir Charles Thompson, and several others.

The Sittin' In With record label was in Atlanta, Georgia. I was appearing at the Royal Peacock in Atlanta. Steve Shoals was the president of RCA Victor when they gave up the race music. He flew into Atlanta, and he told me they were discarding the blues line. After he told me I was talking to Cecil Gant along with Johnny Martin, a disc jockey at WERD in Atlanta. We were all drinking. After our conversation, Johnny told Bob Shad about RCA dumping their race records. Bob asked Johnny if anybody in Atlanta had been on RCA, and Johnny told him I had been on RCA. Bob Shad said, "Where in the world is he?" So Johnny sent Bob Shad over to me at the Savoy Hotel, 239 Auburn. He said, "Hey—do you want to make a recording session for me?" So then I had to write some more songs before I could leave Atlanta because he wanted to record those songs at WGRT in Atlanta. That's where we recorded the next big hit, which was "Nothing Seems Right."

Most of the musicians, I met them. Louis Jordan is from down in Arkansas. He was about six miles from me at Wheatley, Arkansas. I did meet Jim Jackson, who made "Kansas City Blues," one of my favorite numbers—"I'm goin' to Kansas City, honey, where they don't allow you." When I was going to school, the little girls would make me mad; I'd sing this to little girls who quit me. She'd send me a note, "I'm up in the cherry tree turning round and round, I'm not say quittin' but I'm just jumpin' down." A little girl wrote me that note. She's here in Chicago now! [*Laughs.*] She wrote me that note, and I went around the school singing "I'm going to Kansas City!"

I had the privilege to meet Jimmy Yancy, but I never met Crippled Clarence. I met Pinetop Smith, but I never met him in Chicago. He used to go on tour. I got as far as Texas when I was playing with Bessie, and that's when I met Pinetop Smith. I met Charlie Spand, too. He had the tune "Soon This Morning." I saw Blind Blake and before Charlie Christian joined Benny Goodman; I met Charlie out there, too. Blind Lemon Jefferson, the one in Texas, I know where he's buried because John Lee Hooker took me to see his grave. I was in Lubbock, Texas, and we went up to see his grave. Dr. Clayton? I knew him and I liked him. He called me his son. He loved his alcohol. If I had known he was in the speakeasy the night that I went looking for him, I probably would have saved his life, because he froze to death in a ditch right behind that place. And when I did go out, I walked right by him—and didn't know it until later. I never will forget this, the day I was sitting in my living room. I just came from Joe Hughes on Sixty-Third Street. We were out all night because I wasn't working. That was when Japan bombed Pearl Harbor and they had released that record. Somehow, they got it out and got it to the radio stations in Chicago here. And after they announced they bombed Pearl Harbor that's when Clayton came out with this thing, "The Japanese flew over Pearl Harbor, dropping bombs by the ton." And you know Sunnyland Slim and Clayton—they were the best of buddies—Sunny and Doc. Sunny could sing just like him, and he mocks him every once in a while now.

I got sick of Chicago and went down to Memphis and goofed off with Presley for—I don't know how long. The biggest thing we did was goof off together. He'd always come by and stay at the house. You know, he couldn't have any privacy at his house, and he got tired of people. And after he knew me and found out—this was after I started playing harmonica again, and Presley loved harmonica! He never had a harmonica in his band, but he'd sit and listen to me play it all day if I'd play. We used to get in the car. He'd get somebody to drive, and he and I would just play harmonica. I'd play harmonica for him, and we'd drive all over Memphis, Tennessee. We'd go into places to eat, and they didn't want to serve me until he snatched his dark glasses off. Then they wanted to feed me when they found out I was riding around with Elvis Presley. I had a friend who lived right across the street on Elvis Presley Boulevard—it ran right by his house. He had a music store there, and I bought all my guitar strings and harmonicas and everything else right there at his store—Mike Ladd. We were over there one day and started jamming. Elvis happened to be at home this particular day, and that day I was playing guitar, jamming and clowning, and he heard that guitar and came over there and wanted to know who was playing. All the guys were in the back. So he came back and he introduced himself, and from then on, whenever he was in Memphis, we were together more than likely. Whenever he'd be traveling, sometime he'd stop over wherever I was to see me. That's how well I knew Elvis. And I have a dog right now that he gave me, Rocky. He brought him over one night. I was appearing up in Fayetteville, Arkansas. He came by this particular night. It was raining like mad and he had this towel under his arm and he brought me this little dog in the towel. I still have him.

I was a little disgusted after I had to give the saxophone up. I don't play it anymore because I hemorrhage when I blow. I wasn't doing much of anything because I was despondent. My wife told me one day, "You sit around and you look like you don't have a friend in the world. You can't play a saxophone. Couldn't you play a guitar?" What was she talking about—I didn't know how to play a guitar. "Well, you could always try—you learned to play a saxophone." I told her I'd think about, but I didn't think any more about it [*laughs*]. I was sitting in the room one night, just sitting there. My wife said, "Do you want to talk to me?" "Yeah—I'll talk to you. What do you want to talk about?" "Do me a favor. You've got some money here that you've been hiding. I know where it is—it's under the corner of the rug. Why don't you take some of that money, go down to Wurlitzer, and get a guitar? Get one of those guitars, bring it back, and you can learn to play it." So the next morning I went down to Wurlitzer's, walked in and was looking at guitars. My wife thought I was going to get an acoustic guitar, but I walked right by that. I always did have a champagne taste and a beer pocketbook. I walked down to Epiphone and Gibson, the popular guitars. Man, they had a pretty blonde Epiphone. I took one look at that thing and said, "That's me! I'm going to get that." I told the guy what I wanted, and he said, "You know, you've got to get the amplifier with that." I said, "Yeah, I want it all." He set it out and told me what it cost. "I haven't got that much money—I can go by home and get it." He said, "Are you working anywhere?" "Yeah—I'm at Wendigo Construction here in Chicago." "Well, wait just a minute." He called and then came back. "You don't have to go home—you can just take the guitar with you." At that time during the 1950s, that guitar costs me $500 then. I'd never had one in my hand! I went walking in and set it down in the room at home. My wife looked at it, but she didn't pay it too much attention at first—until I put the bill on the bed. When I put the bill on the bed, that's when we went to war! "Oh, my God! Why didn't I go with you?" Now,

Big Bill had one he played overseas, because at that time you couldn't play a box from here overseas unless you had a device to change the current. Now, Bill finds out that I've got the guitar. Bill was a hell of a guitar player, and so Bill came over. Bill, Tampa, Maceo, they were all coming over to see a guitar like that. They all wanted to get their hands on that guitar and play with it. My wife says to me, "You've got to learn to play this thing." I said, "No—I'm going to take it back." She and Big Bill were very tight, and she called Bill. "Bill said, "NO—he's not going to take it back." Big Bill knew the guy that I bought the guitar from. Bill went down—he didn't call him—he went down and talked to the guy. He said, "Now when he comes back tell him you'll give him $50 for it." I went in with the guitar and he told me—and I told him, "Man, you got to be crazy! I'll take it back home and set it in the corner and let it stay!" "That's what you'll have to do because the best I can give you for it is $50." So I got back home with it, and Big Bill came. He used to call me Little Boy. "Well, Little Boy, get that thing out and let's see what we can do with it." I got it out and Boom-Boom-Boom. I couldn't play a thing on it. Bill said, "You'll have to read your book." And then he began to show me different chords. I got to the place I could make them. But then when I got into the thing, I didn't want anything that would hurt my hands—and that's what it was doing, naturally: it was making my hands sore—and that's when I knew I was going to give it away! My wife told me one night, "I've got news for you. You're going to play that thing or I'm going to hook the guitar around your neck and you're going to wear it for a watch fob—one or the other!" [*Laughs.*] Then I got down to it, and I began to practice like mad.

Bill came by, and he'd been borrowing it. He came by, and I was playing a record and trying to play along with it. I noticed him sitting up smiling. That night he called me: "Hey, Little Boy—I got to borrow your guitar, but I need you to come along and set it up." I didn't catch on. "Come on out, get out of the house. I've got a job over there." He had taken a job over at the Zanzibar, Sixteenth Street and Ashland, but he took it for me—not for him. He'd been trying to get me to play in public, but I wouldn't do it. He talked with the manager over at the Zanzibar and told him what he was trying to do. We went over and I hooked the guitar up, and we sat and had a few drinks. Bill said, "Hold on—I've got to go to the bathroom." So he went to the bathroom and he never came back! The rest of the boys showed up. They had a boy there named Pie Face: he was a heck of a piano man. But Bill didn't show. When time to start came, the boys played a few tunes, but then the manager came up and said, "Wait a minute here boys—where's your guitar player? I'm paying for a guitar player, but I don't see one up there. If you want to get your money, you better get a guitar player up there." So the boys were saying to me, "Hey—come on." And I was saying, "No! You're not going to get me up there and make a fool out of myself. I can't play guitar good enough to be in public." "Oh, yes, you can. You come on up here." The manager spoke up: "I'm going to tell you one thing—you better just get up there and hold it!" [*Laughs.*] "Because if you don't, these guys aren't going to get any money. Suit yourself!" I was feeling bad, but I was mad enough at Bill to kill him. So I got up there and did just what he told me: I took that guitar and held it. Finally, the manager came back and said, "Hold it, fellows. I can't have this junk. I'm paying for a guitar player, and I don't have one. I'm a man short, and you're going to be looking for your money. I'm going to have to call you down." Everybody was in on this but me. The fellows in the band got pitiful, "Arbee, if you just play a little bit. Play whatever you can play on it. That way we can get paid." Then I started making chords on the guitar, and once I started making the chords, it all fell in place. I could feel it. Then I started making a few runs, and once they got me started, we were all right. Bill had a black Cadillac parked right by the door. I looked up, and Bill's stepping out of this black Cadillac. The guys that owned the place were holding up their hands. I played the rest of that gig. [*Laughs.*] I've been playing guitar and harmonica ever since.

Collenane **Cosey**

One of the most popular artists in rhythm and blues was Louis Jordan. During a sixteen-year span (1938–1954) with the Decca label, Louis recorded more than two hundred sides—including more than forty hit recordings. In 1992, Bear Family, a German record label, released an eight-CD set with everything that Louis recorded for Decca. One night on the program I played a side from the set called "Ration Blues," and the phone rang immediately. The voice on the other end said, "You know, my mother wrote that song, "Ration Blues," and we've been trying for years to find a copy of it. She wrote the tune, but we never owned a copy of the record." The guy on the phone was Pete Cosey, a well-known guitar player on the Chicago scene whose studio work crossed genre—from Etta James, Fontella Bass, and Minnie Riperton to Miles Davis and Herbie Hancock. He also had the misfortune to be the guitarist on a series of landmark blues misfires produced by Marshall Chess as he attempted to update the sound and the audience for a pair of the Chess label's classic blues performers, Muddy Waters and Howling Wolf. Pete explained that his mother entered a songwriting contest sponsored by the Decca label. His mother submitted the song "Ration Blues" and won the contest. We made arrangements to send his mother a taped copy of her winning tune, and she agreed to come on the air and tell the story of the whole episode.

Collenane Cosey died in 2010 at age one hundred.

Record label for "Ration Blues." Photo courtesy Steve Cushing.

■ ■ ▪

I was writing songs before, ballads, and I did a lot of things for school—silly songs for kids. I'm sort of a potboiler. I go from the sublime to the ridiculous. My husband was a musician. Originally, he was a violinist, but there was no money in that, so he asked his dad if he could switch over to saxophone—which he did. He traveled all over the world. He spent half his life over in Europe. He played with Jimmie Noone—he even played with Duke one time. He was with Red Saunders for a long time. He used to play with Earl Hines. He didn't do too much recording. As I say, he was in European jazz clubs. They liked that hot jazz. He knew Django Reinhardt and those people. There was a contest. Decca Records held a contest. It was through the *Chicago Defender*. There was an ad and an application for the contest. Louis Jordan wanted a new song. He'd had so many hits, and he was looking for something new. So this was very timely. It was during World War II, during the time of rationing—everything was being rationed. Everything was in short supply—meat, potatoes, coffee, sugar, gas. We had these little tokens and you could get so much meat—forty ounces of meat. That had to last you a week and then you'd get a bunch of tokens for the next forty ounces. You hear that in the words to the song. So I went to this store searching all over Chicago trying to get some meat for my family, and there was none. I went into a neighborhood store—a foreign neighbor—and tried to get some meat. In very broken English this lady said, "We don't wait on strangers." Here I am, a stranger in my own hometown. It was the same with the sugar and everything else. In the meantime, this contest was announced. So I put all these things together and made fun of the whole darn thing

I didn't write blues. My husband taught me how to write blues. What I had would never have passed I'm sure: it was too tame. When he gave me the idea, I sat down on the streetcar one morning when I was going to work and wrote it on the streetcar in about fifteen minutes.

The thoughts were all building up, and I put them into words. I sent that in as my song. It took about a week or ten days for them to get back to me and tell me my song was the winner. There were seventy-five contestants, and they called me and said I'd won. The prize was a $75 bond and the contract. I was supposed to get a ninth of a ninth on that particular record—if you can imagine how much that would be. I only got one payment from them, and I was so disgusted with the whole thing I said the hell with it. Another thing—at that time the records were made of rubber, and there weren't enough. The stores had a backlog of two and three thousand in every store. Nobody could get it. It was just sold out. It was listed in *Downbeat* and *Billboard* for I don't know how many weeks, but the shortage of material made the record unavailable. That's how that particular one came about—"The Ration Blues."

Did you get any other work from that?

Eddie "Cleanhead" Vinson asked to have some songs done, which I did—"Luxury Tax Blues," that also was in the offing—I wrote that one and "Bonus Pay." My brother-in-law was a songwriter, and we worked together on that one. "Gal, You Need a Whippin'"—I did that one because I had heard somebody beating up his wife—like I say, I'm a potboiler. I take an idea and build around it. We'd had a little record company going at the time, the Cool label; Louis Jordan got the "Gal, You Need a Whippin'." We recorded it with a fellow named Beard—Harold Beard. He did a fine job of it. Louis Jordan was slated to pose for the publicity picture and give us a send-off. Next thing I know, he took it and jumped the gun on us. The company wanted me to write for them, but I was so angry about what they did, I just forgot about it. I sued them and got a few paltry dollars out of it [*laughs*]. I actually did a song that I was going to give to Bing Crosby. It was called "Boogie-Woogie Popcorn Man," but like I said, I was just disgusted. I've got plenty of songs—they're just buried. One thing—I'm really glad Pete listened to your program and heard the record. It means I finally have a copy after all these years. . . .

Roosevelt **Sykes**

Roosevelt Sykes was a blues original, a pianist who was not so much a piano technician but a singer/songwriter who happened to play piano. His true strength was as a composer of blues lyric. During his forty-year career (1929–1977) he recorded more than four hundred sides—including such classics as "44 Blues," "Sail On, Little Girl," "Highway 61," "Night Time Is the Right Time," "Sunny Road," "47th Street Jive," and many more. His lyrics were often wry reflections on blues life and black life in general—"D.B.A. [Damned Black Ass] Blues," "3–6 & 9 Blues" (known as "the Shit Roll," for you numbers players), and "Under-Eyed Woman"—all classics of the blues environment. He served as influence to other notable bluesmen, including Memphis Slim, Sunnyland Slim, and Eddie Boyd. In December 1981 the Jazz Institute of Chicago decided to present a blues piano double bill, featuring both Little Brother Montgomery and Roosevelt Sykes, at the Blackstone Hotel. This was a mistake, if you wanted to see Sykes at his best. Little Brother was by far the better pianist technically. Sykes was only too aware of this and was always intimidated by having to appear back to back with Brother. It put a real damper on his breezy performance persona—but it did bring him to town. I made arrangements to pick

Roosevelt Sykes. Photo courtesy the Robert G. Koester Collection.

him up at the Blackstone that afternoon and bring him to the studio for an interview. He was just putting on the finishing touch, splashing on some English Leather when I showed up. Roosevelt was fun to talk with in the studio. I remember that as we sat across a table from each other, he would reach over, emphasizing a point by pecking his index finger into the back of my hand and speaking in hushed tones, as though he were confiding personal secrets that never before had been told. I recall that at one point in the conversation I ask him about being a Muslim: there was a popular social trend among African Americans during the 1930s, when many converted, at least temporarily, to Islam. Sykes had at one point adopted the name Roosevelt Sykes Bey and had a PR photo sporting a turban. He immediately danced back from this subject and refused to answer any further questions about it—a curious reaction to a benevolent question. Sykes's career was so long that, as an interview host, I didn't know quite where to start. This interview is short—but short as it is, it's one of my favorites.

This interview was recorded in December 1981. Roosevelt Sykes died July 17, 1983.

■ ■ ▪

I was born in 1906 in West Helena, Arkansas; that's where I was raised at. It's on the west side of the river, ninety miles south of Memphis. My auntie was a little type of pianist. I could hit some chords. My granddaddy had an organ, and I would always work on that when I was twelve or thirteen years old. But I couldn't play what they did around the joints. When I got older, I got a chance to see these fellows playing the joints and watch what they did. I saw a guy by the name of Jesse Bell, and I took his piano style. He was just a regular guy, and his club was right in the neighborhood. Everybody around there would try to play that style. It was a gambling house with a lot of tables in there—tables for gambling, not for drinking. So I saw Jesse Bell, and I liked his style. Of course, it was a long time before I could get in the joint, so I stood by the door, and every time two or three would go in there, I'd get a chance to see in there. It was a swinging door, and I could see way in there. But after I got a little older—say, about eighteen—they said, "Well, you can come in here now. In fact, we'll give you a job. You want to play here?" Ever since I was thirteen years old, I stayed on the road and I didn't need no train fare. If a train came along and it was going where I wanted to go, I'd just hop on it. Nobody would bother me. That's how I traveled a lot and met all kinds of people and learned a lot. I'd hop freight trains to different parts of the country.

What can you tell me about Lee Green?

That Lee Green was a great guy. He was a great piano player, and he wasn't much older than me. We were great friends, and we'd run together all the time, and then he started getting in on some of the same stuff I was trying to play. He died. He was running, trying to catch a train, and he got too tired. He ran in about four or five or ten coaches down. When he did finally get on he was panting, trying to catch his breath, and he died.

Did you know Jesse Johnson well?

Jesse Johnson had a music store, and there was a big theater right in front of his store—the Booker Washington Theater, I think it was, in St. Louis. This was in 1929. He'd sell records and play records in the store. He had a piano in there, and every time I'd go by, I'd play a piece. He was a talent scout for the OKeh record label. And when I'd play, he'd come by and say, "Hey, that's all right. You play pretty good. Play it again like that." So I played, and he said, "I'm going to see if I can't get you a recording in New York." And I said, "Noooo—not no records. I can't play good enough for that. There's too many good people playing. I'd be ashamed." [*Laughs.*] But he talked me into it. He said, "You come over here Monday and I'll get the tickets and take the train and go to New York." So we stayed there and recorded. Back in those days, there weren't any tape recorders so you could hear yourself. You couldn't hear the way you sound. But they played the record back, and I said, "That's how I sound—that's me." It was strange: "That's the way I talk? That's the way I sound? That's me!" It sounded funny to me, and I thought, "Wow—that sounds kind of lonesome—like somebody died or something." And Jesse was saying, "That's good, Roosevelt—people are going to buy that!" I just said, "I been playing that ever since I was a kid." I made four numbers. The first I made was "The Forty-Four Blues"—and it was a big hit!

Who wrote, "The Forty-Four Blues"?

Who started it? Well now, that's impossible to say. They call it "Forty-Four Blues"—there weren't any words to it. When I heard it, I learned it and I wrote words to it. "I walked all night"—I wrote that myself and sang it. When Little Brother made his, it was the "Vicksburg Blues"—it wasn't "The Forty-Four Blues." But they don't know where it came from—no, they don't know. It's just like the sun: it wasn't there, and all of a sudden there it is—and it looks good. They don't know where it came from, but it's there. They can tell you, but they don't know—Noooo!

I see in the discography that you played behind Edith Johnson on record. What can you tell me about that?

Edith Johnson—that's Jesse Johnson's wife. She made records, and when she recorded, I played piano behind her on "The Honey Dripper." That's why they call me the Honey Dripper. She made "The Honey Dripper," but I was the piano player on it. And they started calling *me* the Honey Dripper—and that's the professional name I have today from way back. Edith said, "You aren't supposed to be the Honey Dripper." She wrote the words, but I played the piano on it. That's why they call me that—schoolkids and everything. Now, if someone's got a piece of candy or he's eating some ice cream and he calls me the Honey Dripper, I say, "Yeah, man—what do you want?" But if he hasn't got anything, I say, "Call me Roosevelt, that's my name."

That was just one of the names that you used down through the years . . .

And then there's Easy Papa Johnson—that was tricky, you know? My nickname was Dobby—and my grandfather's name was Bragg, so on the record they used the name Dobby Bragg. And I had a brother named Willie Kelly. My father had got another woman named Kelly that he was going with before he met my mother. So when I got up big enough to make records, I had a contract with this record company and another contract with another record company; I said I'm going to make my name on this contract Willie Kelly.

I saw a photo of you wearing a turban. Were you a sheik way back when?

Sheik was before that word sharp came out. That's a guy who dresses good all the time. You watch what you put on when you go out—you got your hair combed up and everything. Go out with your hair uncombed? Uh-uh! You got to comb your hair and shave and everything. That's what they mean when they say sharp—sharp means you're dressed. Sharp is the word these days; it means you stay well-dressed. That's what a sheik meant—you stay sharp all the time. "That cat stays sharp, man!" That means the same thing. People today don't really know that—but that's what that is. A lot of guys who were sheiks had women, and their women were prostitutes. They dressed well, and they had four or five women giving him their money. He'd tell those women what to do, and then he'd get in with somebody in the law and help the women out. He always knew what to do, where to go to get these women out if they got arrested.

When did you come to Chicago?

I came to Chicago about 1936, and I stayed here all the time. I left in 1962. The promoter would take us down to Tampa Red's and rehearse the songs. I knew Tampa well. We'd play together, and I'd go over to his house—me and Big Bill, we'd all rehearse at his house. He had a piano and kept it in good shape. Couldn't too many people play with me because I had my own style, but I could show whoever was in my band what to do. I took music lessons once in Chicago because I was planning to be a band leader and I wanted to know what to tell the people in my band what to do—B-flat, F-sharp, D minor—I wanted to know what those were, and I wanted to know so I could tell the guys and explain it to them. Then I could get my band sounding like I wanted. My teacher said, "Hit D-flat major!" And I said "I don't know . . ." and she said, "Hit that key right there—bap! That's it!" I say, "Well, I been playing that all the time." "Well, that's it." So all the things she showed me—I was already playing, but I didn't know the name of it. "What do you call it?" "I don't know." But I could play it. Lots of time I had my own band—other times I'd play with friends of mine. I had my band for a long time—about fifteen or twenty years. I had ten pieces, and we worked all over the country. December 22 will be fifty-two years in the music business for me.

Can you describe for folks today what the Cootie Crawl was?

That's a dance where people would be moving slow and dragging their feet—that's what they call the Cootie Crawl. But you'd dance slow with the girl—you wouldn't swing out like we do today. That's why you do it [*laughs*] because you're so close, you're almost one! [*Laughs.*]

Index

Abe Lincoln Hair Straightener, 128
Abrams, Sherman, 91
Aces, The, 36
Adams, Beryl, 115, 116, 122, 123
Adams, Jojo, 103, 105
African Methodist Episcopal (AME) Church, 76
AFTRA (American Federation of Television and Radio Artists), 85
Aimee Semple McPhearson Temple (Los Angeles), 71
Alcoholics Anonymous (AA), 112
Alexander, Robert, 167
Allen, Hortense, 138
All Nations Pentecostal Church, 88
Altheimer, Josh, 210
Amen (television program), 72
American Friendship Club, 157
Ammons, Albert, 124, 180
Ammons, Gene, 144
Amos 'n' Andy (radio program), 71, 72
Apollo Theater (New York), 30, 86, 108, 122
Archia, Tom, 105, 132
Aristocrat Records, 109
Armstrong Louis, 155, 179, 208
Arnie's (night club, Winona, MN), 127
Arnold, Billy Boy, 205
Ashby, Irving, 28
Ashley, Ernest, 115, 121, 122, 125
Assemblies of God, 92
Augie's (night club, Minneapolis), 128
Azusa Street Experience, 92

Baby Face Leroy, 198
Baby Grand Club, 108
Bailey, Bill, 137
Bailey, Pearl, 137
Bakker, Jimmy and Tammy, 92
Ball, Lucille, 138, 146
Barge, Gene, 89
Barnett, Charlie, 27
Barns, Emory, 49, 50, 69, 70, 72
Barry Brothers, The, 137
Bartel's (restaurant), 124
Basie, William "Count," 54, 104, 210
Basin Casino, 125, 152
Bass, Fontella, 217
Bass, Goodman, 146
Bass, Ralph, 141
Bates, Lefty, 103
Batista, Fulgencio, 32
Beard, Harold, 219
Bear Family Records, 217
Beck, August, 205
Bell, Jesse, 221
Bell, Mother, 83, 84
Below, Fred, 36, 39
Bennet, Tony, 26
Benson, Al, 89, 156
Berry, Ken, 147
Bethlehem Healing Temple (Chicago), 95
Bethune, Mary McLeod, 60
Biddy Mulligan's Blues Club, 39
Big Maceo Merriweather, 173, 198, 199, 215

Billboard magazine, 211, 212, 218
Black and White Records, 141
Blackstone Hotel, 180, 220, 221
Blackwell, Francis Scrapper, 19, 22
Blair, Archie, 165
Blake, Blind, 166, 190, 208, 213
Bland, Bobby Blue, 108
Bluebird Records, 168, 203
"Blues Before Sunrise" (song), 17, 20
Blues Before Sunrise (radio program), 17, 47, 131
Blues on Halsted, 170, 202
Blythe, Jimmy, 166
BMI (Broadcast Music Incorporated), 85
Bolden, Buddy, 163
Booker Washington Theater (St Louis), 222
Bostic, Joe, 97
Boyd, Eddie, 162, 175, 220
Bracken, Jimmy, 90
Bragg, Dobby, 223
Brass Rail (tavern, Chicago), 156, 178
Breckinridge, Paul, 53
Brim, John, 162
Brockman, Gale, 133
Bronzeville, 155
Broonzy, Big Bill, 16, 173, 204, 210, 214, 223
Brown, Hilliard, 115, 116, 125, 132
Brown Mule Chewing Tobacco, 13
Brunswick Records, 167
Bryant, Louise, 137, 146
Bryant, Willie, 155
Buck and Bubbles, 137, 154
Buckley, Dick (Chicago deejay), 25
Bumble Bee Slim, 18
Bunch, William (Peetie Wheatstraw), 19
Bunker Hill Music (Memphis), 10
Burns, George, 71
Burton, Cherie, 48
Butler, Jerry, 90
Butterbeans and Susie, 155, 186

C & A Hotel, 194
Calender, Red, 28
Call, Bob, 166, 211
Calloway, Cab, 154
Camp Meeting Choir, 104
Candacy, Miss, 169
Capital Lounge (Chicago), 123
Capital Records, 27, 32
Caravans, The, 91
Carnegie Hall, 97
Carol, Judy, 146
Carr, Leroy, 17, 19, 20, 23, 24, 204
Carr, Maureen, 22
Carter, Benny, 146
Carter, Bob, 145
Carter, Vivian, 90
Carver, George Washington, 59
Castel, Carlos, 28, 30
Cats 'n Jammers, 114, 115, 118, 121, 123, 125
Cayou, Red, 165
CBS Radio Network, 47, 58
CBS Television, 88
Charles, Ray, 26
Checkerboard Lounge (Chicago), 40
Chess, Leonard, 44, 89, 105, 106
Chess, Marshall, 212
Chess, Phil, 89
Chess Records, 88, 89, 109, 217
Chez Paree (night club, Chicago), 28, 31, 32, 33
Chicago Blues (film), 187
Chicago Defender, 155, 218
Chicago Theater, 154
Chicago White Sox, 31
Chilton and Thomas (Claire Chilton and Maceo Thomas) dance team, 154
Chitlin Circuit, 30
Chocolateers, 155
Christian, Charlie, 213
Chudd, Lew, 142
Church of God in Christ (COGIC), 75–78, 80, 81, 83, 84, 86, 88, 92, 93, 95

Civic Opera House Chicago, 106
Clark, Jimmy (Memphis Jimmy), 199, 200
Clayton, Buddy, 190
Clayton, Peter "Dr.," 171, 173–75, 198, 204, 213
Cleveland, Rev. James, 85
Club Congo, 156
Club DeLisa, 104, 105, 117, 119, 124, 132, 136, 137, 140, 142, 152, 153
Cokeliss, Harley, 187
Cole, Fats, 110
Cole, Marie, 28, 34
Cole, Nat King, 25, 26, 28, 69, 114, 124, 153
Coleman, George, 6
Coleman, Jesse "Monkey Joe," 168
Collins, John E., 28
Columbia Records, 96, 199
Comfort, Joe, 28
Committee 100, 157
Como, Perry, 29
Cook, Carol, 147
Cooke, Sam, 86, 89, 153
Cool Records, 219
Cooper, Ralph, 155
Cootie Crawl, the, 224
Copacabana (New York), 28, 32
Copenhagen snuff, 13
Corea, Chick, 29
Cosey, Collenane, 217
Cosey, Pete, 217, 219
Cotton, James, 41
Crosby, Bing, 219
Cruddup, Arthur "Big Boy," 205
Crune, Leroy, 89
Cushing, Steve, 17

Dandee, Cecil, 53, 69, 70, 72
Daniel Boone Woolen Mills, 83
Davenport, Charles "Cow-Cow," 166
Davenport, Lillian, 166
Davis, Wild Bill, 145

Davis, Bobby, 43
Davis, "Blind John," 162, 174, 201
Davis, Martha, 145
Davis, Miles, 217
Davis, Mother Marion, 92
Davis, Sammy, 31, 154
Davis Sisters, 85
Day, Ike, 178
Dean, Dolphus, 117
Decca Records, 86, 88, 96, 145, 173, 217, 218
Dee Gee (night club, Chicago), 117, 118
DeJohn, Harold, 165
DeLisa, Mike, 142
Delmark Records, 4
Desdune, Clarence, 165
Desilu Playhouse, 146
Desilu Workshop, 147
Dickerson, Althea, 167
Dickerson, Carol, 134
Dixon, Jesse, 89
Dixon, Willie, 89
Doggett, Bill, 145
Dolphin, John, 84, 88
Domino, Fats, 142
Donnelley, Elliott, 157
Dorsey, Prof. Thomas "Georgia Tom," 89, 167, 208
Douglas School, 150
Downbeat magazine, 218
Down Beat (night club), 146
Dozier Boys, 106
Dozier, George Iverson, 117
Dr. Jordan and his Midnight Minstrels, 209
Duncan, Al, 89
Dupree, Champion Jack, 23, 24
Du Sable Hotel, 103, 139
Du Sable Lounge, 103
Dyer, Sammy, 132, 138
Dyerettes, The, 138
Dyett, Walter, 144

Eagle, Peter, 96
Earl Theater (Philadelphia), 30
Easler, Haddie, 53
Easton, Amos (Bumble Bee Slim), 18
Edmonson, Estelle, 146
Edwards, Moanin' Bernice, 185
El Grotto (night club, Chicago), 119, 121, 136, 137
Elkinson, James Lewis, 68
Ellington, Edward "Duke," 60, 115, 126, 146, 154, 155, 218
El Morocco Hotel, 104
Elry, Jesse, 19
Elsewhere (blues club, Chicago), 202
Epiphone guitar, 214
Erlanger Theater, 121
Evans, Bill, 29
Ezell, Will, 166

Fagan, Bo, 190
Fagner, Harry, 165
Fast Western, 180
Favors, Rev P. R., 83, 87, 93
Fitzgerald, Ella, 31
Flame Club, The, 199
Flemming, Ray, 205
Fletcher, Dusty, 126
Floral Park Cemetery (Indianapolis), 23
Florence's (blues club), 9
Flynn, Michael, 35
Ford, Tennessee Ernie, 146
Ford, Friday, 169
Ford, Henry, 32
47th Street, 149
Foster, "Baby Face" Leroy, 198
Foster, Paul, 89
Foxx, Red, 6
Franklin, Edward Lamont "Guitar Pete," 18, 22
Franklin, Flossie, 17, 21
Franklin, Rev. C. L., 87, 89
Franklin, Rev. Thomas, 18
Franklin, Sylvester, 18

Fredrick Bros Inc., 205
Freeman, Grady, 35
Friar's Club (Los Angeles), 71, 72

GAC (General Artists Corporation), 30, 123
Gale Agency, 212
Galloway, Sigmund, 96
Gant, Cecil, 102, 212
Garroway, Dave, 122
Gay, Preacher Donald, 82, 83, 87, 93
Gay, Evelyn, 82–91, 95–97
Gay, Geraldine, 82–87, 95–97
Gay, Mildred, 82–85, 87–89, 93–95
Gay, Mother Fannie Parthenia, 94, 95
Gay, Robert, 83, 94, 95
Gayten, Paul, 163
Gelatin Casino (Philadelphia), 31
Georgia Smart Set, 168
Gerri's Palm Tavern, 155
Getz, Stan, 31
Gibson guitar, 11, 214
Gillespie, Dizzy, 29, 94, 144
Gillum, Jazz, 204
Glenn, Charlie, 132, 133, 136, 140
Goldberg, Sammy, 105
Goodman, Benny, 213
Goreau, Lorraine, 95
Grand Terrace/Sunset (night club), 104, 132, 137, 153
Grand Theater, 166
Grant, Charlie, 189
Grapevine (highway), 55
Gray, Charles, 142
Gray, Harry, 96
Gray, Henry, 82
Gray, Jim (Chicago deejay), 26
Grayson, Bobby, 192, 103
Grayson, Kenneth, 102, 108, 109
Grayson, Melvin, 101, 111
Grayson, Paul, 102
Green, Charlie, 141
Green, Imogene, 89

Green, Lee "Pork Chop," 167, 222
Green, Lil, 155
Greene, Bill, 143, 144
Greene, Irving, 124
Greer, Sonny, 126
Griffin, Gloria, 95
Griffin, Tommy, 168
Grimaldi, John, 42
Grimler, Earl, 127

H & T Club, 203
Hammond, John Sr., 204
Hampton, Lionel, 132
Hancock, Herbie, 29, 217
Harmonicats, 124
Harris, Charley, 28
Harris, Homer, 196
Harris, Sid, 176
Harrison, Jester, 72
Hartman, Johnny, 144
Hatch, Wilbur, 146
Hathaway, Donnie, 90
Hauser, John, 133
Heidt, Horace, 71
Helfer, Erwin, 162, 163
Henderson, Fletcher, 142, 153, 179, 210
Henderson, Horace, 153, 210
Herring, Emelda, 52
Hickman, Sylvester, 115, 116, 126
Hicks, Minnie, 167
Hill, Chippie, 155
Hill, Luther, 144
Hines, Bobby, 10
Hines, Earl, 29, 118, 121, 132, 133, 153, 155, 218
Hodges, Johnny, 115, 117
Hogan, Marty (Chicago deejay), 26
Hollywood Rendezvous (blues club, Chicago), 41
Holt, Red, 90
Holy Angels Church, 111
Hooker, John Lee, 213
Hopkins, Claude, 132, 155

Howard Theater (Washington D.C.), 30
Howling Wolf, 5, 36, 194, 217
Hudson, Leroy, 90
Hughes, Joe, 145
Hunky Dorey (deejay), 14
Hunter, Ivory Joe, 105

Idlewild, MI, 151
I Love Lucy, 146
Illinois Central Railroad, 85, 92
Imperial Records, 142
Impressions, The, 90
Inkspots, The, 70, 71, 152

Jackson, August, 86
Jackson, Jesse, 157
Jackson, Jim, 212
Jackson, Lee, 8
Jackson, Mahalia, 93, 95, 102
James, Elmore, 198
James, Etta, 217
Jaxon, Frankie "Half-Pint," 153
Jaycox, Martin, 89
Jazz Institute of Chicago, 220
Jazz Record Mart (Chicago record store), 17
Jeeter, Claude, 91
Jefferson, Blind Lemon, 118, 190, 213
Jeffries, Jim, 152
Jimmy's Palm Tavern, 104
Jockey Club (Winona, MN), 127
Joe Kelly's Quiz Kids (television show), 88
Joe's Deluxe Club, 119, 124
Joe's Music Café, 145
John, Easy Papa, 223
John Gaston Hospital (Memphis), 13
John Marshall Law School, 147
Johnson, Bunk, 163
Johnson, Eddie, 132, 133, 140, 142
Johnson, Edith, 222
Johnson, Ernest "44 Kid"/"Delco Robert"/Flunky, 167
Johnson, Jack, 152

Johnson, Jesse, 222
Johnson, Joe "Ziggy," 132
Johnson, Lonnie, 199, 203
Johnson, Pete, 124
Johnson, Raymond, 165
Johnson, Robert, 171–73, 175
Joint Negro Appeal, 157
Jones, Clarence, 166
Jones, Curtis, 162, 175
Jones, Floyd, 162
Jones, Gladys O., 51
Jones, Johnny "Little," 168, 199
Jones, Mahalia S., 42
Jones, Nat, 115–17, 132, 140, 142
Jones, Theautry "T," 42
Jones Home (orphanage), 153
Jordan, Charlie, 174
Jordan, Louis, 122, 123, 145, 168, 212, 217–19
Joseph H. Cohn Vanity, 151
Joy, Leonard, 96
Joyland Revelers, 165
Jubilee Showcase (television program), 91
Just Mahalia Baby (book), 95

Kaiser, Kay Orchestra, 65
Keegan, Walt, 110
Keene, Paul, 145
Kelly, Willie, 223
Kennedy, President John F., 33, 34
Keyhole, The (night club), 110
KFFA radio station, 171
Kimbal, Lloyd, 132
King, B. B., 6, 171
King, Eddie, 155
King, Rev. Martin Luther, 73
King Biscuit Time (radio program), 171
King Records, 60
King Tuts (night club), 166
Kirby, George, 137
Knight, Jim, 155
Knowling, Ransom, 174, 211
Koester, Bob, 17, 180, 187

Kramer, Worth, 51, 61
KRNT radio (Des Moines), 27

Laibly, Art, 167
Laine, Frankie, 71
Lambert, Adam, 121, 122
Lane, David, 205
Lane, George, 135
LaPalm, Dick, 25
Larkin, Milt, 122, 135
Lawry's Restaurant (Chicago), 86
Lee, Peggy, 27, 31, 32
Lee, Sister, 88
Lewis, Meade Lux, 180
Lewis, Ramsey, 89
Life magazine, 3
Lightning Flashes, The (dance team), 155
Lily's, 202
Lindsey, Nettie, 168
Ling, George, 140
Lindstrom's (night club, Boston), 31
Little, Milton, 75
Little Miss Cornshucks (Mildred Cummings), 104, 115, 117, 131, 142
Little, Robert, 75, 81
Little Son Joe (Ernest Lawler), 10, 11, 173
Little Walter Jacobs, 36, 41–44, 171, 175, 177, 198
Local 47 Musicians Union (Los Angeles), 147
Local 208 Black Musicians Union (Chicago), 43, 96, 115
Local 210 Musicians Union (Chicago), 43
Local 767 Black Musicians Union (Los Angeles), 147
Locke, Abb, 3, 4, 5, 7
Lockwood, Robert Jr., 16, 41, 170, 171
Lofton, "Crippled" Clarence, 162, 213
Long, Johnny, 125, 132, 155
Long Tall Friday, 165
Los Angeles Dodgers, 31
Louis, Joe (boxer), 60, 140
Louis, Joe Hill, 14, 16

Lowe, Mundell, 212
Lubinsky, Herman, 84, 85, 88
Lucy Show, The, 146
Lunceford, Jimmy, 155
Lutcher, Nellie, 27

Mabon, Willie, 162
Mack and Mack, 154, 155
Maddock, Red, 115, 116, 126
Magic Sam, 194
Magic Slim, 9
Magid, Lee, 85
Majors, Eddie, 163
Mallard, Sax, 105
Manee, Ed, 176
Manner, The (night club, Minneapolis), 129
Markham, Charlie, 136
Marshall Fields (Chicago department store), 25
Martin, Bill, 117
Martin, Bob, 164
Martin, Dean, 31, 146
Martin, Joe, 164
Martin, Johnny, 212
Martin, Miles, 209
Martin, Sara, 183, 186, 208, 209
Martin's Corner (night club), 105, 106
Marvin, Lee, 14
Mason, Bishop Charles Harrison, 77, 78, 80, 81, 92, 93
Matinee Club (Memphis), 197
Mayberry R.F.D., 147
Mayfield, Curtis, 90
Mays, John, 117
McCullen, George, 165
McGee, Rev. F. W. Jr., 75, 81
McGee, Rev. F. W. Sr., 75, 76, 80, 93
McGee, Henry Wadsworth, 80
McGown, Ginni, 146
McKay School, 154
McKinley, L. C., 199
McNeil, Claudia, 137

Meadows, Al, 50, 53
Melody Mill Club (LaCrosse WI), 127
Melotone Records, 167
Melrose, Franklin, 205
Melrose, Lester, 20, 173–75, 199–201, 203, 204, 207, 210, 211
Melrose, Walter, 205, 206
Memphis Cotton Sales, 10
Memphis Jimmy, 199, 200
Memphis Minnie, 9, 173, 199
Memphis Slim, 162, 173, 197–99, 220
Mercury Records, 115, 123, 124, 126
Metropolitan Theater, 149, 153, 155
MGM Records, 205
Midnight Musicals, 93, 94
Miller, Alex Rice (Sonny Boy Williamson II), 38, 210
Miller, Johnny 28
Millinder, Lucky, 146, 212
Mills Bros, The, 70, 72, 123, 152
Mimms, T. S., 210
Mississippi Industrial College (M.I.), 35
Mitchell, Billie, 155
Mocombo, The (night club), 105
Modernaires, The, 70
Moke & Poke, 137
Montgomery, Dicey, 163
Montgomery, Eurreal "Little Brother," 116, 162, 163, 220
Montgomery, Gunzie, 163
Montgomery, Harper, 163
Montgomery, Leon, 163
Montgomery, Olivia, 163
Montgomery, Willie, 163
Moore, Gatemouth, 103, 105
Moore, Oscar, 28
Mormon Tabernacle Choir, 58
Morrison, Charlie, 138
Morton, Ferdinand "Jellyroll," 166, 204
Mr. Freddy, 118
M Squad (television program), 14
Muddy Waters, 36, 38, 40, 43, 155, 196, 199, 200, 217

Murad, Jerry, 124
Musician's Forum, 90
Myers, Bob, 40
Myers, Dave, 36–39
Myers, James, 40
Myers, Louis, 36–40

NAACP, 157
Nash, Herman, 86
NBC Television, 31
Neeley, Lee Charles, 89
Newborn, Phineas, 29
Noble, Gene, 211
Noone, Jimmie, 166, 218

Oberstein, Eli, 168
Oden, James, 204
Okeh Records, 167, 183, 222
Old Town School of Folk Music, 82
Oliver, Joe "King," 165, 166, 179
Oliver, Paul, 3
125 Club, 121
Ordower, Sid, 91
Other Place, The, 112
Otis, Johnny, 121
Otto's Restaurant, 201
Overstreet, Ester, 52, 53
Owl Theater, The, 166

Packing House, 91
Palmer, Doc, 168
Palmer, Edmund, 168
Palmer House, 150
Papa Lord God, 164
Paramount Records, 167
Parham, Tiny, 166
Parker, Charlie, 132, 134
Parker, Herman, Jr., 38
Parker, Rev. B. M., 77
Parks, Rosa, 73, 74
Parrish, Jay, 133
Patterson, Bishop O. J., 78
Patterson, James, 202

Paul Quinn College, 76
Payne, Odie, 178
Payton, Dave, 165
Peacock Records, 108
Peer, R. S., 182
Pepper's Lounge (blues club, Chicago), 43
Peterson, Oscar, 29, 31
Petty, William, 96
Phillips, Brewer, 8, 9
Piano Man (night club), 202
Pijon, Walter "Fats," 165
Piper, Vernon "Scotty," 149, 152, 158
Piron, Armund, 163
Plantation Club (Chicago), 198
Poole, Mother Mattie, 95
Portillo, Caesar, 96
Pot, Pan and Skillet (dance team), 137
Prairie Home Companion, 115
Presley, Elvis, 139, 197, 207–9, 213, 214
Prince, Wesley, 28
Providence Hospital, 157
Pryor, Snooky, 162
Pullum, Joe, 185

Quick, Eddie, 155

Raff Club (Memphis), 197
Rag Doll, The (music club, Chicago), 26
Rainey, Gertrude Ma, 118, 153, 202
Raitt, Bonnie, 16
Rawls, Lou, 153
RCA Victor Records, 167, 168, 202, 211, 212
Reed, A. C., 11
Reed, Leonard, 155
Reese, Della, 85
Regal Theater (Chicago), 26, 30, 120, 121, 149, 155, 166
Reily, Bud, 91
Reiner, Paul, 141
Rhinehart, Django, 218
Rhodes Hotel, 173

Rhumboogie, The (night club), 119, 132, 133, 135–37, 139, 140
Rhythm Willie, 153
Rich, Buddy, 178
Richmond, June, 126
Rick's Café American, 180
Riley, Judge, 174, 201, 211
Ringling Bros. and Barnum and Bailey Circus, 150
Rio, The (night clubs, Argentina and Brazil), 31
Riperton, Minnie, 217
Rip Top (Loomis Gibson), 164
Ritz Hotel, 104, 110, 121
Ritz Lounge, 104, 106, 121, 210
Riverside Recording Studios, 9
Roberta Martin Singers, 95
Roberts, Bishop William, 78, 92
Roberts, Oral, 92
Robinson, D. Q., 145
Roby, Don, 108
Rocco, Maurice, 123
Rogers, Jimmy, 8, 198
Rogers, Willie, 89
Rollins, Sonny, 94
Roosevelt, Eleanor, 65
Roosevelt, Franklin D., 151, 197
Roseland Ballroom, 132
Ross, Jackie, 89
Royal Peacock (night club), 212
Royal Theater, Memphis, 11
Rush, Otis, 4
Russ & McCain, 137
Russell, Nipsy, 108
Rust College (Holly Springs, MS), 35

Samuels, Art, 114–16
Samuels, Bill, 114, 115, 118–20, 123–27, 129
Samuels, Elliot, 114
Samuels, Geneva "Gin," 118, 121
Samuels, George, 121
Samuels, Georgia, 121
Samuels, Shelly, 115, 116, 125
Samuels, Shirley, 127, 129
Samuels, William Burroughs, Sr., 116
Sands (Las Vegas), 30
Satterfield, Louis, 89
Saunders, Red, 152, 218
Savoy Ballroom, 125, 149, 155
Savoy Records, 84, 108, 212
Scott, Jesse, 137
Scott, Ken, 43
Scott, Mabel, 137
Scotty (clothing store), 151
Scruggs, Irene, 167
Seals, Frank, 182
Sears, Zena, 211
Settles, Rev Glenn, 47, 51, 52, 53, 56, 57, 59, 61, 69
708 Club (Chicago), 41, 155
Shad, Bob, 212
Shayne, Freddy, 118
Shoals, Steve, 212
Shockley, Dorothy, 18
Shore, Dinah, 93
Shurman, Dick, 3
Silver, Horace, 29
Sinatra, Frank, 32
Singer, Hal "Cornbread," 212
Sittin' In Records, 212
Skinner, Frank, 165
Slack, Freddy, 146
Slater, Duke, 152
Small, Clarence, 48, 49
Smith, Bessie, 182, 186, 202, 207–9, 213
Smith, Clara, 186
Smith, Clarence "Pinetop," 166, 213
Smith, Henderson, 115–17, 133, 140, 141
Smith, Ivy, 166
Smith, Elder Lucy, 88
Smith, Mamie, 153, 180, 208, 209
Smith, Tab, 212
Smith, Rev. Utah, 93
Smothers, Otis "Smokey," 170
Soul Stirrers, 89
Softwinds, 29

Southern Troubadors, 168
Spand, Charlie, 166, 213
Spann, Otis, 161, 168
Spearman, Martha, 53
Stairway to the Stars, 155
St. Charles Hotel (New Orleans), 168
Steele, Larry, 138
Step Brothers, The, 152, 155
Stevens, Bill, 205
Stidham, Arbee, 207
St. Louis Jimmy (James Oden), 204
Studebaker John, 42
Sullivan, Ed, 31
Sunbeam Records, 131, 142–44
Sunny & Sunny, 137
Sunnyland Slim, 16, 162, 169–71, 175, 199, 204, 213, 220
Swaggart, Jimmy, 92
Swan Silvertones, 91
Swanson, Petite, 145
Sykes, Nelson, 156
Sykes, Roosevelt, 11, 15, 16, 18, 19, 149, 167, 198, 220, 221
Sylvio's Lounge, 198

Tampa Red, 167, 173, 194, 198, 202, 203, 208, 210, 211, 215, 223
Tate, Erskine, 125, 155, 166
Tatum, Art, 29
Tavares, Sparky, 30, 32, 34
Taylor, Hound Dog, 8
Taylor, Koko, 89
Tharpe, Sister Rosetta, 83, 84
Thomas, George W., 166, 179, 180, 182–84
Thomas, Hersal, 166, 179, 180, 183–85
Thomas, Hocial, 166, 179, 180, 183–85
Thomas, Lucy, 182
Thomas, Octavia, 184
Thomas, Queen, 185
Thomas, Rufus, 11, 197
Thompson, Buck, 132
Thompson, Butch, 115
Thompson, Sir Charles, 212

Thompson, Sonny, 90, 121, 126
Three Dueces (night club), 121
Tibbs, Andrew, 101, 104, 108
Tiffanee (night club, Los Angeles), 28
Toni's Tavern, 198
Top & Bob (dance team), 104
Torme, Mel, 26, 27
Tracey, Dick, 37
Triangel Club, 199
Tropicana (night club, Havana), 31, 32
Truman, President Harry, 66
Tucker, Luther, 41
Turner, Annie, 168
Turner, Big Joe, 123
Tuskegee Airmen, 59
Two-Gun Pete, 3–7
211 Club, 156
Tyner, McCoy, 29

University of Illinois at Navy Pier, 26
University of Wisconsin at Madison, 18
Urban League, 157
USO, 59

Valois Cafeteria (Chicago), 82
Vaughn, Coony, 164, 168
Vaughan, Sarah, 31
Veeck, Bill, 31
Vendome, 166
Victor Records, 183
Vincent, Ozzie, 90, 91
Vincson, Walter, 168
Vinson, Eddie "Cleanhead," 219
Violinaires, The, 89
Vocalion Records, 18, 167, 203, 204
VS&P Railroad, 164

WAAF radio (Chicago), 25
WAIT radio (Chicago), 26
Walgreen's drug store, 152
Walker, Leander, 205
Walker, Reuben, 166
Walker, T-Bone, 138–41, 190

Wallace, Alfred, 175
Wallace, Matt, 182
Wallace, Sippi, 179, 180, 183
Waller, Thomas "Fats," 166, 167
Washboard Sam, 210
Washington, Dinah (Ruth Jones), 102, 137
Washington, Harold, 153, 157, 158
Washington, Sylvester "Two-Gun Pete," 3–7
Waterman, Dick, 16
WBBM radio, 122
WBEZ radio, 202
WCCO television (Minneapolis), 126
WCFL radio (Chicago), 26, 88
WDIA radio (Memphis), 11, 14, 15
Weatherford, Ted, 166
Wells, Junior, 36–41, 43
Wendell Phillips High School, 102, 144
WERD radio (Atlanta), 212
Wesley, Willie, 202
Western Electric, 111
WGAR radio (Cleveland), 51, 61
WGN television (Chicago), 96
WGST radio (Atlanta), 211
Wheatstraw, Peetie, 19
White, Ellison, 68, 70, 72
White's Emporium, 124
Whitman Sisters, 155
Wildroot hair creme, 31
Wiley, Arnold, 166

Wiley, Irene, 166
Williams, Big Joe, 210
Williams, Clarence, 183, 204, 209
Williams, Fess, 155
Williams, J. Mayo "Ink," 167, 173, 174, 202
Williams, Joe, 26, 33, 104, 123, 153, 155, 210
Williamson, John Lee (Sonny Boy Williamson #1), 16, 177, 198, 203, 204, 210
Wilson, Eudell, 165
Wilson, Quinn, 133, 140, 145
WIND radio (Chicago), 26
Wingmen, The, 68, 70, 71, 72
Wings Over Jordan Choir, 47, 48
Winstrup's (nightclub, Boston), 32
WLOK radio, 14
Woods, Charles, 19
Wohlmuth Tailors, 151

Yancy, Jimmy, 212
Yazoo Records, 20
Young, Chester, 142
Young, Harry, 142
Young, Johnny, 8
Young, L. D., 90
Young, Lee, 32
Young, Lester, 32

Zanzibar Club, 198
Zenith Radio, 26
Zimmerman, Todd, 48

STEVE CUSHING has hosted *Blues Before Sunrise* for forty years. He is the author of *Blues Before Sunrise: The Radio Interviews* and *Pioneers of the Blue Revival*.

Music in American Life

Only a Miner: Studies in Recorded Coal-Mining Songs   *Archie Green*
Great Day Coming: Folk Music and the American Left   *R. Serge Denisoff*
John Philip Sousa: A Descriptive Catalog of His Works   *Paul E. Bierley*
The Hell-Bound Train: A Cowboy Songbook   *Glenn Ohrlin*
Oh, Didn't He Ramble: The Life Story of Lee Collins, as Told to Mary Collins
   Edited by Frank J. Gillis and John W. Miner
American Labor Songs of the Nineteenth Century   *Philip S. Foner*
Stars of Country Music: Uncle Dave Macon to Johnny Rodriguez
   Edited by Bill C. Malone and Judith McCulloh
Git Along, Little Dogies: Songs and Songmakers of the American West
   John I. White
A Texas-Mexican *Cancionero*: Folksongs of the Lower Border   *Américo Paredes*
San Antonio Rose: The Life and Music of Bob Wills   *Charles R. Townsend*
Early Downhome Blues: A Musical and Cultural Analysis   *Jeff Todd Titon*
An Ives Celebration: Papers and Panels of the Charles Ives Centennial
   Festival-Conference   *Edited by H. Wiley Hitchcock and Vivian Perlis*
Sinful Tunes and Spirituals: Black Folk Music to the Civil War   *Dena J. Epstein*
Joe Scott, the Woodsman-Songmaker   *Edward D. Ives*
Jimmie Rodgers: The Life and Times of America's Blue Yodeler   *Nolan Porterfield*
Early American Music Engraving and Printing: A History of Music
   Publishing in America from 1787 to 1825, with Commentary on Earlier
   and Later Practices   *Richard J. Wolfe*
Sing a Sad Song: The Life of Hank Williams   *Roger M. Williams*
Long Steel Rail: The Railroad in American Folksong   *Norm Cohen*
Resources of American Music History: A Directory of Source Materials from
   Colonial Times to World War II   *D. W. Krummel, Jean Geil, Doris J. Dyen,
   and Deane L. Root*
Tenement Songs: The Popular Music of the Jewish Immigrants   *Mark Slobin*
Ozark Folksongs   *Vance Randolph; edited and abridged by Norm Cohen*
Oscar Sonneck and American Music   *Edited by William Lichtenwanger*
Bluegrass Breakdown: The Making of the Old Southern Sound   *Robert Cantwell*
Bluegrass: A History   *Neil V. Rosenberg*
Music at the White House: A History of the American Spirit   *Elise K. Kirk*
Red River Blues: The Blues Tradition in the Southeast   *Bruce Bastin*
Good Friends and Bad Enemies: Robert Winslow Gordon and the Study of American
   Folksong   *Debora Kodish*
Fiddlin' Georgia Crazy: Fiddlin' John Carson, His Real World, and the World of
   His Songs   *Gene Wiggins*
America's Music: From the Pilgrims to the Present (rev. 3d ed.)   *Gilbert Chase*
Secular Music in Colonial Annapolis: The Tuesday Club, 1745–56   *John Barry Talley*

Bibliographical Handbook of American Music *D. W. Krummel*
Goin' to Kansas City *Nathan W. Pearson Jr.*
"Susanna," "Jeanie," and "The Old Folks at Home": The Songs of Stephen C. Foster
    from His Time to Ours (2d ed.) *William W. Austin*
Songprints: The Musical Experience of Five Shoshone Women *Judith Vander*
"Happy in the Service of the Lord": Afro-American Gospel Quartets in Memphis
    Kip Lornell
Paul Hindemith in the United States *Luther Noss*
"My Song Is My Weapon": People's Songs, American Communism, and the Politics of
    Culture, 1930–50 *Robbie Lieberman*
Chosen Voices: The Story of the American Cantorate *Mark Slobin*
Theodore Thomas: America's Conductor and Builder of Orchestras, 1835–1905
    Ezra Schabas
"The Whorehouse Bells Were Ringing" and Other Songs Cowboys Sing
    Collected and Edited by Guy Logsdon
Crazeology: The Autobiography of a Chicago Jazzman *Bud Freeman,
    as Told to Robert Wolf*
Discoursing Sweet Music: Brass Bands and Community Life in Turn-of-the-
    Century Pennsylvania *Kenneth Kreitner*
Mormonism and Music: A History *Michael Hicks*
Voices of the Jazz Age: Profiles of Eight Vintage Jazzmen *Chip Deffaa*
Pickin' on Peachtree: A History of Country Music in Atlanta, Georgia
    Wayne W. Daniel
Bitter Music: Collected Journals, Essays, Introductions, and Librettos
    Harry Partch; edited by Thomas McGeary
Ethnic Music on Records: A Discography of Ethnic Recordings Produced in the
    United States, 1893 to 1942 *Richard K. Spottswood*
Downhome Blues Lyrics: An Anthology from the Post–World War II Era
    Jeff Todd Titon
Ellington: The Early Years *Mark Tucker*
Chicago Soul *Robert Pruter*
That Half-Barbaric Twang: The Banjo in American Popular Culture *Karen Linn*
Hot Man: The Life of Art Hodes *Art Hodes and Chadwick Hansen*
The Erotic Muse: American Bawdy Songs (2d ed.) *Ed Cray*
Barrio Rhythm: Mexican American Music in Los Angeles *Steven Loza*
The Creation of Jazz: Music, Race, and Culture in Urban America *Burton W. Peretti*
Charles Martin Loeffler: A Life Apart in Music *Ellen Knight*
Club Date Musicians: Playing the New York Party Circuit *Bruce A. MacLeod*
Opera on the Road: Traveling Opera Troupes in the United States, 1825–60
    Katherine K. Preston
The Stonemans: An Appalachian Family and the Music That Shaped Their Lives
    Ivan M. Tribe

Transforming Tradition: Folk Music Revivals Examined   *Edited by Neil V. Rosenberg*
The Crooked Stovepipe: Athapaskan Fiddle Music and Square Dancing in Northeast
    Alaska and Northwest Canada   *Craig Mishler*
Traveling the High Way Home: Ralph Stanley and the World of Traditional
    Bluegrass Music   *John Wright*
Carl Ruggles: Composer, Painter, and Storyteller   *Marilyn Ziffrin*
Never without a Song: The Years and Songs of Jennie Devlin, 1865–1952
    Katharine D. Newman
The Hank Snow Story   *Hank Snow, with Jack Ownbey and Bob Burris*
Milton Brown and the Founding of Western Swing   *Cary Ginell, with special
    assistance from Roy Lee Brown*
Santiago de Murcia's "Códice Saldívar No. 4": A Treasury of Secular Guitar Music
    from Baroque Mexico   *Craig H. Russell*
The Sound of the Dove: Singing in Appalachian Primitive Baptist Churches
    Beverly Bush Patterson
Heartland Excursions: Ethnomusicological Reflections on Schools of Music
    Bruno Nettl
Doowop: The Chicago Scene   *Robert Pruter*
Blue Rhythms: Six Lives in Rhythm and Blues   *Chip Deffaa*
Shoshone Ghost Dance Religion: Poetry Songs and Great Basin Context
    Judith Vander
Go Cat Go! Rockabilly Music and Its Makers   *Craig Morrison*
'Twas Only an Irishman's Dream: The Image of Ireland and the Irish in American
    Popular Song Lyrics, 1800–1920   *William H. A. Williams*
Democracy at the Opera: Music, Theater, and Culture in New York City, 1815–60
    Karen Ahlquist
Fred Waring and the Pennsylvanians   *Virginia Waring*
Woody, Cisco, and Me: Seamen Three in the Merchant Marine   *Jim Longhi*
Behind the Burnt Cork Mask: Early Blackface Minstrelsy and Antebellum
    American Popular Culture   *William J. Mahar*
Going to Cincinnati: A History of the Blues in the Queen City   *Steven C. Tracy*
Pistol Packin' Mama: Aunt Molly Jackson and the Politics of Folksong
    Shelly Romalis
Sixties Rock: Garage, Psychedelic, and Other Satisfactions   *Michael Hicks*
The Late Great Johnny Ace and the Transition from R&B to Rock 'n' Roll
    James M. Salem
Tito Puente and the Making of Latin Music   *Steven Loza*
Juilliard: A History   *Andrea Olmstead*
Understanding Charles Seeger, Pioneer in American Musicology
    Edited by Bell Yung and Helen Rees
Mountains of Music: West Virginia Traditional Music from *Goldenseal*
    Edited by John Lilly
Alice Tully: An Intimate Portrait   *Albert Fuller*

A Blues Life *Henry Townsend, as told to Bill Greensmith*
Long Steel Rail: The Railroad in American Folksong (2d ed.) *Norm Cohen*
The Golden Age of Gospel *Text by Horace Clarence Boyer; photography by Lloyd Yearwood*
Aaron Copland: The Life and Work of an Uncommon Man *Howard Pollack*
Louis Moreau Gottschalk *S. Frederick Starr*
Race, Rock, and Elvis *Michael T. Bertrand*
Theremin: Ether Music and Espionage *Albert Glinsky*
Poetry and Violence: The Ballad Tradition of Mexico's Costa Chica *John H. McDowell*
The Bill Monroe Reader *Edited by Tom Ewing*
Music in Lubavitcher Life *Ellen Koskoff*
Zarzuela: Spanish Operetta, American Stage *Janet L. Sturman*
Bluegrass Odyssey: A Documentary in Pictures and Words, 1966–86 *Carl Fleischhauer and Neil V. Rosenberg*
That Old-Time Rock & Roll: A Chronicle of an Era, 1954–63 *Richard Aquila*
Labor's Troubadour *Joe Glazer*
American Opera *Elise K. Kirk*
Don't Get above Your Raisin': Country Music and the Southern Working Class *Bill C. Malone*
John Alden Carpenter: A Chicago Composer *Howard Pollack*
Heartbeat of the People: Music and Dance of the Northern Pow-wow *Tara Browner*
My Lord, What a Morning: An Autobiography *Marian Anderson*
Marian Anderson: A Singer's Journey *Allan Keiler*
Charles Ives Remembered: An Oral History *Vivian Perlis*
Henry Cowell, Bohemian *Michael Hicks*
Rap Music and Street Consciousness *Cheryl L. Keyes*
Louis Prima *Garry Boulard*
Marian McPartland's Jazz World: All in Good Time *Marian McPartland*
Robert Johnson: Lost and Found *Barry Lee Pearson and Bill McCulloch*
Bound for America: Three British Composers *Nicholas Temperley*
Lost Sounds: Blacks and the Birth of the Recording Industry, 1890–1919 *Tim Brooks*
Burn, Baby! BURN! The Autobiography of Magnificent Montague *Magnificent Montague with Bob Baker*
Way Up North in Dixie: A Black Family's Claim to the Confederate Anthem *Howard L. Sacks and Judith Rose Sacks*
The Bluegrass Reader *Edited by Thomas Goldsmith*
Colin McPhee: Composer in Two Worlds *Carol J. Oja*
Robert Johnson, Mythmaking, and Contemporary American Culture *Patricia R. Schroeder*
Composing a World: Lou Harrison, Musical Wayfarer *Leta E. Miller and Fredric Lieberman*
Fritz Reiner, Maestro and Martinet *Kenneth Morgan*

That Toddlin' Town: Chicago's White Dance Bands and Orchestras, 1900–1950
    Charles A. Sengstock Jr.
Dewey and Elvis: The Life and Times of a Rock 'n' Roll Deejay   *Louis Cantor*
Come Hither to Go Yonder: Playing Bluegrass with Bill Monroe   *Bob Black*
Chicago Blues: Portraits and Stories   *David Whiteis*
The Incredible Band of John Philip Sousa   *Paul E. Bierley*
"Maximum Clarity" and Other Writings on Music   *Ben Johnston,
    edited by Bob Gilmore*
Staging Tradition: John Lair and Sarah Gertrude Knott   *Michael Ann Williams*
Homegrown Music: Discovering Bluegrass   *Stephanie P. Ledgin*
Tales of a Theatrical Guru   *Danny Newman*
The Music of Bill Monroe   *Neil V. Rosenberg and Charles K. Wolfe*
Pressing On: The Roni Stoneman Story   *Roni Stoneman, as told to Ellen Wright*
Together Let Us Sweetly Live   *Jonathan C. David, with photographs by
    Richard Holloway*
Live Fast, Love Hard: The Faron Young Story   *Diane Diekman*
Air Castle of the South: WSM Radio and the Making of Music City
    Craig P. Havighurst
Traveling Home: Sacred Harp Singing and American Pluralism   *Kiri Miller*
Where Did Our Love Go? The Rise and Fall of the Motown Sound   *Nelson George*
Lonesome Cowgirls and Honky-Tonk Angels: The Women of Barn Dance
    Radio   *Kristine M. McCusker*
California Polyphony: Ethnic Voices, Musical Crossroads   *Mina Yang*
The Never-Ending Revival: Rounder Records and the Folk Alliance
    Michael F. Scully
Sing It Pretty: A Memoir   *Bess Lomax Hawes*
Working Girl Blues: The Life and Music of Hazel Dickens   *Hazel Dickens and
    Bill C. Malone*
Charles Ives Reconsidered   *Gayle Sherwood Magee*
The Hayloft Gang: The Story of the National Barn Dance   *Edited by Chad Berry*
Country Music Humorists and Comedians   *Loyal Jones*
Record Makers and Breakers: Voices of the Independent Rock 'n' Roll Pioneers
    John Broven
Music of the First Nations: Tradition and Innovation in Native North America
    Edited by Tara Browner
Cafe Society: The Wrong Place for the Right People   *Barney Josephson,
    with Terry Trilling-Josephson*
George Gershwin: An Intimate Portrait   *Walter Rimler*
Life Flows On in Endless Song: Folk Songs and American History   *Robert V. Wells*
I Feel a Song Coming On: The Life of Jimmy McHugh   *Alyn Shipton*
King of the Queen City: The Story of King Records   *Jon Hartley Fox*
Long Lost Blues: Popular Blues in America, 1850–1920   *Peter C. Muir*

Hard Luck Blues: Roots Music Photographs from the Great Depression
  Rich Remsberg
Restless Giant: The Life and Times of Jean Aberbach and Hill and Range Songs
  Bar Biszick-Lockwood
Champagne Charlie and Pretty Jemima: Variety Theater in the Nineteenth Century
  Gillian M. Rodger
Sacred Steel: Inside an African American Steel Guitar Tradition   *Robert L. Stone*
Gone to the Country: The New Lost City Ramblers and the Folk Music Revival
  Ray Allen
The Makers of the Sacred Harp   *David Warren Steel with Richard H. Hulan*
Woody Guthrie, American Radical   *Will Kaufman*
George Szell: A Life of Music   *Michael Charry*
Bean Blossom: The Brown County Jamboree and Bill Monroe's Bluegrass Festivals
  Thomas A. Adler
Crowe on the Banjo: The Music Life of J. D. Crowe   *Marty Godbey*
Twentieth Century Drifter: The Life of Marty Robbins   *Diane Diekman*
Henry Mancini: Reinventing Film Music   *John Caps*
The Beautiful Music All Around Us: Field Recordings and the American Experience
  Stephen Wade
Then Sings My Soul: The Culture of Southern Gospel Music   *Douglas Harrison*
The Accordion in the Americas: Klezmer, Polka, Tango, Zydeco, and More!
  Edited by Helena Simonett
Bluegrass Bluesman: A Memoir   *Josh Graves, edited by Fred Bartenstein*
One Woman in a Hundred: Edna Phillips and the Philadelphia Orchestra
  Mary Sue Welsh
The Great Orchestrator: Arthur Judson and American Arts Management
  James M. Doering
Charles Ives in the Mirror: American Histories of an Iconic Composer
  David C. Paul
Southern Soul-Blues   *David Whiteis*
Sweet Air: Modernism, Regionalism, and American Popular Song
  Edward P. Comentale
Pretty Good for a Girl: Women in Bluegrass   *Murphy Hicks Henry*
Sweet Dreams: The World of Patsy Cline   *Warren R. Hofstra*
William Sidney Mount and the Creolization of American Culture
  Christopher J. Smith
Bird: The Life and Music of Charlie Parker   *Chuck Haddix*
Making the March King: John Philip Sousa's Washington Years, 1854–1893
  Patrick Warfield
In It for the Long Run   *Jim Rooney*
Pioneers of the Blues Revival   *Steve Cushing*
Roots of the Revival: American and British Folk Music in the 1950s
  Ronald D. Cohen and Rachel Clare Donaldson

Blues All Day Long: The Jimmy Rogers Story   *Wayne Everett Goins*
Yankee Twang: Country and Western Music in New England   *Clifford R. Murphy*
The Music of the Stanley Brothers   *Gary B. Reid*
Hawaiian Music in Motion: Mariners, Missionaries, and Minstrels
    James Revell Carr
Sounds of the New Deal: The Federal Music Project in the West   *Peter Gough*
The Mormon Tabernacle Choir: A Biography   *Michael Hicks*
The Man That Got Away: The Life and Songs of Harold Arlen   *Walter Rimler*
A City Called Heaven: Chicago and the Birth of Gospel Music   *Robert M. Marovich*
Blues Unlimited: Essential Interviews from the Original Blues Magazine
    Edited by Bill Greensmith, Mike Rowe, and Mark Camarigg
Hoedowns, Reels, and Frolics: Roots and Branches of Southern Appalachian Dance
    Phil Jamison
Fannie Bloomfield-Zeisler: The Life and Times of a Piano Virtuoso
    Beth Abelson Macleod
Cybersonic Arts: Adventures in American New Music   *Gordon Mumma,
    edited with commentary by Michelle Fillion*
The Magic of Beverly Sills   *Nancy Guy*
Waiting for Buddy Guy   *Alan Harper*
Harry T. Burleigh: From the Spiritual to the Harlem Renaissance   *Jean E. Snyder*
Music in the Age of Anxiety: American Music in the Fifties   *James Wierzbicki*
Jazzing: New York City's Unseen Scene   *Thomas H. Greenland*
A Cole Porter Companion   *Edited by Don M. Randel, Matthew Shaftel,
    and Susan Forscher Weiss*
Foggy Mountain Troubadour: The Life and Music of Curly Seckler   *Penny Parsons*
Blue Rhythm Fantasy: Big Band Jazz Arranging in the Swing Era   *John Wriggle*
Bill Clifton: America's Bluegrass Ambassador to the World   *Bill C. Malone*
Chinatown Opera Theater in North America   *Nancy Yunhwa Rao*
The Elocutionists: Women, Music, and the Spoken Word   *Marian Wilson Kimber*
May Irwin: Singing, Shouting, and the Shadow of Minstrelsy   *Sharon Ammen*
Peggy Seeger: A Life of Music, Love, and Politics   *Jean R. Freedman*
Charles Ives's *Concord*: Essays after a Sonata   *Kyle Gann*
Don't Give Your Heart to a Rambler: My Life with Jimmy Martin, the King
    of Bluegrass   *Barbara Martin Stephens*
Libby Larsen: Composing an American Life   *Denise Von Glahn*
George Szell's Reign: Behind the Scenes with the Cleveland Orchestra
    Marcia Hansen Kraus
Just One of the Boys: Female-to-Male Cross-Dressing on the American
    Variety Stage   *Gillian M. Rodger*
Spirituals and the Birth of a Black Entertainment Industry   *Sandra Jean Graham*
Right to the Juke Joint: A Personal History of American Music   *Patrick B. Mullen*
Bluegrass Generation: A Memoir   *Neil V. Rosenberg*
Pioneers of the Blues Revival, Expanded Second Edition   *Steve Cushing*

Banjo Roots and Branches   *Edited by Robert Winans*
Bill Monroe: The Life and Music of the Blue Grass Man   *Tom Ewing*
Dixie Dewdrop: The Uncle Dave Macon Story   *Michael D. Doubler*
Los Romeros: Royal Family of the Spanish Guitar   *Walter Aaron Clark*
Transforming Women's Education: Liberal Arts and Music in Female Seminaries
   Jewel A. Smith
Rethinking American Music   *Edited by Tara Browner and Thomas L. Riis*
Leonard Bernstein and the Language of Jazz   *Katherine Baber*
Dancing Revolution: Bodies, Space, and Sound in American Cultural History
   Christopher J. Smith
Peggy Glanville-Hicks: Composer and Critic   *Suzanne Robinson*
Mormons, Musical Theater, and Belonging in America   *Jake Johnson*
Blues Legacy: Tradition and Innovation in Chicago   *David Whiteis*
Blues Before Sunrise 2: Interviews from the Chicago Scene   *Steve Cushing*

The University of Illinois Press
is a founding member of the
Association of University Presses.

———————————

University of Illinois Press
1325 South Oak Street
Champaign, IL 61820-6903
www.press.uillinois.edu